S0-BNF-957

Reviews

"A valuable resource! Harris-Johnson's guide will assist in improving the lives of many of today's African-American youth."

—Ann Burns, Editor, *Library Journal*

"*The African-American Teenagers Guide to Personal, Growth, Health, Safety, Sex and Survival—Living and Learning in the 21st Century* by Debrah Harris-Johnson is a great aid to teens and all of us who continuously go through life's challenges. The excellent coping methods give elements in life young people need to Stay Strong."

—Terrie Williams, President, Terrie Williams Agency and Author, *Stay Strong: Simple Life Lessons for Teens*

"*The African-American Teenagers Guide to Personal Growth, Health, Safety, Sex and Survival: Living and Learning in the 21st Century* provides countless tips and hints on all subjects that are important to teens. Harris-Johnson also provides information to parents wishing to better help and understand their children."

—Tamika Barns, Book Reviews Editor, *Foreword Magazine*

FOUR STAR REVIEWS
★ ★ ★ ★

"Harris-Johnson's *African-American Teenagers Guide* is just what we needed. When it comes to providing information to teens (and their parents) about getting through the teenage "time tunnel," she leaves no stone unturned and discusses all the challenges of personal growth head on! It is the ultimate guide to growing up! A must-have for every school, every library, and every teen-occupied household."

— Yvonne Rose, Author
Is Modeling for You? The Handbook and Guide for the Young Aspiring Black Model

"Harris-Johnson aims to give African-American teenagers the ultimate comprehensive guide to life...the text is readable, educational and motivational. Many teenagers will find this guide nurturing and empowering."

—*Today's Librarian*

The African-American Teenagers Guide to Personal Growth, Health, Safety, Sex and Survival

Living and Learning in the 21st Century

By Debrah Harris-Johnson

Amber Books
Los Angeles, CA   Phoenix, AZ

The African-American Teenagers Guide to Personal Growth, Health, Safety, Sex and Survival

Living and Learning in the 21st Century

by Debrah Harris-Johnson

Published by:
AMBER BOOKS
1334 East Chandler Boulevard, Suite 5-D67 Phoenix, AZ 85048
Email: amberbk@aol.com   Website: www.amberbooks.com

The publication is designed to provide accurate and authoritative information in regard to the subject matter covered. It is sold with the understanding that the Publisher is not engaged in rendering legal, accounting or other professional services. If legal advice or other expert assistance is required, the services of a competent professional person should be sought.

AMBER BOOKS are available at special discounts for bulk purchases, sales promotions, fund raising or educational purposes. For details, contact: Special Sales Department, AMBER BOOKS, 1334 East Chandler Boulevard, Suite 5-D67, Phoenix, AZ 85048, USA.

Library of Congress Cataloging-In-Publication Data

HARRIS-JOHNSON, DEBRAH
The African-American Teenagers Guide to Personal Growth, Health, Safety, Sex and Survival: Living and Learning in the 21st Century / by Debrah Harris-Johnson - 1st Edition
    p. cm
Includes index
Summary: A guide to understanding the world and how to live in it successfully, discussing safety, survival, sex, money, time, and responsibility.
ISBN 0-9655064-4-4

1. Teenagers — United States — Life skills guides — Juvenile literature (1. Life skills.
2. Conduct of life.)   I. Title.

HQ796.H3515
646.7'00835–dc21

                                                99-29200
                                                CIP

First Printing July 2001
10 9 8 7 6 5 4 3 2 1

Contents

Acknowledgments

To God, I give thanks and praise. It has been by His hand that I have written.

Completion of this book required the cooperation, support and prayers of many individuals. Heartfelt thanks to my mentors, Carroll and Bettie Gibbs, Lutricia Bridgeforth-Madison, Charles Berrin, Jackie Hawkins and Magaji Bukar; my special friends, Paula Valentine-Wilson, B. Dilla Buckner, Jeannette McLaughlin, Linda Barnes-Pratlow, Jo Ellen Deutsch, Janice and Al Lynn, Bob Weck, Judith Richardson, Wilma Purcell, Mildred Flowers, Betty Wilson, John Macklin, Lisa Fiedorek, Katherine and John Dowd; my mother, Doris Harris, sister, Wanda Harris-Johnson, brother, Eddie Harris, Jr.; my in-laws, Lauretta and Pete Foggie, Gloria and Aaren Harbin, Lajuan Allen, Charles, Charleene and Jazmyne Johnson; my Godmothers, Mildred Britton, Clarice Ellis and Jennie Sightler; and, in spiritual memory of my guardian angels, Ann Queen, Eddie Harris, Sr., James Queen, James Nathaniel Queen and Alex Britton.

A warm and caring thanks to all of my neighborhood daughters and sons who weathered the challenges of growth; especially, Thomas, Kim, Crystal, Karr-Neia, Cynthia, Rick, Sean, Oscar, Chris, Louie, Tracy and Tiffany.

And, grateful thanks to my literary confidant, Regina Thomas, and publisher, Tony Rose for sharing in my vision and turning it into a tangible reality.

I am also indebted to the many others who gave their unselfish gift of time and constant encouragement. You know who you are and I truly give you my thanks.

A Special Acknowledgment:

Tony Rose, Publisher and Editorial Director
Samuel P. Peabody, Associate Publisher
Yvonne Rose, Senior Editor
Lisa Liddy, Cover and Interior Design
Joe Liddy, Proofreader
Wayne Summerlin, Cover and Interior Photographs
Mike Armstrong, Interior Photographs
Wayne Parham, Interior Photographs
Walik Goshorn, Interior Photographs

As always the Publisher gratefully acknowledges those whose time, patience, help, and advice have contributed to the success of our literary efforts:

Erline Belton; Philip and Anjie Herbert; Felicia Rose and Kate Saylor; Florence Price; Regina Thomas; Elnora Marie Fleetwood- Miles; Yvonne Marie Fleetwood; Lloyd and Lamurel King; Kevin Anthony Fleetwood, Jr.; John and Mildred Seagraves; Kay Bourne; Cassandra Latney; Therese Fleetwood; Jamila White; Wayne Summerlin; Lisa Liddy; Rodney J. McKissic; Alfred Fornay; Carolyn Herbert; Tom "Satch" Sanders; Samuel P. Peabody; Darryl and Lorraine Sanders; Mrs. Muriel Waller; Mack Lee; Terri Simmons, PhD.; Terrie Williams, Kendal and Revola Minter, Yvonne Rose; Donna Beasley, founder of the Chicago Black Book Fair and Conference; the IBBMEC; the Nation's African-American bookstores; our wholesalers and distributors; the black media; and to Debrah Harris-Johnson for writing a truly great and timeless book for teens and parents.

Dedication

*In loving appreciation to my husband, Leland,
my children Leland, Jr. and Christine;
my grandchildren, Olivia and LeeAnn.
For all you've done for me...this is for you...and,
may we continue to dance together.*

Foreword

Your teen years are your most challenging years. You are faced with decisions that can and will affect your entire life. Choosing to be involved or not to be involved in tempting circumstances, such as sex, violence and crime can be life altering decisions, which could end up in pregnancy, death or imprisonment. On the other hand, education, time management and hard work can lead you on a path toward professional leadership and a successful career. Yes, your future is dependent on how you journey through your teen years.

During this time, you will experience many hormonal changes. Your body will complete its growth cycle and shape you into the image of the woman or man that will carry you through adulthood. Some people, because of ignorance, may not see you as the graceful, wonderful and special person that you are. In fact, some people will see you as an adult and, particularly if you are tall or muscular, may be threatened by your appearance. As an African-American teen you might be faced with special challenges. In some instances, it may not be who you are, but rather what you look like that that causes people to prejudge you. This could be because of racial prejudices or just because of the many negative images that have been seen of you in magazines, newspapers, movies and on television.

You have many serious choices to make and if you haven't yet started, reading this book will help you to begin the process. Your mind is a vessel, which can hold unlimited information, countless images and all the dreams that you can dream. Why not make that a positive thing!

During this time, you need special guidance, and it's here for you. *The African-American Teenagers Guide to Personal Growth, Health, Safety, Sex and Survival—Living and Learning in the 21st Century* by Debrah Harris-Johnson teaches you how to understand yourself and relate to your family and friends. It teaches you various ways to explore and take advantage of activities in your community and those nearby. It teaches you how to: study seriously and excel in school, nurture your mind and body by thinking healthy and positively, maintain a comfortable home by cooking and cleaning properly, deal with safety, sexual issues and survival, find a job or start your own business. It also teaches you how to handle peer pressure and associate with positive friends.

This book was written especially for you—the African-American teenager! To make your reading experience more fulfilling, share the book and your thoughts with your parents and friends. After reading it, you should be able to determine the role that each topic means to you, personally and how it can affect your future. Remember, the choice is yours—making the wrong one can instantly change the path of your life, shattering your goals and dreams; but making the right one can put you on a path that can be rewarding, fulfilling and successful.

—Yvonne Rose, Author
"Is Modeling for You? The Handbook and Guide for the Young Aspiring Black Model"

Preface

Pride prods the writing of this preface. Pride in a woman who is a parent, grandparent, neighborhood Mom, literary talent and entrepreneur.

The African-American Teenagers Guide to Personal Growth, Health, Safety, Sex and Survival was in the making well over 10 years ago. The author saw a need for this instrument as the days of "it takes a village to raise a child" seemed to be rapidly dissolving, back then and even more so, today.

These are times when social nuances are evolving very quickly. A lot of African-American teens, in particular, are being thrust forward with little guidance. Parents are not completely at fault. Likewise, society should not have to shoulder all of the blame. Teens simply live in an age that is ever-changing. This Guide looks at those changes and identifies common sense solutions. It is comfortable reading written in a non-dictatorial style about topics so personal that only the reader would be able to appreciate its importance. This one-step book has been written for African- American teens who are at a major phase of their growth. It is their index to healthy living in a new age of change.

The author is our Mother.

Christine E. Johnson
Leland Johnson, Jr.

Introduction

Are you having a rough time being a pre-teen or teenager these days? Are there times when you feel frightened, frustrated or simply confused? Have you experienced moments when you wished the word "responsibility" was **not** in your vocabulary? Does handling or making decisions, completely on your own, make you feel uncertain about your judgement? If so, then this Guide is for you.

The African-American Teenagers Guide to Personal Growth, Health, Safety, Sex and Survival was designed to give you a few hints and tips to use on your journey toward adulthood. Each section has been carefully molded to provide you with specific tools so that you can comfortably discover ways to improve the you— you— wish to be.

There are suggestions, activities, amusing quotations and an assortment of common sense comments that are sure to stimulate your senses. Quite a bit of straight-talk has also been included. In fact, you might even be offended about some of the subject matter. You are advised, therefore, to simply review the material with an *open mind*. Afterall, while you may not have experienced a number of the situations referred to in this book, it is very likely, that you know family members, friends or even coworkers, who have.

Use this Guide as a "coping" tool. It does not have all the answers! Its purpose is to help you become more aware of yourself and begin giving serious thought to your own health and safety, family values, education, employment, workplace ethics, and alternative life style challenges as you prepare to enter the adult-arena. And, while only the basics have been presented in this book, it is the author's hope that those who read it will take the time and make the effort to dig a bit further, for the benefit of their own well-being.

Good luck on your journey toward adulthood!

Debrah

Chapter 1
Take a "Close" Look at Yourself

The first step in your plan for personal growth is to take an **honest** look at yourself. In this section you get a chance to do just that. You will be able to look at your many strong points. Tips are provided to help you find ways to strengthen those areas you feel need a bit more improvement. Also included are numerous life-altering experiences which will require a meaningful amount of endurance on your part. And, by the end of this section, be prepared for a surprise. You just might discover that your level of self-confidence is beginning to rise!

Me, Myself and I

"I know **myself** better than anybody else!" is a phrase that almost everyone says over and over. In fact, you have probably said this many times, too. But, do you really believe this?

For starters, you know your name, address, telephone number, social security and driver's license numbers. You know where you attend school and your grade. You are familiar with important telephone numbers including your parent's job and calling 911 to reach either the police or fire department in case of an emergency.

Do you know your blood type or whether you are allergic to certain foods or medications? This information, of course, is important in case you are in an accident or some other emergency situation. What makes you **feel** happy? Does being alone bother you? Do you readily volunteer to be on committees at school, church or in your community? Are you able to easily make a list of the things you do **very** well? Do you feel frustrated about activities you really want to do, but simply cannot?

After reviewing your responses to these questions try answering one more. Can you name **one** person who knows **absolutely** everything about your thoughts, private feelings, fears, goals or secrets? Sure you can. It's you!

Giving some more thought to the real you involves looking even closer. Everyone (including you) plays different roles or wears several hats in their lifetime. Your roles (or hats) would include, for example: being a family member, student, friend, neighbor, athlete and perhaps a co-worker. Consider how you see yourself in each of these roles and how you think others see you. Begin with the questions which follow.

- What are some of the things that make me feel good?
- What are my favorite leisure activities?
- If I have to fill out an application for a job, what kind of work skills would I list?
- Do I usually feel comfortable or uncomfortable in a group setting with my peers?
- Am I as organized a person as I think I am?
- If I could change some things about myself, what kind of changes would I make?
- Do I see myself as more of a leader than a follower?
- Can others depend on me?
- Do I think my family sees me as a person who is capable of making a mature decision?
- Am I a person my friends can trust with their secrets?

This is a pretty good time to write your responses down and review them. Look them over very carefully. You might even want to add several more to this list. Remember, this is **not** a test. There are no right or wrong answers. The only rule to follow is to be "honest" about your responses. Then, decide that **today** will be the day you put your energies into action and work on improving the "you" you wish to become.

"Taking an honest look at myself is the first step toward strengthening my weaknesses!"

Feeling Good About "Me"

How you feel about yourself is referred to as "self-esteem." According to Webster's Dictionary, the word "esteem" means having a good opinion about a person, regarding that person as valuable and having respect for her/him. Once you add the word "self" in front of "esteem", a whole new meaning takes shape. Now, it is personal. It is all about you and no one else. So, a newer definition would be: "Self-esteem is the good opinion I have about myself, how valuable I see myself and how much respect I have for myself."

There are several traits (or characteristics) of a person who believes their level of self-esteem is either high or low. People who feel good about themselves have high self-esteem. Those who have a rather negative image are considered to have low self-esteem. Keep in mind that this is a **feeling**. It can be determined more often by what you **do** (your actions or reactions to different situations) than by what you **say**.

You would typically be considered a person who has high self-esteem if you:

- Feel a sense of pride about the things you do
- Handle situations or problems on your own
- Can comfortably accept responsibility for those things that go wrong
- Can remain calm during frustrating periods
- Look forward to new challenges
- Have the ability to guide (influence) others
- Are not afraid to share how you feel (your emotions) with others.

3

Someone with low self-esteem would tend to:

- Run from (avoid) tense, uncomfortable or distasteful situations
- Be unsure of themselves in what they do
- Feel alone and unliked by others
- Be so insecure about themselves that they frequently put the blame for their mistakes on someone else
- Be more of a follower than a leader because they are afraid to act on their own
- Get easily irritated with themselves
- Feel a sense of helplessness
- Keep their real feelings hidden from others.

What level of self-esteem do you have? Is it "high" or "low?" If you think you are somewhere in between, which of these areas do you need to work on, first?

"Absolutely perfect people only exist in books!"

Whatever level you feel you fit in, there is always room for improvement. Think positive! Begin by making a "things-to-do" list. Chose things that will make you feel better about yourself. Your list might include, for example:

- ❑ "Volunteer" to give a presentation.
- ❑ "Be the comforting ear" to a friend who needs to talk.
- ❑ "Start" a conversation with someone you feel does **not** like you. (Wouldn't it be just awful to find out that person really did like you, afterall?)
- ❑ "Admit" to someone that you made a mistake and apologize. (If the mistake was something which caused that person to feel hurt, don't forget to ask what you can do to make them feel better!)
- ❑ Say—"**No**" when you feel it is necessary. (And, don't feel guilty about your decision!)

Make-up a special form like the one below. On it list those areas you think need more improvement.

To Improve My Level of Self-Esteem

(Sample: ***My area of weakness*** = *"I avoid introducing myself to others"*; ***My plan for improvement*** = *"I will work on my shyness and introduce myself to one of the new students in my class, tomorrow!"*)

My area of weakness	My plan for improvement
1.	
2.	
3.	
4.	
5.	

Start believing in yourself. Only entertain thoughts that whatever you attempt to do, you will aim at doing your very best—not just the first time, but every time!

Coping Concerns

A significant portion of an African-American teen's personal growth involves knowing how to cope with different situations. Loosely defined, coping means either "managing" or "handling." There are not a whole lot of people who have a problem coping with *pleasant* experiences. It is the *unpleasant* experiences that pose a problem.

How competent are you with coping (or handling) uncomfortable situations? Consider those situations which often make you feel embarrassed, cause you to think "twice" about asking for help, provoke you to show anger, distaste or annoyance.

There are many areas of real importance which could have been included in this section. The following, however, are probably the most troublesome for anyone to comfortably handle—regardless of their age.

Adapting to Changes

Everyday life occurrences can bring on changes. Many of these changes will be pleasant. A good majority, on the other hand, may be challenging. To successfully cope with changes will depend on your ability to comfortably adapt or adjust to a particular situation.

Changes come in many forms. As an African-American teenager, you will find yourself needing to adapt frequently to changes and obstacles. There will be times when you have to face attending a new school, making new friends and learning your way around a new city. As you get older you will have increased levels of responsibilities at home, school and on a job. Special relationships (girl-friend/boyfriend stuff!) will bring out feelings you never noticed before. Sudden illnesses (yours, a family member or friend) will prompt you to re-think and re-evaluate what you view as really important in life. Added to this brief list is divorce and death. Both, for obvious reasons, will more than likely be the most uncomfortable changes for you to confront.

Your level of self-esteem plays a big part in how you handle changes in your life. There are also human factors involved like your personality, maturity and level of common sense. Your method of adapting might be taking the time to look at both sides **before** making a decision about what to do, searching for ways to make things better for yourself, and accepting the fact that you have no control over certain situations. In some instances, it is perfectly okay to simply move on with caution! If you are a bit shaky in the confidence-arena, then you can expect to shy away from even *trying* to adapt! You will, for example, sit by and expect others to make decisions **for** you and be absolutely miserable when the result is not what you had in mind and be too afraid to take matters **back** into your own hands.

Did you know that you **can** take matters **back** into your own hands? You can if you remember to respect and abide by the wishes and/or rules of your parents, school officials and job supervisors. Yes, it will be a little hard and probably uncomfortable. But, if you can have a discussion that is not threaded with disrespectful tones, a lack of manners or a willingness to listen as well as talk (listening to what they have to say and sharing your side), a mutual agreement **can** be reached by **both** sides. You will not know if this is even possible, unless you try!

> *"Life is a continuous circle of change,*
> *re-evaluating and problem solving!"*

Asking for Help

Sometimes you will need to seek the advice of others. Talking to someone will make you feel less "alone" and more confident. Discussing an idea or problem with someone can also minimize feelings of frustration, stress and worry. Asking for help and getting it also leads to solutions. Keep in mind that not all solutions will be exactly what you want. It will be up to you to decide if a solution makes you feel uneasy, will require you to make too many compromises, or feels workable and worth taking a chance.

It is always wise to ask for help from a person that you trust. Choose someone who makes you feel comfortable. Make sure she/he is not the kind of person who cannot keep a secret—secret! Consider asking an adult for help. Afterall, adults have had more experience and can suggest *workable* solutions because they may have gone through the same situation themselves.

Some adults you might want to talk to are: parents (yours or a friend's), a favorite teacher, the school counselor or nurse, a doctor, pastor or call one of the toll-free hotline numbers advertised on television. Still another alternative would be to contact one of the hospitals in your area.

Tell the hospital operator: "I am **'x' years old**. I have a problem that I need to discuss with a counselor or doctor. Can you help me?" By saying this, the hospital operator will have a better idea of who she/he needs to connect you with for help. Be prepared to answer any questions you might be asked. If you are comfortable giving your name, that's fine. But, usually, it is only necessary to share this information with either the doctor or counselor.

> **Note:** The hospital operator probably will not ask you for your name or address. She/he might, however, ask for your telephone number. At some hospitals (hotlines, too) the operator's notes will have "Caller #000, time, date, purpose of call and telephone number".

Asking for help is not hard to do. Simply tell the person you have a problem and need to talk. Let them know you value, trust and feel comfortable with them and **want** their help. After describing the problem, be courteous enough not to interrupt them when they are sharing their opinions and advice. You may not like what they suggest. It is also possible that after having talked with them, you still need to talk to someone else. If so, go ahead and contact someone else. It is perfectly all right to do this. In some instances, a second opinion will turn out to be more along the lines of what you had in mind at first. Don't forget to say "thank you". Remember also to let the person know you intend to give their comments and suggestions serious thought before **you** make a decision about what to do.

*"Asking for help can result in answers
you might not want to hear!"*

Bargaining

Positive use of bargaining skills can strengthen your sense of commitment. Making a bargain with someone means that you agree to give or do something in return for something else. Bargaining is similar to negotiating a deal or making an agreement. It can also be a very useful tool for coping with conflicts.

You can make a bargain with family members, friends, classmates or even co-workers. One example of bargaining might be to agree to help a friend with a school project if they will setup your new computer. Make a bargain with your parents to do extra chores so you can stay past your usual curfew time to attend a special dance. Agree to switch shifts with a co-worker if she/he will do the same for you the following month.

While making a bargain may sound easy on the surface, this is not always true. Many people have trouble keeping their word. Some also have problems making a commitment (or promise). To over-come these obstacles will take practice, patience, a clear under-standing of what you want and the willingness to give your time and energy to obtain it. This is also true for the other person you are making the bargain with. If they do not feel the same way, then there can be no bargain! Only an honest person and one who keeps her/his word will succeed with this skill. And, if both sides cooperate, everyone involved can be a winner.

> **Note:** Negative use of bargaining skills can lead to inap-propriate actions. So, under no circumstances is it wise to make a bargain with someone that has the appearance of being illegal, unhealthy or harmful to you or others.

Consequences

There is not a whole lot that can be said about coping with conse-quences. To explain it quite simply: you make a decision (or choice) to do something and whatever happens afterwards is the result of your actions. Handling positive consequences is usually not a problem. But, if your decision is to do something negative, chances are pretty good that the result (or consequences) will also be negative.

To avoid facing the unpleasant consequences of your decisions, keep the following in mind.

- Sharpen your decision-making skills. Have a clear under-standing about what the situation is, look at more than one way to handle it, and select the one you feel is best.

- Aim for results that will not be harmful or unhealthy for your well-being or that of others.

- Be prepared to accept whatever happens as a result of your decision.

Dealing With Difficult People

Difficult people are those who make you feel uncomfortable, unsure of yourself, and sometimes, threatened. They are people who can be abusive, intimidating, unable to listen, uncaring, usually use guilt tactics to get their point across, cannot be trusted and enjoy being the center of attention (even if it means in a negative sense). Do you know a few people who fit this description?

To deal with these people, you need to put on a bit of insulation. Here are a few insulation covers for your protection.

☐ Remember that difficult people are difficult because **they** have a problem. So, take what they say and do, seriously.

☐ Remain calm and try not to add fuel to their flames by feeding into their abusive, threatening and intimidating behavior. (They like to *challenge* others!)

☐ Become an "active" listener. Active listening means you hear what is being said, understand what you are hearing and, at the same time are able to think (process) beyond what the person is actually saying. If you listen closely to their abusive remarks, you will probably be able to "hear" and understand the basis for these remarks.

Example: You are a B+ student in Biology and the difficult person (who happens to be in the same class) is barely making a C. You might hear comments from her/him like: "So, I guess you think you are really something. It must be nice hearing Ms. Harbin give you so much praise in class, today. Well, you're not! In fact, if I were as fat as you are, didn't go out on dates and had the kind of pimply skin you have, I guess I would have enough time to be really good at Biology, too!"

As an active listener you might hear that this person: (1) feels a sense of envy about the praise you received in class, (2) probably really likes Biology but does not have as firm a grasp as you do, and, (3) can only vent her/his frustrations by striking out at you in an abusive and hurtful manner.

> **Hint**: This is one of those situations when "walking away" and not making any comments would be appropriate!

❑ Do not take abusive, insulting or hurtful comments too personally. Again, remember that this person is the one with the problem. You did not create it. You do not have to correct it. And, you do not have to use your valuable time to counsel (or help) this person get through their problem.

❑ Be assertive and give only non-threatening responses. Difficult people constantly seek threatening and abusive comments for fuel, so that they, in turn, can *continue* giving these kinds of abuse to others.

❑ Ask "specific" questions. Not, "Why are you so mad?" Try instead to ask: "Why are you so upset because Ms. Harbin singled me out, today?" A specific question will usually take the difficult person off-guard for a few moments. And, if there is an audience (which there usually is) they will back down just a bit. In the heat of an argument almost everyone has trouble answering a specific question. But, for the difficult person, it is even harder because they have to admit out-loud what is really bothering them. Quite often, many will simply make a final abusive remark and walk away.

❑ Avoid, as best you can, any and all physical confrontations. Unfortunately, some incidents of pushing, shoving and/or hitting will occur. This is another challenge tactic that some difficult people like to use.

Should you be threatened with the possibility of a physical confrontation seek assistance from a higher authority. At school it could be the principal or a teacher. On the job contact a supervisor.

If there is not enough time to get assistance, you will have to rely on your own physical strength. Try to defend yourself without the aid of any props (guns, knives, glass, etc.). What is important to remember is, should the situation reach this stage, your goal should be to "temporarily" stop your attacker—not, bring an end to a life!

Embarrassment

Some of the examples which follow might sound silly. Try, however, to imagine yourself going through these situations!

It would be embarrassing, for example, to bump into a glass door you thought was open. It would be embarrassing, when you are playing basketball to accidentally slam-dunk the ball in your opponent's basket! Wouldn't you feel embarrassed at the library when your stomach suddenly decided to make loud noises? How embarrassed would you be in a restaurant when you accidently spill your glass of water on the table and the other guests? These things do happen and there is no advance warning.

Embarrassing situations can make you feel a sense of being ashamed and out of control. While embarrassing situations are awful, keep in mind that you do not have to feel bad enough to cry, run out of the room, give a public apology or pretend it was the person standing next to you! Embarrassing situations happen to everyone, so you are certainly not alone.

> *"Worry gives a small thing a big shadow."*
> *—Swedish Proverb*

There are ways to cope with embarrassment. The next time you are faced with an embarrassing situation quickly do the following:

- ❏ Immediately close your eyes.

- ❏ Silently and slowly count to 100 by ten's.

    Hint: Counting backwards **can** force you to concentrate **more** on the numbers than on the situation!

- ❏ Take about three deep breaths in a comfortable "inhale" and strong "exhale" motion.

- ❏ Silently repeat the following: "This moment of embarrassment has already happened and is now—over. So, I will not waste my valuable time worrying about it!"

- ❏ Open your eyes and go on with what you were initially doing.

This quick exercise may sound like it will take 2-3 minutes, but it really only lasts about 60 seconds. Try it!

There will often be times when *others* embarrass you. Naturally, these situations will make you feel even worse. In order to cope, attempt to:

❑ Stay calm.

❑ Avoid wasting time thinking about the reasons "why" that person would say or do such a thing to you.

❑ Consider the possibility that she/he did not think you would be embarrassed by their comments or actions.

❑ Resist the urge to do to them, what they did to you.

❑ Make an effort to let that person know you did not appreciate what was said or done. Then, politely ask her/him never to do this to you again.

❑ Maintain your composure. If you don't, you might cause another situation that **could** be even more embarrassing than the first one!

❑ Rely on your sense of humor and common sense to get you through the situation. Remember: this is a situation that was caused by someone else—not you.

❑ If necessary or should you really feel the need to do so, simply walk away. A quick change of scenery might be just what you need for a few moments to regain your composure!

"Use laughter as a positive tool...it is
healthy, reduces stress and has a calming effect!"

Empowerment

At some point you will want your parents to give you the authority or power to handle situations on your own. You want to know that they are really listening to you and value your opinion about a decision you make that will affect you. As one expert put it: "A sense of personal power is absolutely essential to a person's ability to function responsibly and independently. It is the first line of defense against feeling helpless and victimized, and it is a key component of self-esteem. Empowerment is necessary for...self-caring behaviors, such as just saying no" (Bluestein).

Parents will not readily give you the level of personal power you want. What you must first do is show them by your actions that you are capable of handling this kind of power. They will be looking for signs. Some of these signs include: honesty, responsible behavior at home and school, how dependable you are and whether or not you act in a mature manner.

Your parents can empower by offering you choices about things that matter. They can give you the opportunity to make mistakes, re-think what happened and make the necessary adjustments to correct those mistakes. In a way, what you will be doing is managing yourself. And, without the proper proof shown to your parents, you can almost always forget about receiving any form of empowerment from them. Work on this area. The rewards can be very satisfying for you and your parents!

Handling Problems

Having to handle problems will almost always make you feel uneasy. To feel better and more confident, you have a couple of choices:

- Find a way to eliminate the problem.
- Find a way to handle the problem in a manner that feels "comfortable" to you.

Attempt to be prepared for the unexpected. Keep in mind that many situations are either small, slightly important, or are **very** serious. Some will require you to give a *special* amount of time and attention. Go ahead and schedule the amount of time you think will be needed. You, afterall, might be the **one** person who has the responsibility to find a resolve. So, don't be afraid to be responsible enough to make a decision and act on it.

"To pretend that a problem does not exist,
is fertilizer for its growth!"

Everyone copes with problems differently. You might, for example, handle a problem one way. Using the same problem, however, your friend might handle it in a completely different manner. In other words, both of you are different individuals, have different levels of patience and will look at the same situation from a different angle. But, the final result would be the same—a workable resolve was found.

Wouldn't it be nice to be able to visit the Library and check-out an "Answer Book" that listed **all** the problems a person would have to face in their lifetime? Well, no such book exists! So, while you are waiting for this book, try using the following "Ask and Analyze" method for problem-solving, instead.

Problem Solving: Ask and Analyze Method

1. Is this **really** a problem?

   If your answer is "no" then perhaps you simply over-reacted to an uncomfortable situation. If you answered "yes" then give the problem its appropriate weight of concern. Is it a serious problem, very serious or urgently in need of a solution? Write your comments on a sheet of paper. Put these notes away for a few hours or even a couple of days. Go back and re-read your notes. If you still feel the situation is, indeed, a "problem" go on to the next step.

2. How can this problem be handled?

   Consider as many sides of the situation as you can. Did you do something to cause the problem? Should you seek help by talking to someone about it? Who should you talk to? Would it be better to leave it alone and hope it will eventually disappear? If you do not try to resolve it, will someone you care about be hurt? Will you be hurt? Does it have to be handled immediately? Do you have a little time to think about "how" to handle it?

   After giving these questions consideration, decide how you intend to develop a solution. List several choices that you think would be the best way of handling the situation. Now, go to the next step.

3. List three ways to handle this problem.

   After looking at the problem from several different angles, select three approaches you feel are "workable." Pick **one**! Select the one choice you feel is a clear and reasonable way to resolve the problem.

4. Use the approach you selected!

   You might find that your first choice was wrong. Perhaps the end result you hoped for simply did not happen. Rather than become frustrated, keep in mind that everyone makes mistakes. Many people are often guilty of using poor judgement, or simply did not have a clear understanding of the situation to be handled. So, do not get upset! Instead, try another alternative. Re-think your second and third choices. Use the same steps you used before. If necessary, begin again, and list three "new" alternatives.

What is important in handling problems, is to *focus* on whether or not there is a problem. You then need to take steps to either eliminate the problem or reduce it to a level that you can comfortably handle. Next, figure out a way to accept the fact that this particular situation may **not** be within your control. If you cannot do anything about it, simply leave it alone and adjust as best you can.

> **Tip**: If the problem is either life-threatening or will cause emotional or physical harm to you or someone else, seek professional help immediately!

Looking out for your own well-being, after all, is your responsibility and should be a first priority on your list of things-to-do.

As a final note, many of the problems you will be faced with, are not unique to your age-group, not unfamiliar to your parents, and, in many instances, *cannot* be resolved by you. Try depending on (and trusting) your inner feelings, using common sense and d *ignoring* any *pressures* your peers might be placing upon you. In fact, be **very** selective about who you talk to about your problems.

Insults

Insulting others is impolite, discourteous, and inconsiderate. It can also be perceived as abusive and inappropriate. Handle insulting remarks from others with tact, poise and a smile. (Keep in mind that the "smile" will be a bit hard to pull off—but, do the best you can!) Walk away, avoid showing anger or embarrassment and **do not make any comments**. By doing so, you give a message (without saying a word) that they have offended you. Do not waste your valuable time making a scene. It will be by your actions that the insultor will be taken "temporarily" off guard and probably won't know what to do next! And, should this same individual decide to do this again, repeat your action. At some point, she or he should get the message that their actions are not quite producing the end result they were aiming for!

Multiple Moves

Moving to a new area can be very stressful. Facing a move once or twice is bad enough, but if your family is in the military or your parents' jobs require frequent moves, this can be even worse!

Moving interrupts friendships. It can make you feel disoriented. You may even find that you are ahead in certain subjects at school or behind in others. You will also experience frustration having to find your way around the city. While everyone reacts differently to moving there are sure signs that indicate you may be having a problem coping. Some of these signs are: feelings of depression, changes in your appetite, withdrawing from others (want to be alone for long periods of time), a drop in your grades, being irritable and not sleeping well. If you notice that you are experiencing these kinds of signs, perhaps you need to talk to someone. Try talking to your parents, first. If this is not possible, then make arrangements to talk to the school counselor, nurse or the principal.

The more frequently your family moves, the more unsettled you can become. But, it does not have to be that way. Getting involved in the relocation plans with your family can help you feel more a part of this activity and lessen your level of stress. Do some research. Try to get maps, newspapers and a *Yellow Pages Directory* from your new city **before** the move. Share this information with your parents and the rest of your family. Quite a bit of the information you need to gather can be sent to you by calling or writing the Chamber of Commerce in the city where you are moving. They have a set of "welcome" materials which includes bus/train schedules, a directory of local schools, churches, hospitals and shopping malls.

Keep this in mind: moving can be a positive growth experience, can lead to increased self-confidence and does not have to be so awful, after all!

Name-Callers

There are a number of people who will constantly call you negative, derogatory and hurtful names. These people fall under the category of "name-callers." Many name-callers, like difficult people, probably need to feel a sense of power. They make up names or yell out uncomfortable and insulting comments that they feel will be hurtful and degrading to you, especially in front of others. For instance:

"Here comes the class clown!"

"Welcome! We knew you were on your way because we felt the floor vibrate!"

"Now that I know your secret to staying thin, how many pounds of food did you leave in the bathroom this time?"

"Betty-Bad-Breath, would you kindly sit over there instead of next to me?"

"Hey, Adopted Andrew, did you find out why your real parents dumped you at an orphan home?"

"Four-Eyes, when do we meet your seeing-eye dog?"

"So, Lame Legs, do you take those metal sticks with you on dates, too?"

"We were just talking about getting sun-burned. But, I guess you people don't know anything about that, right?"

"You know, you remind me of the woman who played in the movie *Imitation of Life*. Have you ever tried to pass for white? I think you could if you wanted to!"

These kinds of cruel remarks create hurtful memories. But, what can you do if these remarks and name-calling are aimed at you? Two helpful hints are available if you are mature enough to handle them.

1. Ignore and make absolutely **no** comment to the person making the remark or name-calling. By ignoring this person on a consistent basis, they will eventually stop. Why not? If it is obvious that they are not bothering you, why should she/he continue?

2. Simply, walk away! You will, as far as they can tell, have defeated their purpose, which was to hurt you (probably in front of others). Let them be the one to look foolish in public!

   Tip: Once you get home and in the privacy of your bedroom, have a good cry for how hurt you really feel. Then, the next morning go on as usual without a hint to anyone, particularly the name-caller, that what she/he said has made any impact on you at all!

Peer Pressure

Peer pressure can make you feel just awful. It can make you feel so uncomfortable that you simply give in and go along with the crowd. Depending on the activity, you could get into a lot of trouble. Stay alert! Really listen to the kinds of invitations your peers are extending. Remember to respect your health. Protect the well-being of your mind and body. You are an individual who can make choices to engage in right versus wrong conduct. Where peer pressure is concerned, your **first** priority should always be—you!

Prejudices

Not everyone is exactly like you or like you want them to be! You show prejudice when you tell an ethnic joke, call or talk about others using rude and crude names related to their race, age, weight, height, physical challenge status, religion or sexual preference. If you find yourself in a group setting where people are talking about someone in a manner you feel is distasteful, there is no need for you to laugh or be supportive for the sake of "fitting in". This is especially true if these comments or jokes make you feel "uncomfortable". Whenever you get the chance, politely leave their presence. To do this you might, simply say: "Sorry, guys, I thought I could stick around, but I've got to go and I'll see (or talk) to you tomorrow!" Then, **immediately** leave. This will be a more than appropriate manner to get away! Consider taking some private time to re-evaluate those who were **making** the offensive comments. Keep in mind, that the others **may** or **may not** have felt as uncomfortable as you did. They probably did not have enough confidence in themselves to do what you did—take a polite exit!

Should you be **really** questioned about your exit by the person who initiated the insulting remark/joke, try saying: "I don't think what you are saying is especially funny. Obviously you don't know a few of the details about *my* background. If you did, I'm sure you wouldn't have shared those jokes while I was sitting here!" And, that should be the end of that!

> **Tip**: It doesn't matter whether or not you have any relationship to the subject matter that they are making jokes about. Once you leave, however, you will at least have planted a seed of "suspicion" which will make the joke-teller and the others think again, the next time!

About the Handi-capable

Handi-capable people are people who are physically-challenged. They are people who go about their daily routine in a wheelchair, on crutches, may be missing a leg or arm, might be blind or are hearing impaired. Like you, they attend school, work, have goals, value their level of self-esteem, are family members, have friends, neighbors, co-workers, attend church and, when you look at it, are not a whole lot different from you. For many people, their sense of prejudice seems to surface when they come into immediate contact with a handi-capable (or challenged) person. In fact, they tend to feel so uncomfortable that they allow their prejudices to show. Suddenly, their **real** level of insensitivity becomes very obvious to others. They tell jokes and make very inappropriate comments. Sometimes they share these comments while the person is present. Or, they make these comments behind that person's back. But, they simply cannot help themselves. This is their problem.

Below is a short list of "don'ts" when in the presence of handi-capable (or physically challenged) persons:

■ Don't stare.

■ Don't try to help unless they have asked for your assistance. If you have offered to give assistance and been told "yes" go ahead and help. Or, if there is an obvious emergency and you must provide whatever assistance is appropriate at the time, don't wait for permission.

■ Don't ask "What happened?", or "How do you usually handle this or that task"? These kinds of questions are very personal and more than inappropriate to ask unless you know the person very well.

■ Don't yell or talk loudly to a person who is deaf. It only takes a gentle tap on her/his shoulder to get their attention. Typically, they can read lips, so your loudness will only bring unnecessary attention to the two of you. Be patient enough and willing to repeat yourself if your friend indicates they did not understand what you were saying. When talking in a group, position yourself so that your non-hearing friend can be included. (*Let your manners show!*)

> **Special Note:** If you have a relative or friend who has a guide dog, **under no circumstances should you try to play with or distract the dog**! It is, afterall, their dog's responsibility to provide certain kinds of services to its companion. Playing with or distracting the dog could reduce the amount of assistance that their dog was trained to provide.

About the Overweight

Overweight people are often perceived to be over-eaters. This is not always the case. There are any number of medical, emotional or physical disorders that could be the cause.

> **Hint:** This also works in the reverse. Not all "thin" people are thin by choice!

Some medical professionals (Kemper) believe: "Excessive body weight compounds many health problems. It stresses the heart, the muscles, and the bones. It increases the likelihood of...many other problems. Excess weight makes breathing more difficult. Additional weight slows you down, makes you less effective in personal encounters, and lowers your self-image. Over-weight people are hospitalized more frequently than are people with normal weight; they have more gallbladder problems, more surgical complications, more cases of breast cancer, more high blood pressure, more heart attacks, and more strokes."

Keep these facts in mind the next time people around you are sharing "fat" jokes or starting rumors about someone who is overweight. Ask yourself this question: "Why would anyone make insulting remarks about (or in the presence of) this person?" Is it possible that there is a "personal basis" involved with their prejudice about overweight people? Think about it!

About Those of Different Races, Religions and Sexual Preferences

Many of your family members, friends, classmates, neighbors and co-workers will be from a different ethnic background than yours. Think about this for a moment. How important is it to you that there is a *difference*? Will this difference keep you from being friends? Will your relationship with this person be harmful to you or them on a physical or emotional level? Have you been watching too many movies? Has this caused you to view someone in a negative way? In real life, do you feel "uncomfortable" when certain people are around you because of their race, religion or lifestyle?

This list could go on and on but let's stop here. Did you answer "yes" to at least 4 of these questions? If so, it is quite possible that you are a prejudiced person. What you need to do at this point is:

- Admit to yourself that you have a sense of prejudice about certain ethnic groups, people who are not of your faith, or those who prefer a lifestyle that you consider to be inappropriate.

- Make a decision to re-think and re-evaluate your real feelings.

Everyone has the right to exercise their freedom of choice. Don't you? But, it might be a good idea to consider those choices that are **not** within most people's control. Were you given a chance to select the race you wanted? At the age of one, were you prepared to say: "I don't want to go to a Baptist Church, I would rather go to a Catholic Church?" After having experienced a loving family relationship that involves either a two-mom or two-dad relationship, do you feel less "loved" or "cared-for"?

This very short list of questions is provided to stimulate your thoughts. As you can see, there are numerous thoughts that could be added to this list. The bottom line, however, is, to go with your feelings, **know** what you want, take the necessary steps to accomplish your goals, "stick by" your convictions (what you *feel* is right for you) and take the necessary steps and/or actions that are needed to make **you** feel comfortable! Nope! It will not be easy. You will have to endure a bit of pain and much discomfort. But, eventually, like everything else, it will smooth out and what you are looking for will happen!

Punishments

Being punished by your parents is their way of giving you a penalty for misbehavior (wrong conduct). Their purpose is to minimize the chances that whatever you did will not happen again. In other words, a punishment is intended to make you think "twice" about misbehaving. The next time you are scolded, lose privileges or get sent to your room, accept it in a mature manner. Look at your punishment as a learning experience and vow never to repeat that wrong conduct again.

Right and Wrong Conduct

On the subject of right versus wrong conduct, it is suggested that you "let your morals show!" In other words, let the way you *act* tell others that you *know* the difference between right and wrong behavior.

Do not participate in activities which you feel fall into the category of "wrong" conduct. Give those who extend an invitation, a courteous (yet, firm) "no, thank you!" response. Decide, instead, to do the right thing for the right reasons. Remember, you don't have to feel pressured into doing something that makes you feel *uneasy.* And, allow your *instincts* and *common sense* to over-rule feelings of temptation to do something wrong. By consistently saying "no" to these invitations for inappropriate conduct, those who extend the invitation will eventually get the message—and leave you alone!

Self-Forgiveness

No one can receive benefits from feelings of shame, disappointment, or self-hatred. Everyone makes mistakes, uses poor judgment and goes through periods of regret. No one is perfect. And, today, is a great day to begin forgiving yourself. It will take a lot of patience and practice, but you can do it. While you do not have control over the past, you can pull strength and knowledge from past experiences—today—for a better tomorrow!

Temper Control

Everyone gets angry and it is perfectly all right. What is not all right, however, is to become *so* angry that you lose your temper. This is not acceptable behavior. It keeps you from doing what you have to do and makes you feel terrible. Losing your temper can also cause you to needlessly harm another person or even yourself.

The next time you feel you "might" lose your temper, try: looking away, counting to ten, taking a walk, reading a book, humming, whistling, washing your hands with warm water or taking a shower. Do anything that would be considered positive, healthy or time-consuming. What you need is to *quickly and temporarily* take your mind off of whatever has upset you. The few moments you spend doing something else will give you a chance to calm down. Once you have calmed down, the urge to lose your temper will then begin to fade away.

Winning and Losing

Sometimes you win, sometimes you lose. Winning, and knowing how to handle success, is usually not a problem. It is being able to deal with losing that brings on troublesome feelings. Make it a point to be as good a "loser" as you are a "winner". Be proud that you tried and did your **very** best.

Avoid getting angry at yourself or others if you lose. Resist the temptation to place the blame on someone else. Don't waste time feeling sorry for yourself. Instead, look *forward* to the next challenge. Keep in mind that even when you lose, you win—because you almost always learn something new from each attempt you make. It is also a good idea to get into the habit of being a *courteous* loser. Congratulate the winner!

"Mature persons rarely show disappointment in public!"

Divorce Dilemmas

Does this sound familiar? Your parents are, or soon will be, divorced. This decision was made without even discussing it with you. Some of your friends' share stories about what will happen to you when your parents split-up. Their stories aren't very pretty. In fact, some are rather scary! How does all of this make you feel? What kind of life changes lie ahead? Are step-sisters or brothers in your future?

Mixed Feelings

Your parents' divorce is sure to be an unnerving experience. As one expert (Hyde) put it: "feelings of sadness, hurt, anger, and anxiety are common at the time a family is coming unglued". For some, a first reaction to the news might be guilt. *"What did I do to cause this to happen?"* Another reaction could be feelings of abandonment. You might, for example, wonder if the remaining parent will someday do the same thing and leave you totally alone.

Along with this bag of mixed feelings come periods of utter confusion. You won't know who you are more angry with. Frustration will set in once you figure out that you have absolutely no control over their decision to divorce. You may even feel embarrassed around your friends.

Be on guard because you will have to endure many of these feelings. Remember, however, that your parents divorce each other; they do not divorce you!

Shared Time

The divorce is final. One parent gets to keep you at home. The other one receives visitation rights. Both share you on a scheduled basis.

It is quite possible that living with only one parent will make you feel uncomfortable. Levels of responsibility may increase. There will be new house rules to follow. Those scheduled visits with the other parent will sometimes cause you to feel irritated. The packing, unpacking, checking the calendar and watching the clock will initially make you want to scream! As terrible as all of this sounds, you can and eventually will get past this newness. You might even discover that many of the changes are not as bad as you thought.

Another side of shared time involves your parent's set of feelings. It is especially important to have a sense of how the parent you are living with might be feeling. Divorce is difficult for parents, too. Some parents suffer from fear, loneliness, isolation, guilt, failure and other negative emotions. "Many single parents feel overwhelmed with the responsibilities (of) earning money, paying bills and handling all the everyday matters that were once shared by two people. Some discover that they have little time for themselves and this makes them depressed." (Hyde)

Like you, the parent you are living with has to get accustomed to a different lifestyle. And, like you, they too will adjust—in time.

Step Status

Where do you stand if the parent you are living with decides to remarry? This could be a good change. Imagine gaining an additional parent who shared many of the same interests you have in a particular sport, outside activities or a favorite hobby. It might also be a bad change for you! But, what can you do to find out? Here are a few questions to consider concerning your future step-parent.

- Do I like her/him?
- Does she/he make my parent happy and content?
- Do I feel she/he will try to take the place of my other parent?
- Will I have to worry about how my other parent will feel when she/he hears about the remarriage?
- Am I going to have to follow a lot of new and inconvenient house rules?
- Will my parent love me less if there are other children involved?
- Do I want my parent to remarry? Why or why not?

After giving serious thought to these questions, take a moment to discuss your feelings with the parent you are living with. Make it a point to include your future step-parent in the discussion. Positive communication between the three of you is important. (Do not forget to include step-sisters/brothers, as well!) This will be a necessary step for everyone involved.

"Divorce is not always an undesirable change!"

Accepting Death

Death, like divorce, can be difficult to understand and even harder to accept. Both deal with the loss of someone you love, respect or deeply appreciate. Everyone handles these life crises differently. What tends to be similar, however, are the kinds of feelings which seem to surface. Expect to feel, for example, sadness, anger, loneliness and guilt. Add to this list confusion, frustration and helplessness. These are very strong and draining emotions. Acceptance of what you cannot change is certain to bring out a level of weakness you have never experienced before. And, handling these emotions will require you to put a self-healing plan into action.

The Ultimate Loss

Unlike divorce, death is a final loss. There are no visitation rights involved. You will never see that person again. The only cushion of comfort will be your memories.

Losing a family member will be the hardest loss to accept. This is especially true if the family member is a parent, sister/brother or grandparent. You have, after all, had them in your life for quite some time. Your daily routine and lifestyle is structured around them. Their demise will shatter what once was a set and workable pattern. Experiencing the death of a friend will really be unsettling. Was she/he about your age? Fear will seep into your thoughts. No longer will you look at death happening to someone who is old or very sick. *That could be me!*

Another loss you might not think about is the death of a pet. Your pet is a companion. Its role is to bring you comfort, a sense of happiness and unconditional (no strings attached!) love. This loss can be very painful regardless of your age. Aside from sadness and anger, you might feel guilty as well. Many "what-ifs" will come to mind. *What if I had taken better care of my pet? What if I had remembered to close the gate so my pet could not escape and run into the street? What if I had given more attention to regular vet visits?*

Coupled with the "what-ifs" will be periods of jealousy. It will be difficult not to feel jealous of family members, friends or neighbors who have pets. Those who, like you, have a special fondness for animals and constantly want to talk about them. Listening to them will probably make you even more miserable. Since they may not be aware of how uncomfortable you are, simply tell them. By doing so, you give them the opportunity to help you through these feelings until you become strong enough to accept this loss.

Unfortunate Causes

Death can occur as a result of any number of health-related causes. Age and gender (female or male) are not always a main factor. And, race, religion or social status do not always play a major role. Some of these causes include: cancer (breast, colon, prostate), contracting AIDS, heart diseases, meningitis (an illness that affects the brain and spinal cord), pneumonia and abnormal usage of illegal drugs.

Accidents happen without advanced warning. When an accident occurs you feel shocked, scared and stunned. Common accidental deaths involve cars, planes, drownings and fires. A few not-so-common accidents are being struck by lightening, causes resulting from a tornado, hurricane or even hypothermia. Hypothermia happens when body temperatures drop below normal. "It occurs when the body loses heat faster than heat can be produced by muscle contraction and shivering. It can quickly lead to unconsciousness and death if the heat loss continues" (Kemper). Whether common or uncommon, accidental deaths can really make you feel helpless, numb and disoriented.

Murder is taking the life of someone on purpose or while another crime is being committed. It happens everyday. It happens very often. It can happen to practically anyone. It does not matter if the person is rich or poor, healthy or sick, young or old. It can happen to someone you know like a family member, friend, teacher or neighbor. It can happen to others you do not know on a personal basis such as a public figure, an entertainer or a sports celebrity.

Murder can occur as a result of a drive-by shooting, a stabbing, being in a building when a bomb explodes or being given a lethal amount of drugs. A murder can also happen anywhere. For example, at a bank, store or at home when a robbery takes place, walking across the parking lot to your car, boarding a school bus, sitting in church, standing around chatting with schoolmates and simply being around when a disgruntled employee decides to open fire on anyone in sight because she/he was just fired. In short, if someone's agenda includes murder, no one is safe anywhere! Besides feeling shocked and caught completely off guard, you might also feel defenseless and very vulnerable. The key to handling the news about a murder is to find healthy ways to cope with your feelings.

The most tragic kind of death is suicide. Some people kill themselves because they are depressed, feel unloved and lonely or because of the painful loss of a family member or friend. Many people select suicide as their way of coping with a difficult life situation. Suicidal people feel there is no reason to continue living. Not a whole lot can be said about your feelings when this kind of death occurs. It pretty much depends on how close you are to the person who commits this terrible act. Be prepared, however, to have a rather heavy bag of mixed feelings to be worked on for your own well-being.

The Grief Process

Grief is not something you can catch like a disease. There are, therefore, no miracle medications that can stop you from grieving. Your natural instincts just seem to kick in and often you are not even aware of what is going on. The grief process goes on for quite a while but there comes a time when it will end.

The grief process typically has three different stages—numbness, disorganization and reorganization. For your own well-being, you will need to go through each of these stages completely. "During the initial stage of grief (numbness) you may feel as if you are involved in a bad dream which will soon be over. The second stage is disorganization—loss of appetite, sleep (and) constant weeping are all indications of the pain you feel; other symptoms of grief include feelings of tightness in your throat, shortness of breath, the need to frequently sigh and extreme fatigue. With the final stage (reorganization) you gradually weep less, sleep and appetite are being restored—you care, once again, about yourself. You are calm, but you may still have terrible days. As time passes such days will occur with less frequency" (Temes).

Do not try to fight the grief process. Allow yourself to go through all of the stages. It is a natural, normal and very essential element for your growth.

For More Thought

To cope with either divorce or death, it is important to remember that you have no control over either one. These situations do not happen because of something you may have done and there is *absolutely* nothing you can do to prevent them from happening. What you do have control over, however, are: (1) accepting the fact that these situations have occurred; and, (2) finding a way to comfortably get through these experiences.

As a healthy suggestion, try using one (or all) of the following:

Talk   "Talk" about how you are feeling! Share these feelings with family members, friends, a school counselor or doctor. Being able to talk about how you feel will make you feel better.

Cry   Whether in public or private, crying is a great stress release. It helps you to let go of some of these feelings.

Write   Record your feelings. Start keeping a journal. Many people only write one or two sentences. Others, write a few paragraphs to even one full page of notes on a daily basis. How long you wish to keep this journal is strictly up to you. Write what has happened, how you feel about it and how you hope to feel the following week, month or year. Forget about spelling, sentence structure or punctuation. Just write!

Be Patient   Practicing patience will not be easy. In fact, it is very hard for many people. But, it is important to at least try. *In time*, the pain will lessen!

Pray   Regardless of your religious preference, take the opportunity to pull from your beliefs in a *higher power*, as a source of strength and comfort. You might even consider meditating or simply sitting quietly and thinking soothing thoughts.

"Sadness can make even the strongest person feel weak!"

Below is an excerpt written by Iyanla Vanzant that paints a pretty fair picture of what this section has had to offer. Read it and reflect on the new you, you wish to become!

"The only way to eliminate stress and pain is to stop doing the things that create it. It is easy to see what others do to us while we forget the drama we create for ourselves. How? Take your pick: The need to be right. Lack of life purpose. How we think others see us. Trying to fix the world. Dishonesty with self and others. Accepting someone else's truth. Seeking material wealth over spiritual values. Doing it alone. My way is the right way. Fear of the future. Negative thought patterns. Trying to prove yourself to others. Anger over the past. Telling other people what to do. It all boils down to not knowing who we are."

"When I know me, I stop doing what's not good for me!"
—Iyanla Vanzant

Chapter 2
Think "Healthy"

Making sure you are a healthy person is your responsibility. It is probably the most important part of your personal growth. Since it is so important, you need to get into the habit of thinking healthy. This will take dedication, a little practice and lots of patience. But, you **can** do it! You will also need to make plans for how you intend to be (and stay) physically, mentally, emotionally, socially and spiritually fit. All of these areas, when combined, make-up a more "healthier" you.

Looking Good

Many people tend to judge others by their appearance. Did you know that appearance is not always limited to what you wear, designer labels, expensive jewelry or physical attractiveness? These trimmings do play a part in how others see you. There are, however, some other areas they look at when looking at you. For example, others look at whether or not your clothes are neat and clean and if you are well-groomed. They even pay attention to how you walk, talk, act and even how you smell!

*"Judging others on first impressions
can cause negative imprints!"*

To ensure that you will *not* be viewed in a negative sense by others, here are some tips you might find helpful.

☐ Make sure you are dressed "appropriately" for all occasions. Wear outfits that are both fabric and color coordinated.

☐ Avoid runs or holes in hose and socks.

☐ Make a special effort to keep your shoes in good condition and polished.

☐ Wear jewelry that will compliment your outfit and not over-crowd it. Gentlemen should refrain from wearing earrings for certain occasions.

☐ Keep your hair clean and well-groomed.

☐ Your nails should be clean and trimmed. (Ladies should refrain from wearing "bold" nail polish for certain occasions. Gentlemen need to keep in mind that an occasional manicure is not an "un-masculine" thing to do!)

☐ Ladies should use "light" applications of makeup. (Refrain from "bold" lipsticks and eye makeup for certain occasions.) Gentlemen need to be well-shaven.

☐ Perfume, cologne or after-shave lotion should be applied in "modest" amounts.

☐ Avoid chewing gum, eating candy, smoking or talking loudly on certain occasions.

Added to this list is a reminder that attention to personal hygiene is a **must**! Without daily bathing, brushing your teeth and applying deodorant, you endanger your health and may cause others to feel uncomfortable in your presence. Remember, how others see you is important. Be sure you are looking your "best" the first time and every time.

"You never get a second chance to make a good first impression!"
—Ivory Soap Commercial

In the list provided above, reference is made to "certain occasions." These occasions would include, for instance: going on a job interview, attending church, going to a wedding, representing your school or job at a conference, going to a college interview or dinner at a fancy restaurant. Give some thought to other "occasions" where attention to your appearance might be important.

Whenever you are in doubt about what to wear, ask an adult. That adult might be a parent, an older sister/brother, a neighbor or even your school guidance counselor. You only need to tell them what the occasion/event is and ask for their opinion about what to wear. If you feel comfortable with that person, then you can also feel confident about their opinion and suggestions.

Hygiene and Grooming

Routine hygiene habits and grooming are beneficial for good health. Always maintain a clean body, hair and teeth; remove excessive facial, underarm and body hair; use appropriate skin care products and deodorants daily. Do not forget to give some attention to your hands and nails. Your nails should always be clean and filed neatly. You can do this yourself, but for a treat, why not have them done by a professional every three months? Use lotions or creams that will keep your hands soft and moist. Some of us tend to get "ashy." Be sure to use hand and body lotion on your hands, elbows, legs, and knees—and if necessary, carry some with you for touch-ups.

> **Tip:** Do not let the summer months show others that you forgot to give a little attention to your feet in the winter!

Skin Care Basics

Models always seem to have such healthy looking skin. Have you ever wondered what they do? According to one professional model (Rose) "your skin is a reflection of your general health...and whether you wear make-up or not, a regular skin care regimen is essential." This expert's suggested regimen (routine) includes using your favorite line of products along with the following tips:

❑ Daily cleansing should be done with a cleansing cream or lotion. (Avoid using a bath soap. Bath soaps do not penetrate the surface of the skin for deep cleaning, and they often leave a greasy film on the skin.) Apply the cleanser to the nose, forehead, cheeks and chin, massaging upward and outward in gently rotating motions with fingertips. Remove the cleanser with a clean damp face cloth or sponge.

❑ After cleansing, rinse your face thoroughly with cool water. Blot your face dry with a white tissue.

❑ Next, apply a freshener or toner for normal or dry skin, or an astringent for oily skin, using a cotton pad or ball. This is used in order to remove excess soil or oil remaining on the surface of your skin. (Ask the cosmetics expert where you purchase your products.)

❑ Moisturizing is vital, in order to maintain soft, healthy skin. Whether your skin is dry or oily, it should be moisturized in order to attain a proper balance and to retain the skin's emollients.

❑ Your lips need extra protection, too. After applying your moisturizer, you should use lip gloss or vitamin "A".

Check Your Wardrobe!

A good wardrobe is a workable one. Build a wardrobe based on the basics. Solid colors are a must for your basic wardrobe! You will need a solid white blouse/shirt, black, brown and navy slacks.

> **Tip**: Buying suits in these colors would be more cost effective. For even greater savings search for suits that come with an extra skirt or slacks!

Sweaters in these colors make great wardrobe stretchers, so add a couple to your list. Now, purchase items that can be mixed and matched with these basics.

Keep quality in mind. Natural fabrics like cotton, linen, wool and silk last longer. Add other colors, prints, textures, tones and even an occasional "fad" item. What colors work for you? Do not forget about your shoes. Again, basics are best. Be sure you have at least one good pair of both black and brown shoes that can be worn in any season. And girls, your *have-to-have* accessories include: jewelry, scarves, ties (with matching hankies) and belts.

Know what looks best on you. Stick to those colors and styles that enhance your good looks. With a little creativity, knowing what looks best on you and an eye for a bargain, pulling an appropriate outfit together for certain occasions should be a cinch!

"Fads have a short life-span!"

Clothes Care Tips

Always check the labels! Did you know that care labels are required by law (in the United States) on all wearing apparel except shoes, caps, hats and gloves? In general, what you will find on these labels are:

- Washing or dry-cleaning instructions;
- Water temperatures and dryer settings;
- Iron settings; and,
- Whether or not bleach is safe to use or if only non-chlorine bleach can be used.

Giving close attention to care labels can ensure longer wear of your garments. Let's focus for a moment on footwear.

Experts suggest that you polish leather shoes and boots on a regular basis using either shoe cream or paste wax. Be sure to carefully match the colors. Polishing is easy. "First wipe the shoes, then apply cream or paste with a clean cloth or applicator, rubbing gently in a circular motion. Finish by buffing to a gloss, using a separate brush for different colors. With paste wax, buff with a towel or soft cloth" (Kindersley). That's all there is to it!

> **Hint**: Want to make some extra money? See how many of your friends are willing to pay you a few dollars to do their shoes. You might be surprised!

Conflicts

Be prepared for a little friction between you and your parents! There will be times when your parents don't quite accept what you are wearing, your "newest" hair color or hair style (did you shave your head!?). When the discussion comes up, don't get upset.

Don't yell, be offensive or disrespectful. Instead, try to compromise. Attempt to find a workable solution that both of you can accept. During these discussions everyone needs to honestly listen to each other and be willing to "bend" a little. By doing so, it is quite possible that both of you can walk away a winner. If necessary, make a written agreement. It does not have to be really involved. Below is a sample to get you started. Just fill-in the blanks.

Our Statement of Agreement

This is an agreement between _____(your name)_____ and _____(your parent(s)_____ . We agree to do (or stop doing) the following:_____(1)_____, _____(2)_____ and _____(3)_____ for the next (include a timeframe—number of days, weeks, etc.) .

We agree that should either one of us violate this agreement, we will immediately take time to re-think, re-talk and revise this "Statement of Agreement".

It is also agreed that if we are **not** able to abide by this agreement, we will seek help from someone who is not a family member.

Now, both of you simply sign the agreement. Do not forget to put the date. And, remember to keep it in a safe place. Having things put on paper can be very useful. It means that there is no question about what each of you have agreed to do. It also means that there is a level of trust in each other.

> **Hint**: Remaining *calm* and being *respectful* are the two most important elements in this type of discussion!

Health Alert

Having good health is a necessary ingredient for your physical, mental, emotional and social well-being. Here is a recipe you might want to try.

Preserving My Health

Ingredients:

> 1/3 cup of concern
> 1/3 cup of planning
> 1/3 cup of maintenance

Directions:

Mix all the reasons you can think of for being healthy, with the many activities and goals you wish to pursue. Add to this, a list of things you can do to be and stay healthy. Now, very carefully, fold in good hygiene habits, and periodic medical/dental visits until the mixture becomes a smooth "routine."

Serves One: You!

Staying healthy is your job. Know your body and what is normal for you. Pay close attention to any body or mood changes. Watch what you eat. Keep track of when it is time to get a physical examination, see your dentist, or have your vision checked. Include the "Sensible Sevens" on your plan for staying healthy.

Sensible Sevens

1. Eat well-balanced meals as often as you can. Don't forget about drinking plenty of water and milk, eating an assortment of fruits and vegetables, and watching the kind of snacks you consume.

2. Try to remain calm, most of the time. Stress can make you sick!

3. Be smoke-free and avoid being in the same space with smokers. Second-hand smoke is unhealthy, too.

4. Don't drink alcohol or do drugs. Both can cause serious health problems.

5. Have only good feelings and thoughts about yourself. Thinking positively can raise your self-esteem and help your body to maintain a much healthier level.

6. Have a physical examination at least once a year.

7. Visit your dentist and eye doctor every six months or at least once a year.

Special Health Concerns

Be aware of your health risks. As an African-American you are at risk for heart disease and stroke, high blood pressure, diabetes and cholesterol problems. Since age is not always a factor it is important to find out as much as you can about your family's medical history.

Here is another area of concern. Are you living with a parent or another family member who has a mental illness? If so, read on. The American Academy of Child and Adolescent Psychiatry says:

"Mental illnesses in parents represent a risk for children in a family. These children have a higher risk for developing mental illnesses than other children. The risk is particularly strong when a parent has one or more of the following: an anxiety disorder, schizophrenia, alcoholism or other drug abuse, or depression. Risk can be inherited from parents through the genes."

The experts feel that "an inconsistent, unpredictable family environment (can) also contribute to psychiatric illness in children. Mental illness of a parent can put stress on the marriage and affect the parenting abilities of the couple, which in turn can harm the child."

Stay alert to these special health concerns. Talk to your family about their medical history. Ask lots of questions so you will be more informed about your own health risks.

Visiting the Doctor

If you absolutely **despise** going to the doctor, dentist or getting an eye examine, welcome to the club! Many people (adults included) feel the same way.

It is always wise to be a prepared patient. Be on time and take insurance information with you. Know the purpose of your visit. Have a list of questions you intend to ask. Depending on the purpose of your visit, some of the questions you might want to ask are:

- What is wrong with me?
- Is it a common problem?
- Can you tell me what the words (any words you don't understand) mean?
- What do I need to do now?
- What should I do at home?
- Is there anything I shouldn't do?
- When do I need to see you again?
- If medication is prescribed ask: How will this medicine help?
- Does it have any side effects I should look out for?
- Are there certain foods or beverages that should be avoided while I am taking this medicine?

Listen carefully to what the doctor has to say. Plan to do what she/he advises. After all, if you do not intend to follow the doctor's instructions, why bother going in the first place? Remember that these visits are for **your** benefit. So, go and don't put up a fuss!

Visiting the Dentist

It is recommended that you go the dentist every six months for both a regular examination and cleaning. In the meantime, should you have any of the following problems, go to your dentist immediately!

- ❑ If your gums bleed.
- ❑ If your gums are red, swollen or tender, or if pus is present.

❑ If your teeth are loose, appear to be moving apart or there are changes in the way your teeth fit together when you bite.

❑ If you have a toothache.

Tip: Some crunchy foods can actually clean your teeth naturally. Try snacking on apples, carrots and other raw vegetables!

Eating Healthy

Eating healthy on a regular basis includes:

■ Whole-grain and enriched breads, cereals, and grain products

■ Various vegetables

■ An assortment of fruits

■ Dairy products like milk, cheese, yogurt

■ Meats, poultry, fish, eggs, beans or peas and tofu.

Healthy eaters pay close attention to their weight. Healthy eaters only choose diets that will not harm them physically or cause too much stress. And, they consult a doctor **before** selecting a diet.

According to the U.S. Department of Agriculture's "Dietary Guidelines for Americans", there are some dietary tips you should follow.

❑ Balance the food you eat with physical activity. Maintain or improve your weight.

❑ Choose a diet with plenty of grain products, vegetables and fruits. Complex carbohydrates (grains, vegetables, and starches) and fruits pack the most nutrients per calorie.

❑ Choose a diet low in fat, unsaturated fat and cholesterol.

❑ Choose a diet moderate in sugars. Sugars have little, if any, vitamins, minerals or fiber.

❑ Choose a diet moderate in salt and sodium. For some people, sodium increases blood pressure.

One set of experts (Kemper) offers the following facts about a couple of items that you might find helpful:

Fruits and Vegetables

"Fresh fruits and vegetables are good for you. They provide vitamins, minerals, and fiber and are naturally low in fat. Many fruits and vegetables, contain a lot of vitamins A (beta carotene), and C, especially oranges and other citrus fruits, broccoli, sweet potatoes, winter squash, carrots, spinach, and other leafy greens. As a result, a diet that includes lots of fruits and vegetables helps protect you against heart disease and cancer. Fruits and vegetables are most nutritious when eaten fresh and raw or lightly cooked. When you cook vegetables, steam or microwave them to retain more vitamins."

Fiber

"Fiber has no vitamins or minerals, yet it is important to good health. To increase fiber in your diet:

■ Eat at least five servings of fruits and vegetables a day. Eat fruits with edible skins and seeds (kiwis, figs, blueberries, apples, and raspberries). Eat more of the stems of broccoli and asparagus.

■ Switch to whole-grain and whole wheat breads, pasta, tortillas, and cereals. Check the package. The first ingredient listed should be whole-wheat flour. If it just says wheat flour, it means white flour, from which much of the fiber has been removed.

■ Eat more cooked dried beans, peas and lentils.

■ Popcorn is a good high-fiber snack. However, avoid added oil, butter and salt."

Calcium

"Calcium is the primary mineral needed for strong bones. Calcium is especially important to growing children and women, especially in the peak bone-building years between the teens and early 30s... Teens and adults need 800 to 1200 mg (milligrams) per day. A cup of skim milk has about 313 mg of calcium. Nonfat and low-fat yogurt has 442 mg per cup. Other good sources of dietary calcium include broccoli, greens, kidney beans and low-fat cheese."

Lactose Intolerance

"People whose bodies produce too little of the enzyme lactase have trouble digesting the lactose sugar in milk. Symptoms of lactose intolerance include gas, bloating, cramps, and diarrhea after drinking milk or eating dairy products.

Tips for dealing with lactose intolerance include:

❑ Eat small amounts of dairy products at any one time.

❑ Drink milk only with snacks or meals.

❑ Try cheese, which usually does not cause symptoms. Most of the lactose is removed during processing.

❑ Yogurts made with active cultures provide their own enzymes and cause fewer tolerance problems.

❑ Pretreated milk, enzyme treatments and enzyme tables are available in most stores.

❑ If you cannot tolerate milk in any form, include other calcium-rich foods in your diet.

❑ Severe lactose intolerance may increase your need for calcium supplements. Ask your doctor.

Water

"One easy way to improve your diet is to drink more water. Active people need two quarts of water a day. People who exercise regularly need even more water. If you drink other fluids, you can get by with less, but plain water is best. (Drink an extra glass of water when you wake each morning.)"

Rearrange Your Eating Habits

Many health care professionals agree that along with watching what you eat, it is also important to watch *how* you eat. Breaking old eating habits is just what you will need.

Always go grocery shopping, for example, on a full stomach. If you are hungry, the urge to buy lots of snacks will be great! Put your fork down between bites. The slower you eat, the quicker you will begin to feel full. You can also slow down by chewing each bite 10 times. Do not skip meals. If you do, you'll probably overeat later. Leave the table as soon as you have finished eating. Remove all food you have hidden in several secret places at home or at work. (Don't eat them, give them away!) Only eat at scheduled times and in scheduled places. If you are in the habit of eating in the bedroom while watching television—stop! Instead, make it a practice to eat at the kitchen table, sitting in the same chair and eating at the same time each day. Let family, friends and co-workers in on your plan. With their help, this will be one less habit to break!

Avoiding Germs

Thinking healthy also means taking precautions to avoid getting germs from others. You can get germs from contact with someone who is sick. Many diseases quickly spread to the skin, scalp and eye areas. Colds, influenza and pneumonia are on this list. Generally, the five things you can do to avoid getting or spreading germs are:

- Stay away from those who have contagious skin, scalp or eye diseases.

- Avoid touching articles used by a sick person. If there are a lot of people around you who are sick, either at home, at school or where you work (for example, everyone seems to have either a cold or the flu), be sure to wash your hands as often as possible. Use a napkin or paper towel to handle door knobs, bathroom fixtures, and copy/fax machines. Avoid using their telephones, computer keyboards, typewriters or calculators.

Wear rubber gloves. While it might sound silly, look ridiculous and be an inconvenience, try them. These are the type of gloves many people use when they are washing dishes, polishing silver or using different household chemicals. You can purchase these gloves in most local food stores.

> **Tip**: Baby-wipes are good to have on hand, convenient and sanitary!

While others will, more than likely, think you are acting rather "strange". remember: you are doing what you are doing to protect yourself and stay healthy.

> **Tip**: This is an excellent time to allow your sense of humor to show!

- Make sure that dishes, cooking utensils and linen are properly washed (hot, soapy water and then rinsed with *very* hot water to kill germs).

- Don't be a germ spreader. Cover your mouth or nose when you cough or sneeze. Use plenty of soap and water when you wash your hands.

- Be sure to dispose of the tissues you use, **immediately**. And, once again, wash your hands.

*"With good health, I can do many things;
without it...very few!"*

Fitness Counts

When you think about "fitness" what usually comes to mind are the many activities designed to strengthen, improve or enhance your body. Did you know that your mind, attitude and social awareness also need to be in "fit" condition?

Physical Fitness

Are you physically fit? If so, then you have a strong and healthy body. You are a healthy eater and get an appropriate amount of exercise and sleep. You also stay on the alert for signs of stress so you can protect your healthy body.

Daily exercise (beyond the gym class, of course!) can be a "plus" for a healthier you. Through exercise you will be able to reduce stress, have some fun, stimulate your mind, control your appetite, enhance muscle tone and elevate your self-esteem. Through aerobic exercises, for example, you can strengthen your heart and lungs. This would include taking walks, running, climbing stairs, riding a bike or swimming. Muscle enhancement is important because it strengthens your muscles and reduces fatigue. Try doing bent-knee curl-ups, chin-ups, push-ups and leg-lifts for your abdominal areas, neck, arm, shoulder and legs. Don't forget to "stretch" before and after your exercise routine.

> **Tip:** Stretching can be a benefit. It can also prevent physical injuries!

Pick an activity or plan a set of exercises that you will enjoy doing. Keep in mind that you want to have fun and still reap the benefits of becoming a more healthier you. Don't exercise for too long a period of time, too hard or too often. Set your alarm clock. At the first sign of discomfort, slow down! Schedule daily exercise time for about 15-20 minutes. Begin and end with a 1-2 minute stretch. Make your stretch slow and gradual. Try not to bounce. Hold your stretch for about 10 seconds and relax. When your exercise time is up—drink some water!

Sleep and Rest

You need an ample amount of sleep everyday. The magic number of hours everyone really needs is 8 hours. Since your daily schedule is probably very full, it will not always be possible to get as much sleep and rest as you need. But, when it is time to go to sleep be sure to follow these do's and don'ts:

- **Don't** take sleeping pills.
- **Do** sleep on a firm mattress, not a soft one. (It is better for your back.)
- **Don't** forget to turn off the light, television and your music.
- **Do** make it a habit to get a full 8 hours of sleep at least 3 times a week.

■ **Don't** forget to take a few 10 minute breaks throughout the day to relax. (You might find that these short breaks actually give you extra energy during the day. And, with that extra energy you will probably do more and be naturally tired enough at night to calmly fall asleep!)

Stress

Stress can cause even the most physically fit person to be uncomfortable or sick. Stress surfaces when you have to experience (go through) situations involving changes and demands in your life. Everyone goes through periods of stress. It is simply that part of life which will require you to find a way to adjust to common everyday life events.

Stress can do several things to your body. It increases your heart rate, blood pressure, breathing and amount of perspiration; slows down your digestion; and, cause the pupils of your eyes to dilate. Your body becomes tense. You feel irritable and oversensitive. You might also become offensive, abusive or cruel in what you say or do to others.

Have you ever felt stress about having to give a presentation in front of the class? Did you feel stress on the first day at a new school? Do you feel stress just thinking about taking your driver's test? Did you (or do you) feel a bit stressed about your first date, first job interview or the first time you have to fly instead of taking the train?

There are also life-changing situations that are stressful. For example, the illness of a family member (or you), family problems, divorce or death. (Do you know anyone who, having been faced with a tragic life-changing situation, found themselves homeless for a short period of time?)

These kinds of situations require you to adjust. And, in many instances, you simply are not ready to handle them. In order to be prepared for the unexpected, you need to remember that many situations are correctable, but others will be **absolutely** beyond your control. Remember, too, that it is very important for you to find ways to reduce stress in your life. If you don't, you could experience unnecessary discomfort and harm both your physical and mental well-being.

Stress wears several hats and goes by many names. It quietly creeps its way into your life. It can take on the form of anxiety, strain, tension, burden and pressure (including peer pressure). It attacks you at home, at school, at work, and even during those times you have set aside for **quiet** time. Below is a short list of those things that can cause stress.

- Finding time for yourself
- Your grades
- Your boyfriend/girlfriend, or your children
- Your health
- Your personal safety
- Being laid-off
- Making more money
- Accepting lifestyle changes

With these concerns in mind, there are a number of things you can do. Why not make a plan? Your plan would include, for example, those areas you feel you need to work on in one column. The second column could be your plan of action. Use this form to get started.

My Worry List

My Worry   What I Intend to Do With It!

_____   _____

_____   _____

_____   _____

_____   _____

_____   _____

It is quite possible that you won't know when you are experiencing stress. Some experts (Kemper) believe there are several signs that indicate you are (or beginning to) "stressing-out!".

"You may get a headache, stiff neck, nagging backache, rapid breathing, sweaty palms or an upset stomach. You may become irritable and intolerant of even minor disturbances. You may lose your temper more often and yell at your family (friends, neighbors or co-workers) for no good reason. Your pulse rate may increase and you may feel jumpy or exhausted all the time. You may find it hard to concentrate. When these symptoms appear, recognize them as signs of stress and think of a way to deal with them. Just knowing why you're crabby may be the first step in coping with the problem. It is your attitude toward stress, not the stress itself, that affects your health the most."

Do any of these signs feel familiar?

Stress Reducers

A number of stress-release suggestions are available to help you cope. On the list are: crying, putting your feelings in words (keep a daily or weekly journal), working on arts or crafts, walking, humming, whistling, screaming (in an area that will not disturb others, of course!), or repeatedly pounding the pillow on your bed! Using any of these stress-releasers will definitely make you feel better, calm you down and give you a chance to think clearly. Try these.

Attitude Alignment — Look for positive ways to re-develop how you perceive and re-act to potentially stressful situations. Understand and accept the fact that you are not alone in your feelings and situations. People go through experiences that mirror your own. It is "how" you handle a particular situation—using your own unique strength mechanisms—that separates you from someone else.

Shift Your Thoughts — Become a thought-shifter! Stop thinking about whatever is making you feel tense. Think about something else. Think about something that makes you smile. While this may be only a momentary pause, that short pause could very well calm you down just long enough for you to relax and regain your composure.

Practice Visualization Pretend you are someplace else! On warm sand looking out over the water at sunset. Sitting before a fire at a ski resort. Or, perhaps, riding quietly along a bike trail in the mountains on a cool spring day. Don't be surprised at how *quickly* this short pretending exercise can make you feel more relaxed! Being able to effectively master the art of visualization takes a little practice...so be patient and concentrate. Once you get the hang of it, you will love it!

Walk Away Walking away from the area that is causing you stress for just a moment will allow you to calm down, re-focus and begin again. Or, you might consider just looking away for as little as 60 seconds!

Use Warm Water When you feel tense, your blood circulation reduces. By running warm water (the warmer, the better) over your hands for a few moments, you restore that circulation and can almost instantly feel more relaxed.

Set Aside Some Quiet Time It is **very** important to find "quiet time" for you! Quiet time allows you to settle down. Select a specific amount of time (15 minutes is good and 30 minutes is even better!) Pick a place that has little or no distractions. Remember, **only** use this time to relax!

Do you want a few more ideas?

■ Read a magazine or book (Do you like poetry?)

■ Color a picture in a child's coloring book (don't forget to stay within the lines!)

■ Assemble a puzzle

- Sign up for a yoga class (this can be very relaxing!)
- Go swimming, take up tennis or golfing
- Ride a bike
- Take a dance course
- Write a letter to a friend (no business letters...too stressful!)

Do **not** let your tools for coping with stress include: taking pills, smoking, drinking, overeating or simply not eating at all! Instead, allow your body to calm your mind and your mind to comfort your body. Decide what has to be done for a particular situation. Use exercise to keep fit and ensure that your body and mind are in fit condition so you can handle a particular situation. Again, remember, many of the situations you will have to handle will **not** be within your control. So, find a way to cope that is comfortable for you!

> *"Managing my stress level can significantly improve my physical fitness!"*

Well, it is all up to you! Pick a tip. Select a technique. Use it. Look forward to saying to yourself in the mirror: "Hi...You must be the **un**-stressed me!

Mental Fitness

Getting taller is a clear sign of physical growth. Did you know that there are also signs that show you are growing mentally, too? For instance, your vocabulary increases. This gives you a way to express your feelings in a clearer manner. You begin to think in more logical terms and you start handling problems in a more mature manner.

In general, you are considered to be a "mentally fit" person if you are free from any brain injury or disease which might cause mental distress (or tension, pain, anxiety). You are able to recognize and solve personal problems. You use both good judgment and common sense in making decisions. You are usually, quite alert, eager to learn, and look forward to finding (and using) new and better ways to accomplish your goals. You use several stress-release tools to cope with those unexpected situations that you have to face.

A major key to becoming a more mentally fit person is to think "positively"! By doing so, you will then begin using the process of "tricking" your mind. Your mind and body, typically, work together. So, if the signal you are sending through your mind to your body is positive, then you can almost always expect your body to respond in a positive sense. It is your mind that often triggers (or causes) your feelings to play a major role in your physical comfort or discomfort. With positive thinking you may find it easier to cope with illness, pain and periods of depression.

To overcome the negatives, try actively thinking about positive alternatives and actions. Put these actions in motion. Allow humor, an appreciation of friendships and a sense of love for yourself to take over.

Emotional Fitness

Before moving on to tips about emotional fitness, let's take a moment to grasp what the word *emotion* really means. "Emotion" is merely a fancy word for "feelings." Below is a short list of emotions, its definition and its use in a sentence so you will have a better understanding of what they mean.

Emotions

Admiration A feeling of approval or respect. (Paula feels admiration when she thinks that a person is very good or a thing is very beautiful.)

Anger A strong feeling that a person has toward another person or a thing that opposes, insults, or hurts her/him. (In a fit of anger, Anthony threw a book at his sister.)

Compassion Feeling sympathy for someone else's suffering or misfortune, and having the desire to help. (Wanda had such compassion for the lonely old woman that she visited her in the hospital every day and brought her presents.)

Contempt — A feeling that a person or act is bad, mean, or worthless. (Christine has contempt for people who are cruel to animals.)

Despair — A feeling of *complete* loss of hope. (The family was filled with despair when their house was destroyed by a fire.)

Doubt — A feeling of not believing or trusting. (Al had doubts about the honesty of the man who was trying to sell him a car.) Also: A state of being undecided or unsure. (Janice had doubts about the car Al bought!)

Fear — A strong feeling caused by knowing that danger or pain is near. (Shawn felt great fear when he witnessed a drive-by shooting!)

Grief — A feeling of very great sadness or pain. (Paul's grief about the death of his grandfather was something he will never forget.)

Guilt — A feeling of having done something wrong. (Charlene felt a good deal of guilt after she yelled at the store clerk.)

Hate — To have very strong feelings against or to dislike very much. (Christal hates to drive at night.)

Inferiority — Low or lower in quality, importance, or value. (Aunt Gloria admitted she has always felt that her school work was inferior to her sister's.)

Jealousy — Having envy of a person, or what a person has or can do. (Eddie was jealous of his friend's ability to play tennis so well.)

Joy — A strong feeling of happiness or delight. (Olivia jumped with joy when she saw her birthday present.) Or, a person or thing that causes a strong feeling of happiness. (Tenika is so helpful around the house that she is a joy to her mother.)

Loneliness   Feeling unhappy from being alone. (Lajuan felt lonely on her first day at the job.)

Misery   Feeling great unhappiness or pain. (The flood in Florida caused Doris to feel a lot of misery because she lost her home.)

Modesty   A feeling of not wanting to think too highly of yourself. (Cynthia was very modest when she did not brag about winning the Employee of the Month award at her job.)

Prejudice   A feeling of an opinion that has been formed without careful thought. (Letty showed prejudice when she said she disliked people who were smokers.)

Regret   To feel sorry about. (Lutricia regretted having said unkind things about her best friend.) Or, a feeling of sadness or sorrow. (Marie felt regret about her decision to move to another city.)

Respect   Feeling a high regard or consideration; having a favorable opinion or admiration. (Karr-Niea feels very strong about respecting the rights and opinions of others.)

Revenge   Feeling the need to injure, harm or punish someone to pay back a wrong. (Linda swore to get revenge on those who were spreading gossip about her.)

Selfishness   Thinking only of oneself; not thinking of others. (Leland was selfish when he would not offer to pick-up Marcus from the airport.)

Temptation   Having a feeling or urge to be persuaded to do something that is wrong or foolish. (The fear of

	getting a poor mark tempted Aaren to cheat on her final exam.)

Trust To believe or have confidence in. (We should have trusted, Channel Nine's weather expert, Sheila, **before** going to the beach!) **Or**, (I trust Ann to keep a secret.)

Vanity Feeling too much pride in one's looks, abilities or accomplishments. (Octavia's vanity made her think she was the prettiest little girl in her class.)

Worry To feel or cause to feel uneasy or troubled about something. (Dawn's parents worry when she is out too late.)

As you can see from this brief list, there are many emotions that everyone goes through. An emotionally fit person, however, is capable of controlling their emotions in most instances. They take responsibility for their *actions*. They *accept* the consequences of their decisions. They do not cry, pout or act moody when they cannot get their way. They make a special effort to adjust to situations and when they need help, *know* how to ask for it.

It is a little hard to tell if you are growing *emotionally*. There are, however, a couple of questions you can ask yourself to determine if you are beginning this process.

❑ Do you pretend difficult situations do not exist?

❑ Do you like challenges?

❑ Do you accept the fact that there are some things you can or cannot change?

❑ Do you constantly wish to be the center of attention?

❑ Do you prefer that others satisfy all of your wishes?

❑ Do you accept your physical limitations?

❑ Do you, comfortably, accept criticisms from others?

❑ Do you accept disappointments in a mature manner?

❑ Do you accept unexpected successes without getting too excited?

If you checked at least six of these questions, then you can feel reasonably sure that you are making good progress in your emotional growth. Take a *really* close look at your responses. Keep in mind that the level of your emotional growth includes not only the way you "act" and the way you "think," but also the way you "feel"! Is there room for improvement?

Social Fitness

Are you a socially-fit person? If you are, then you know how to comfortably adjust to most social situations. Loosely defined, a social situation is when you are in the company of one or more people. So, being socially-fit also means that, while you are in the company of others, you know what to say, how to act and when to move on.

Social Settings

Very often the social situation (or setting) you are in will be for enjoyment purposes. You might, for instance, be with others at a party, concert, sports event, having lunch with a few friends or simply engaging in a game of chess. Aren't you in a social situation when you have a conversation with the person sitting next to you on a bus? What about when you are in a classroom, at church or attending a meeting? Can you add to this list those times when you are: in the grocery store (okay, let's say at the check-out counter when you are buying those *must-have* jeans!); having a discussion with a teacher, counselor, pastor, neighbor, co-worker; or, holding a conversation with a family member.

All of these examples are social situations. In order to fit in, you will have to adjust differently to each one.

As a special note, keep in mind that many social situations will not be enjoyable! You might find yourself in the company of others whose intent could cause harm to someone else, to them or even to you. It will be during these times that you need to re-evaluate just how social you intend to be!

Communicating

A key element to fitting-in socially is having good communication skills. Communicating with others comes in many forms. Talking and writing are at the top of the list. When you have a conversation with someone or when writing a letter, your choice of words is important. Others will know you actually heard what they were saying by the comments you make. They will judge you, often imitate you and want you around them. Let's look at some of the do's and don'ts of a person who communicates well.

Good communicators **do**:

- Really listen to what someone is saying by giving their full attention
- Respond appropriately being sure not to offend or disrespect the other person
- Make it a point to see that others feel included, comfortable, safe and respected

They **do not**:

- Criticize others in a manner that would cause emotional discomfort
- Make those in their presence feel threatened or afraid to say what they want to say
- Ask inappropriate questions
- Intentionally insult someone

Did you know that your tone of voice and body language are also forms of communicating? Your tone of voice can send out a number of different messages. If you are talking to someone very slowly and in a low-pitched voice, they might think you are either bored or slightly depressed. A high-pitched voice, speaking rapidly or loudly, on the other hand, could mean that you are excited, being defensive, unsure of what you are saying or angry. Try the following activity. All you need is a tape recorder, concentration and sharp listening skills.

Activity: "My Tone of Voice"

Repeat each of these sentences twice. First, say the sentence using a low-pitched voice and speaking slowly. Repeat the same sentence using a high-pitched voice and speaking rather quickly.

Sentence 1   "Sure, I can handle this."

Sentence 2   "There are two more days before the end of the semester."

Sentence 3   "You need to apologize right now."

Sentence 4   "She never asks me to join in."

Did you notice your tone of voice sending out different messages even though you were saying the same sentence? Others hear these differences, too!

Your body language is a definite signal-sender. You can communicate, for instance (without saying a word) whether you agree, like or dislike a particular comment, activity or situation. Others will be able to tell how you feel by your posture, how you walk and even by your facial expressions.

When someone is talking to you, are you in the habit of constantly looking around, or crossing and uncrossing your arms (your legs?), or tapping your feet? Do you fiddle with your jewelry, scarf, tie, buttons or keep putting your hands in your pockets and taking them out over and over again? When you stand, sit or walk, does your posture show that you are a confident person who has high self-esteem? Do you frown or have a smile on your face when others are talking to you?

> **Hint**: Depending on the conversation, of course, there will be times when either a frown or a smile can be inappropriate!

Make it a goal to become an alert communicator. Be the kind of communicator that you wish others would be for you.

Social Responsibility

Socially-fit people are also socially-responsible. This means that you have reached a level when you feel confident making friends, do not feel uncomfortable in small or large groups and are always considerate about the feelings of others. If you have reached this level, then you:

❑ Pay attention to your appearance. You make sure you are well-groomed at all times and practice good hygiene habits.

❑ Remember to be polite. Saying please, thank you or excuse me are responses you say automatically and naturally.

❑ Make a special effort to please others **without** causing harm or discomfort to yourself.

❑ Easily step forward to introduce yourself to others. Then, going a step further, you feel very much at ease introducing someone to others as a way of making that person feel welcome.

❑ Participate in group activities. You consider being a member of the team more important than being the "star"!

❑ Find ways to resolve conflicts. You attempt to always go at least half-way in ending an argument.

Socially fit people make and keep friends. They experience less stress. They are comfortable to be around and have a healthy image about themselves.

Spiritual Sense

Some sense of spirituality is a needed ingredient for your overall well-being. The term, "spirituality" means different things to different people. To some, it has a religious meaning. It means that you have faith, pray and believe in a higher power on more that one day a week! In fact, part of your daily routine should either begin or end (perhaps both) with prayer or at least moments of silence expressing gratitude to your higher power. For others, having a sense of spirituality are those moments they set aside to experience and enjoy some "aloneness" time.

Taking about 20 minutes to just sit and reflect is all you would need. You could reflect on how thankful you are to be alive. Aren't you grateful that your health is good or getting better? Are you thankful for the strength it took to face and handle many of the problems you had in the past (last night, a week ago, a year ago)? What about how fortunate you are to have family and friends around you who care about you, keep you safe and encourage you to always do your best?

Including *spiritually* in your plan for personal growth offers many pluses. It brings the physical, mental, emotional and social sides of you together in a positive way. It can be a source of strength for you during troubled times. It can also help you feel more confident, reduce stress and make you a much healthier person.

If it is your wish to include spirituality on your plan for personal growth, here are a few suggestions.

- Attend services at your place of worship on a regular basis.

- Get more involved in activities at your church.

- Pull from your beliefs in a higher power for strength, guidance and comfort.

- Set aside some time to think only pleasant thoughts, to pray, meditate or just say "thank you" to your higher power.

  "Prayer is more powerful than a prescription!"

Chapter 3
Take "Control" of Your Time

The element of time can have a strong hold on you. Isn't that how you feel once you begin to run out of it? Wouldn't it be nice to get a firmer grasp on your time? It is possible if you have a plan. Develop a plan which will allow you to become more organized and be able to complete tasks using fewer hours.

> *"Extra time is almost always available*
> *with proper planning!"*

Examine your daily routine. Isn't it packed full of things to do? In fact, it is usually so full you probably cannot figure out what to do first! For example, you have to "juggle" or rearrange enough time to handle school activities and a part-time job. You have to be responsible for taking care of your younger sisters and brothers until your parents come home. Is preparing dinner most evenings your job?

For many, doing a juggling act every day is not unusual. What is unusual is finding a way to do all you have to do in a timely manner. Are you in the habit of putting things off until "later?" If so, then you need to re-think your priorities. Do you regularly feel rushed? Would making a plan and deciding to stick to it help?

What Is Time?

Lots of people (adults included) go through schedule-shock, just like you. "Schedule-shock" is having a list of things that really have to be done, and not knowing how in the world you will be able to finish! Do the hands on your clock scare you? This can bring on all kinds of stress. Time can also make you feel powerless. Why? Because it is absolutely impossible to make time "stand still" or "add" more to it!

Time is divided into moments measured in seconds, minutes, hours, days, weeks, months and years. It cannot be saved like money. It is always used (whether we want to or not) in 60 second portions every minute of every day of our lives. Here is an interesting fact: everyone has the *same* amount available to use. It doesn't matter how young you are, how old you are, what you do for a living or whether you are a student. The important point to remember is that it is *how* you use this amount that counts.

Since time is so valuable, using it wisely is a **must**. Wasting it is **unwise**. With good planning, many of the goals you set can easily be achieved in both an effective and efficient manner.

"Taking time for granted, now, could be a gift lost forever!"

How You Use It

The importance of time is constantly before you. There are specific amounts of time geared to attending school, completing homework assignments, handling household chores, cooking and taking care of younger sisters and brothers. You have pets to care for and errands to run. There are required visits to the library, doctor, dentist and optometrist. Plus, there are an assortment of church, community-related and other outside activities which require you to use even more time. For instance: basketball/cheerleader practice, golf, tennis or dance classes to attend, choir practice, neighborhood collections for-the-needy and, those workshops your parents feel you *absolutely and positively* have to attend!

Many of you work part-time. This takes a big bite out of your time because it means using as much as 4 hours after school or 16 hours on weekends. For some, using these hours to work is perfectly all right. You get a chance to earn money to pay for many of your own expenses like clothes, concert tickets or taking someone out on a date. For others, however, working is a *necessity*. A good portion of their earnings have to be contributed to the family's budget. This is especially true in today's single-parent homes.

If you are wondering, at this point, if there is any time left over for fun and relaxation—the answer is a definite *yes*! Believe it or not, there is a special pocket of available time that belongs *only* to you. It is called your "leisure" time. Only you can use it. Only you can decide *how*.

Let's look at ways you typically spend time on leisure activities. Here is a short list:

- Watching television
- Playing computer/video games (searching the web!)
- Talking on the telephone
- Listening to music
- Attending sports events/concerts
- Going to parties
- Going to the movies

Added to this list is the time you spend at shopping malls. Time spent at the mall usually consists of enjoying the company of your friends, meeting new friends, eating lots of cookies, candy, pizza and whatever fast food specials are being offered that day. What about shopping? Well, you do that, too, eventually! Can you think of a few more that might be added to this list?

How much time do you use on a *weekly* basis? Doing what? For how long? The chart below lists *approximate* amounts of time you might use on a weekly basis. These estimated hours are based on 24 hours per day x 7 days per week, or a total of 168 hours in a single week.

Your Time Use By Activity and Amount

Type of Activity	Estimated Hours Used/Week
Sleeping	56
Leisure, for fun/relaxation	40
Attending School	30
Bathing/Dressing	14
Doing Homework	10
Travel to and from school	5
Miscellaneous	13
Total	168 hours

Below is an explanation of how these approximate figures were calculated.

Sleeping: 56 hours per week

Based on 8 hours/day x 7 days. Let's face it, in order to get 8 hours of sleep a day, you would have to go to bed about 10:00 p.m. each night. For many, this simply does not happen. Some of the things that reduce your sleep time include after-school activities, late starts on completion of homework and early-rise times in preparation to meet the school bus.

Question: How many hours do you really use to sleep?

Leisure, for fun/relaxation: 40 hours per week

Based on 3 hours per day x 7 days a week for watching your favorite television programs; 1 hour per day x 7 days per week for video games; 5 hours per week (usually on either Saturday **or** Sunday) for fun at the mall; and 1 hour per day x 7 days per week for other fun stuff.

Included is some time to bathe and dress, and travel time to and from your destination.

Question: How much time do you use getting ready for a date?

Attending School: 30 hours per week

Based on 6 hours/day x 5 days. Most school systems require attendance for a total of six hours a day from Monday through Friday.

Question: Are you in a work-study program at your school which permits you to attend classes 4 out of 6 hours a day?

Bathing/Dressing: 14 hours per week

Based on 2 hours per day x 7 days per week. If bathing for long periods of time is not a particular joy for you, then you probably spend about 1 hour in the morning and 1 hour at night. (This includes getting dressed for the day and undressing at night.)

How long does it really take you to bathe and dress?

Doing Homework: 10 hours per week

Based on 2 hours per day x 5 days. The more time you spend on homework assignments the better! But, a **minimum** amount of time would be 2 hours each evening.

How many hours do you usually use each evening?

Travel to and from school: 5 hours per week

Based on 1 hour per day x 5 days. Whether you ride a school bus, drive or walk, you probably spend at least 30 minutes getting to school and returning home.

How much travel time do you spend?

Miscellaneous: 13 hours per week

This category includes those activities that might take as little as 10 minutes to as much as 3 hours. It includes for example, your part-time job, required babysitting responsibilities, household chores, or walking the dog.

Question: How much time do you use watching your younger sisters/brothers?

Now, estimate your own time use. Using the same chart add an additional column. A sample is provided below.

My Estimated Time Used Each Week

Type of Activity	Estimated Hours Used/Week	Amount of Time I Spend
Sleeping	56	_____hours
Leisure, for fun/relaxation	40	_____hours
Attending School	30	_____hours
Bathing/Dressing	14	_____hours
Doing Homework	10	_____hours
Travel to and from school	5	_____hours
Miscellaneous	13	_____hours
Total	**168 hours**	**_____hours**

Were you surprised at the number of hours you *really* use each week? Do you still think you need *more* time? If so, look again at your "leisure" hours.

Isn't it possible to simply *borrow* a few hours from this category? Sure you can!

Let's say you plan one Saturday to go to the movies, go shopping and have lunch. This will probably take about 5 hours. Instead of spending the full 5 hours, why not use only 3 of them—just to see a movie and have lunch. The remaining 2 hours could then be added to one of the other categories. Here is another suggestion: plan **not** to watch your favorite television programs for a few nights. Wouldn't this give you a few more hours each week to do something else? Couldn't you decide, instead, to use that block of time to work on an upcoming science project?

Look carefully at what you have to do. Figure out how much time you will need. Then, simply *borrow* what is needed from your "leisure" hours.

Practice setting priorities. What has to be handled, first? second? third? Next, which category needs more hours added to it? Do a bit of calculating. Now, can you comfortably borrow enough time to handle your list of priorities?

See, there **is** enough time, after all!

"Extra time is always available with proper planning"

Ways You Waste It

Almost everyone is guilty of *mis*-using valuable time. In many instances, this happens because you allow certain things to stop you from doing what has to be done. You waste time when you do not plan your time wisely. Putting things off until later is another time wasting habit. Not setting priorities can be a big waste of valuable time. How often have you neglected to do the most important thing, first? Time is often misused when you rush through tasks. In fact, by doing so you only end up having to do them over; and, then have to use even more time! Another waste of time occurs when you allow unexpected visitors and telephone callers to interrupt you. By taking a closer look at these time wasters you may discover ways to avoid them.

No Plan, No Action!

A plan is an outline for actions to be taken. Having a plan is very important. With one you will have a sense of direction. Without one, little can be accomplished. A plan allows you to set goals you hope to achieve. It can serve as a reminder about how you expect to attain your goals and help you stay focused on the timeframe needed to be successful. As an added bonus, by carefully following it, step-by-step, you will probably see a new side of yourself begin to surface. All of a sudden an *organized* you will emerge!

You can make a plan for practically everything you have to do. This could be for the completion of a task that will take as little as 30 minutes or as much as an entire year or even longer. Did you know that business owners, for example, make plans (or projections) about how many customers they intend to have five years in advance? You can make plans for what you have to do on a daily, weekly or monthly basis. Plans can be made for activities involving home, school, work, leisure time and career concerns. And, if you design a workable and comfortable plan, you will see improvement in your physical, emotional and spiritual fitness levels.

Making a plan requires the use of four basic elements: (1) setting a goal (or objective), (2) listing and prioritizing the steps needed to achieve that goal; (3) assigning a specific start time and an end time; and, (4) reviewing the plan (a couple of times) to ensure that it is workable and comfortable.

> **Tip**: A good planner should also include a few "what-ifs" actions to take, just in case!

Keep in mind that making and using a plan will require work, self-discipline and patience. But, it will be worth it!

> *"You delay but time does not!"*
> —*Benjamin Franklin*

Doing It Later

Also on the list of things that cause you to waste time is *procrastination*. Procrastinating is waiting until a later time to do what you should be doing—now!

Procrastinating is not a good idea. It can be harmful to your physical and mental health. It is a waste of today and now. It has a way of making you feel frustrated, bored or incapable of solving problems. Being a person who consistently procrastinates can also be damaging to how others see you. People will shy away from asking you to join in activities because they do not feel they can depend on you to keep your word. In fact, procrastinators tend to make others feel uncomfortable. Is this the image you want others to have about you?

You can overcome the urge to procrastinate. Whenever you feel the urge starting to rise, use a "Yes/No" question approach.

Yes/No to Procrastination

Yes	No	Question
❑	❑	Do I really want to allow this activity to make me feel frustrated?
❑	❑	Does this task have to be handled in one step or all in the same day? *(Most do not!)*
❑	❑	Is anyone depending on me to take care of this project today instead of tomorrow?
❑	❑	If I put off taking care of this task now, will it interfere with a particular leisure activity that has already been planned?
❑	❑	Am I energized enough to tackle this project today?
❑	❑	Is it really important to me to be able to complete this task today instead of tomorrow?

Review your answers very closely. If you look at them carefully, you will be able to determine whether or not to get started today...instead of tomorrow!

The "I's" Have It!

Having to cope with too many "I's" can be a tremendous time waster. The "I's" to avoid or at least comfortably be able to handle are:

Interruptions Unexpected visitors can put a big dent in your time. This also goes for telephone callers. Be straight forward with visitors. Tell them, in a courteous manner, that you appreciate their stopping by and wish you could but can't spare the time right now. Gently, yet firmly, let telephone callers know that they have caught you at an inconvenient moment. Ask them to call back at a specific time or offer to call them back. Handle interruptions as quickly as possible and continue where you left off.

Interferences The oddest things can easily block (interfere with) what you have planned to do. You might be in an area where there is loud music playing. Are you sitting in front of a window that has a great view? Is there a magazine laying around nearby with an article you started but didn't get a chance to finish? Is the television on? If your work space is so cluttered that it causes you to be distracted—for even a few minutes—time is wasted. You also waste time going from room to room gathering needed materials. Be aware of those things that block your planned time and make the necessary adjustments before getting started.

> **Tip**: Looking out a window with a nice view could make you daydream; so, close the curtains!

Intermissions Taking occasional breaks while working on a task or project is a good idea. Short breaks can help re-energize you. Taking longer breaks of 30 minutes to an hour could pose a problem. This amount of time is just too tempting! In fact, it could be so tempting you might decide to delay handling the original task until another day. You will then be back where you started, nothing will be accomplished and frustration will begin to set in. When taking breaks try to: (1) "break short" for success; (2) do stretching exercises; and, (3) only eat healthy snacks.

Intrusions Thoughts have a way of intruding on your concentration. And, during those moments when your concentration is broken, time slips away. Pleasant thoughts are especially hard to handle. These thoughts put you at ease and can lead to prolonged periods of daydreaming. Negative thoughts such as worrying about a troublesome relationship, family problems, grades, promotions, a recent disappointment or a health problem bring on feelings of stress and discomfort. Keep in mind that while you do not have control over when these thoughts will surface, you do have control over letting go of them. Practice letting go by staying focused on the task at hand. If necessary, take a 5 minute break and begin again.

Scheduling Your Time

By definition, a plan is "a method or way of doing something, that has been thought out ahead of time." A schedule is very much like a plan, but this is where exact timeframes are included. To get a better grip on your time, therefore, develop and use a schedule.

Schedules, after all, are not unfamiliar to you. You follow one every day at school or at your job. There are set times, for example, to board the bus, attend classes, and eat lunch. Using a schedule, therefore, should be no problem. And, developing one, will be easy! Consider the following points **before** making your schedule.

❏ It is wise to have a schedule that lists everything you have to do in order of importance.

❏ It is wise to work toward completing each item on your schedule. Make sure that you put a check mark beside each **completed** task. (You will be surprised at how good you will feel seeing the number of check marks begin to add up as you complete items on your list!)

❏ It is wise to keep within the time limits you have designated on your schedule. (If necessary, use an alarm clock!)

❏ It is wise to include time for breaks on your schedule.

❏ It is wise to "carry over" those tasks or activities that were not completed to the next day's schedule. (This might happen a few times. Simply try not to let it happen too often.)

Purchase an appointment calendar. Look for the kind busy executives use. These are usually in book form. It is designed to show a full week at a time. Some are divided to show an entire month at a time. Make sure there is plenty of space to write in. A number of these calendars are divided into 30-minute increments. Visit an office supply store and purchase the type of calendar that best suits your needs. Or, make your own!

"Setting priorities makes scheduling much easier!"

A Good Schedule

In general, a schedule is a tool that helps you to set time limits, complete a number of tasks, be on time and become more organized. A good schedule includes day, date and designated times. It lists activities to be completed in order of importance. It does not have an unrealistic number of tasks to be completed or an under-estimated amount of time for completion. It should be easy to follow and feel comfortable. If you have too many things to be done in a short amount of time, for example, you will end up feeling rushed, frustrated and unproductive. As a special note, having a schedule will only work if you make sure to carry it around with you at all times! Out of sight...out of mind?

There are two additional elements for a good schedule. First, you need to be sure to include "quiet" time. Consider scheduling a 30 minute block of time to be used **only** for relaxation purposes. This could be on a daily basis or once a week. It could be scheduled for when you get up in the morning or just before going to bed. Perhaps a specific day of the week would work better for you. The key is to schedule this time, use it only for relaxation and stick to it. The second element is plugging-in rewards. Review your schedule for end dates and times. Be prepared to give yourself a reward once you have completed a particular project or task. Look forward to that reward and you will find yourself actually motivated to finishing it.

> **Tip:** Be careful to select a reward that is healthy for your body, mind and overall well-being!

"One of these days is none of these days."
—English Proverb

Here is a simple exercise you might find helpful for relaxation purposes:

> Sit in a chair that allows or forces you to sit correctly in a comfortable position. Place your hands in your lap. Close your eyes. Take slow deep breaths. With each breath, tell yourself to relax—by doing so, that "breath" will relax you. As you exhale, tell yourself that all your tension and stress are leaving with that particular breath. Do this for several minutes (3-5 minutes) until you feel your body begin to relax. (**Hint**: Use your alarm clock!)

As a final note, remember that with patience and practice you can discover that there **is** more time available than you thought. So, isn't it about time to stop being afraid of the hands on your clock?

Chapter 4
Become a "More" Responsible Family Member

During the pre-teen, teenage and young adult years, your job is to strive to become a responsible person. This is especially true in your role as a family member. It is about this time that parents start looking for signs that you are beginning to mature enough to be viewed as a responsible individual. They look at how much respect you show toward family members; the amount of respect you have for yourself; whether you are cooperative and helpful; and, they weigh what you say versus what you do.

Are you on the right path toward becoming a responsible family member? Have you started thinking and acting in a rational and mature manner? If not, let today be the first day you show by your actions that their teachings and trust have not gone un-noticed!

The ParentPart

Most family units follow the same pattern. There are parents who have children living with them in the same home. Look at your friends. Does their family unit follow this same basic pattern? While most families look pretty much alike, some do have obvious differences. The most obvious is of course the number of parents in the home and the number of children. Another difference would be that only one parent lived in the home. Perhaps no parents were responsible for the children, and the grandparents or other relatives were the caregivers. Regardless of the structure, one set of experts believe that parents (or parent figures) all share an element of "sameness" where their responsibilities are concerned (Eimers/Aitchison). Below is what they had to say about healthy, unhealthy, and family relationships.

About the "Healthy" Relationship

"...healthy and constructive parent-child interactions (should) lead to warm and loving relationships. This in turn promotes the development of happier, more confident, and more secure children. In short, mutually rewarding family relationships are not just accidents. They are the *result* of *positive* interactions between parents and their children. However, the reverse is also true. Repeated parent-child interactions filled with scolding, tension, accusations, and unpredictable emotional outbursts can strain even the best of relationships...most parents don't want to seem cruel or inhuman...(they) should, instead, take a moment or two to think about how much their children mean to them and how good their child can make them feel...they make you laugh; they make you proud...they care what you think, what you say, what you do, and how you are feeling. They love you, trust you and miss you when you are gone. They probably come to you for just about everything...it's gratifying to be loved and needed like that. It's great to be a parent!"

About the "UnHealthy" Relationship

A key problem area in the unhealthy relationship involves antisocial behavior. "By antisocial behavior, we don't mean shyness or poor manners. What we're talking about here includes a variety of *high-intensity* behaviors performed at the expense of others or their property. Fire-setting, theft, and extreme cruelty are common examples of antisocial behavior. The repeated use of "hard" drugs and/or alcohol also falls into this category. Antisocial behavior is extreme, as well as dangerous. If you notice that your child is beginning to behave in this fashion, staying out very late or all night long, get some professional help right away. The longer you wait, the greater the chances are that someone will get hurt. And, if that happens, you and your child may well find yourselves up to your ears in legal problems."

About the "Family" Relationship

"...let's remember that family life is not always a bed of roses. Children are simply human and, of course, so are parents. And, as we all know, human beings have been known to get in each other's way or on each other's nerves at times. Of course, this happens in some families, more than others...problems will arise... (and) these problems can create resentment, anger, and exhaustion in even the most patient of parents."

These are your parent's guidelines. If it looks like a lot, it is! In fact, many parents feel that being a parent is probably the hardest job they have ever had. But, with your help, it can be a lot less stressful for both you and your parents. Don't be afraid to **work** with them...instead of...**against** them!

Family Structures

A number of different family structures exist these days. There are some who live in a home "...whose mother and father live together, or whose mother and father live apart, or who have only one parent, or whose parent or parents have adopted them, or who live with a parent and a stepparent, or who live with an aunt, an uncle, a grandmother, a grandfather, or other relative, or who have gay or lesbian parents, or who have foster parents" (Harris).

As you can see there are several different family structures. And, it shouldn't be surprising to find out that each has its own set of problems to be faced. Review the family structures which follow so you can get a better understanding about many of the "why's" of how your family operates.

A Mom, A Dad

In both real life and storybook fashion, the typical (or "traditional") family structure has a mother and father living with their children in the same home. For years in a two-parent family, the father always seemed to be considered the authority figure, the parent who made the most money, had a career or specialized job skill, established house rules and who handled miscellaneous repairs, or acting as judge **and** jury where punishments were concerned. Mom, on the other hand, was usually viewed as the caregiver and nurturer. She was the gentle one who stayed at home, worked (maybe) only part-time, cooked, cleaned the house, acted as nurse, chauffeur and homework helper. But, times have changed! Think a moment about the popular television series "The Cosby Family". Both parents had jobs, shared in household chores, raising their children and handled making family decisions from homework helping to giving advice on career planning — together. This same type of teamwork also exists in many of today's two-parent homes. What kind of problems surface in a two-parent home? Practically anything!

Just Mom, Just Dad

While most single-parent homes usually have just a Mom, some have just a Dad. A number of studies show that "the largest number of single parents are those who are divorced, but increasing numbers of people are choosing to give birth or adopt" (Frolkey) without getting married. Living in a single-parent family usually requires the children to be more sensitive to their parent's long list of things-to-do as parent.

Single parents experience difficulty financially because they only have their paycheck to depend on. They have to be able to juggle a job, their personal life and parenting completely on their own. This requires a lot of time and quite a bit of energy. Some experts believe that children in single-parent families have more discipline problems to handle. Boys, for example, seem to find it hard to "accept discipline from their mothers when they are not used to having their mother in that role." Another important area that poses a problem for single parents is how they feel emotionally. Many feel very much alone because they simply do not have the time (or energy) for social or leisure activities. This is, of course, as important for their well-being as yours.

Mom/Mom and Dad/Dad Families

Here is another two-parent family structure. The only obvious difference is that one of your classmates might have two Moms (lesbian women) **or** two Dads (gay men). In this same-sex family structure there are two parents that work, share the responsibility of raising children, making decisions and handling household chores, however, it is not their "parenting" skills that pose a problem for them and their children.

Some people do not approve of lesbian or gay relationships. This lack of approval is often based on their religious beliefs. For others, it is probably because they simply do not understand that it is possible to build a loving, caring and nurturing family structure when the parents happen to be either two women or two men. In order to deal with many of the problems in this family structure, it is necessary for both parents and children to learn and use positive coping skills.

Children, for instance (depending on their age, of course!), have to feel they are living in a loving and caring family environment and be open-minded. What are their parents' responsible for? Several things! It is their job to give, by example, the necessary coping tools that their children need to:

- Not feel different from their friends
- Minimize or eliminate feelings of "shame" for loving, caring and respecting their parents
- Handle episodes of discrimination in a "quick" and "comfortable" manner so that they can go on, and the subject of their having two Moms or two Dads, can be over
- Reduce and/or minimize hurtful comments from others that might surface.

In *Reinventing The Family,* by author Dr. Laura Benkov, "...the tasks for children are to find their strength in the face of obstacles and to sort out their own values in the face of opposition..." This is pretty much what being in a same-sex family structure is all about. The real question to ask yourself is: Am I able and personally strong enough to be a part of this kind of family structure? Are my parents?

Like most of the other family structures discussed, these same questions need to be (and, can **only** be) answered by you — for you. Give them some thought!

Adopted/Foster Families

Whether you are adopted or fostered, your family structure is not that different from either a two-parent or single-parent home. The only real difference is that you are not living with your "natural" or biological parents. Adoption is a permanent placement unlike living in a foster home, which is only for a temporary amount of time. Since the adoptive or foster parents have selected you to be part of their family, this arrangement is very special.

Emotional and behavioral problems are a main concern. Parents have to find ways to cope with their new relationship with the children. Children have to learn to adjust to not only a new set of parents, but in some cases, new sisters, brothers and friends, too. These readjustments are further complicated when the structure is a foster home. Remember, foster homes are only for a temporary length of time. On the list of emotional problems, some children experience feelings of sadness, confusion, aloneness and fear. At some point adopted children begin to become very curious about who their real parents are and the adoptive parents have to make the decision of when to tell them. Foster parents have to contend with children's deep feelings of insecurity and abandonment. It is also not uncommon to see problems arising with lying, stealing and sleep disturbances. The key to coping with these and other difficult feelings and actions depends on the strength of the parents to cope, coupled with a sense of trust and cooperation by the children, to make things work.

Step Families

Every year people remarry and most of them bring their children to the re-marriage. This particular structure is a "blending" of two families. Along with this "blending" comes a number of different conflicts. According to medical authorities, "a new stepfamily faces many challenges. They have no shared family histories or shared ways of doing things, and they may have very different beliefs" (AACAP). Some children feel divided between the parents they live with and the "divorced" parent who lives someplace else. And, since this is a separation, it can cause any number of unhealthy results. There is also the issue of a newly married couple who might not have had enough time to get adjusted to each other **before** taking on the responsibility of raising their new spouse's children. Caring for another person's children can make both the natural parent and stepparent very uncomfortable, insecure and uneasy. In short, this can be especially hard for everyone. Some family members will be openly angry, feel frustrated and powerless simply because they do not know what to do about it.

Discipline is a touchy subject for this family structure. Step parents are often hesitant about using their authority (as parents) to discipline their stepchildren. And, as time goes on, if their lack of discipline is not enforced, behavior problems could begin to occur. One of the biggest problems for step families is money. It is not the lack of money that becomes a problem. Disagreements start over "how much money should be spent on **your** children versus **my** children versus **our** children. One rather unique situation that occurs is when step children begin to feel uneasy about actually "liking" and respecting their stepparent. It is as if they are being disloyal to their natural parent in some way. A major concern of both the parents and children is being able to give and get respect. With time, this **can** happen, but not without a lot of work, patience and understanding from all family members.

Mixed Race Families

According to many experts, the number of mixed race families in America is steadily increasing, due to the rise in interracial marriages and relationships, as well as an increase in transracial and international adoptions.

Their research has shown that multi-racial children do not differ from other children in self-esteem or comfort with themselves. Many tend to be high achievers with a strong sense of self and are tolerant of diversity. A key problem for this family structure concerns the dreaded "discrimination" issue! They are faced with lots of teasing, whispers and stares when they are with their families— just a most uncomfortable feeling.

There are several things that parents can do to help their children cope. They can:

- Talk openly about race, cultures and differences in skin color, hair texture, and facial features.

- Help their children deal with racism.

- Live in a diverse community where the sense of being different is minimized.

- Understand that their children may have feelings of guilt or disloyalty to a parent if they choose to adopt the racial identity and/or culture of one parent.

Did you notice that when you compare this family structure with the others, there really isn't much difference, is there?

Inappropriate Actions

What are appropriate and inappropriate actions? Being a responsible family member means you are a person who is dependable, reliable, and trustworthy. It means you have reached a stage of growth when you: are polite, use proper table manners, can control your temper, respect authority, do not invade the privacy of other family members, do not tease, shout, swear or talk back. It also means you are able and can cope with situations that might endanger the well-being of not only yourself, but others as well. On the "inappropriate" side, there are several actions to be avoided. Listed below are only a few for you to give serious thought.

Judge not my words, for it is my deeds
and demeanor that matter!

Disrespect

If you know and do respect yourself, you will almost always respect others! By being disrespectful means that you do not care about the feelings of others, being polite or even worrying about the consequences which might occur. Some of these consequences might include parental punishments, loss of friendships, being tossed out of school, losing a job or could lead to some level of legal actions. Being disrespectful can be harmful to you on both an emotional and physical level. Keep in mind that the saying: "do unto others as you would have others do unto us" **does** work!

Disruptive Behavior

Acting in a disruptive (or disturbing) manner, over and over again, is inappropriate and can be harmful to you and others. These kind of behaviors include:

- Breaking home or school rules
- Throwing things when you are angry
- Staying out past curfew or running away from home
- Giving threats, starting or getting into fights
- Purposely hurting (or torturing) animals
- Setting fires and damaging property.

Many of these inappropriate actions might require professional attention. If you notice that any of these actions are things you find yourself doing (or thinking) on a continuous basis, seek help from either a parent, school counselor, pastor or medical professional. Remember, your health and overall well-being might be at risk!

Lying

You might be tempted to lie for any number of reasons. Some people use lies to escape being punished, to get revenge, to make others like them or to escape embarrassment. Lying can cause others to mistrust you, disrespect you and keep you from being included in social settings. It can also make family relationships stressful for both you and other family members.

Music and Videos

Watch what you purchase and view! Pay particular attention to music and videos with themes that might be destructive. Some encourage and glamorize drug and alcohol use. Often there are pictures and explicit lyrics presenting suicide as an "alternative" or "solution" as a coping tool. There are even themes that focus on devaluing women, violence toward women, incest, satanism and human sacrifice. How would you feel if your younger sisters or brothers were listening or looking at some of these?

Non-Listening Attitudes

Listening is more than just hearing what a family member is saying. Do you ignore them when they want to talk about something they feel is important? Do you dismiss what they are saying as being unimportant? Are you in the habit of saying "we'll talk about it later" and never do? Non-listening attitudes can make bad feelings creep into any family relationship. Keep in mind that you want others to listen to you sometimes, too!

Stealing

It is always inappropriate to take what does not belong to you. Borrowing a family member's property is only all right if you have their permission. Stealing (taking without permission) from a family member, however, is not all right and shows a lack of consideration for that person's property rights. People steal for many reasons. Would you steal because someone dared you to? Will stealing make you more popular at school with a certain group? Is stealing the only available alternative to getting something you need? Do you consider stealing and getting away with it, an attractive challenge? Did you know that stealing on a frequent basis is a sign of some type of emotional disorder? Think about it!

Communication Hints

One of the secrets to becoming a more responsible family member is being able to communicate with all members of your family. Good communication skills are a **must** on your list for personal growth! With these skills, you will be able to say, act and respond in an appropriate manner with both family members and others. You learn communication skills from many sources. While it begins at home, you also learn from friends, teachers, church, coworkers, social/sport/leadership organizations, community leaders, television, radio and even how-to books from the library.

Without good communication skills you might go through periods of feeling alone, have low self-esteem, lose friends, be ineffective at what you do at home, school or at your job.

There are ways to improve your communication skills. Try avoiding the following:

- Avoid giving orders to others to do what **you** want them to do.
- Avoid giving threats to others that you will do something if they **do not** do what you want.
- Avoid telling others what they **should** do.
- Avoid letting others feel, by your questions or comments, that their concerns are **not** important.
- Avoid making others feel guilty about their feelings and concerns.

Communication skills also include being able to "read" body language. You do not always have to be talking or actively listening to communicate. Sometimes, your facial features, the way you stand, the tilting of your head, crossed or uncrossed arms/legs, or certain hand movements can tell someone (even if they are across the room) how you feel. These are the kind of communication "tip-offs" that should also be avoided.

Try observing others. Have you ever almost known what they were going to say or how they really felt about a particular subject by just observing their body language? To evaluate your own, ask someone to video-tape you (without you knowing about it, of course!) so you can see what kind of gestures you make.

Another communication give-away is your tone of voice. One expert believes that certain "vocal qualities help us to tune into the mood" (Bolton) of the person we are listening to. In other words, we are actually able to figure out that person's emotions! Really look at the following list to determine if you have either observed others or yourself.

The Meaning of My Voice

Tone of Voice	Probable Feeling or Meaning
Monotone voice	Boredom
Slow speed, low pitch	Depression
High voice, emphatic (assertive) pitch	Enthusiasm
Ascending tone	Astonishment
Abrupt speech	Defensiveness
Terse speed (abrupt), loud tone	Anger
High pitch, drawn-out speech	Disbelief

The bottom line is really not quite as simple as many people think! When communicating with others, remember that most people begin learning *how* at home. Watch what you say, how you say it, be careful about your body language and give particular attention to your tone of voice. With all of these elements in mind, you can (hopefully!) be assured that whatever message you intend to give will be accepted and understood by those you are communicating with.

▍**Hint:** Practice, observe and practice some more!

Sure Signs of Responsibility

Signs that you are on the road to becoming more responsible are numerous. Many of these signs begin at home and slowly seep into your outside life. You will find yourself handling home, school and employment tasks without being asked to do so each time. You will automatically resist the temptation to blame others for things that were your responsibility and recognize that it is perfectly all right to make a mistake. You will make decisions on your own, keeping the well-being of your family (and your own) clearly in mind as a priority. You will also accept and follow rules established by family members, school officials or your employer **without** arguing and **with** the use of positive communication skills.

And, as a responsible family member, you will definitely make sure that you are taking care of yourself, first — on a healthy level — by protecting, giving attention to and actively taking charge of your physical, mental, emotional, social and spiritual fitness. By not doing so, you endanger both your family members and others around you.

Let's look at a few more.

Remember to Remember

You are responsible for remembering things—on your own. Should you forget, be prepared to accept or abide by the consequences of forgetting! Have you been guilty of forgetting to do something your parents asked you to do—within 10 minutes or less? Did you forget the promise you made to tutor a friend who had an upcoming exam? Were you supposed to go to work an hour earlier and forgot? Do you often forget where you left your keys? If you think there is no hope for you, think again! Try these tips.

- Be sure you really hear and understand what has to be remembered. Repeat it several times (silently to yourself).

- Write on a piece of paper, what you need to remember. Put these notes in places where you *couldn't possibly* miss them (under your pillow, tied to your toothbrush, inside a shoe)!

- Make a special effort to handle the request (or promise) as soon as possible. (Waiting until a later time **could** be a problem especially if there are time restrictions involved!)

- Make a mental "picture" of *where* you put a particular object. What is located near the object? Was the object placed inside, beside or behind something else?

- Talk to yourself. Say out loud, "I have to remember to return the library book by 4:30 on Wednesday." **or** "I parked the car on Level G and it is three parking spaces from the elevator."

  > **Tip**: Avoid using definite "specifics" like colors, models of cars, building markings, a person's distinctive hair color, etc. These things can change from day-to-day and give you a very difficult (or practically impossible) time with your unique—and specially-designed— memory retention approach!

- Go to the library and get a "memory improvement book" or attend a one-day seminar.

Remember, you **can** be a more responsible person if you remember that you can!

Private Practices

Privacy is a personal privilege. It should and needs to be protected and respected. How would you feel if someone were to open your mail, enter your room without knocking, listen in on your telephone conversation or read your diary? Doesn't this sound like a nightmare? Are these some of the things *you* have done to members of your family? Have some of these *same* things happened to *you*?

While it is true that you live with your parents and must follow their rules, you are still entitled to your privacy. Doesn't this sound great? Well...as great as this sounds, you need to keep in mind that a few more details are also included with this wonderful statement!

Parents want to do the right thing by being "honorable" and **not** snooping in your room, reading your diaries or examining the contents of your bureau drawers. They want to talk to you and resist the urge to stand close simply to smell your breath—in case they suspect you have been smoking or drinking. They also do **not** want to observe your weight increase should you be attempting to hide a possible pregnancy, or constantly watch your behavior, just in case, they suspect you are using drugs. Parents would really like **not** to think about these things. They are too negative. They are too stressful. These are also areas that make them feel like failures in their role as parents. This, in turn, probably promotes some very stressful episodes that both you and your parents have to face. But, with your using the skills and following your plan for "personal growth" even these periods can be handled.

If you do not give your parents or other members of your family a reason to disrespect your privacy or feel uncomfortable enough to "suspect" that there is a reason to "snoop", they probably will not!

Keep in mind that, for some unknown reason...they always seem to know or find out! Think about your experiences or those of your friends. Doesn't this seem to be case? With this in mind, why even try? Re-think, instead, about your choices! If you are **not** hiding anything, then, hopefully, you will be able to convince your family or other family members without any problem. If not, be prepared to be your own defense attorney and prove your case!

Those who invade another person's privacy often *do not* even realize they are doing so! Quite often, in fact, they do not realize how uncomfortable or annoying their actions may be to another person. So, remember that the best way to **get** privacy is to **give** it! Some pointers on privacy to keep in mind include the following:

- Always knock before going into a room and wait for permission to enter.

- Mail that is **not** addressed to you should **not** be opened.

- Listening in on someone's telephone or personal conversation is a sign of bad manners.

- Avoid hanging around when someone is entertaining guests.

- Avoid borrowing someone's personal belongings without first, getting their permission.

> *"Let there be spaces in your togetherness."*
> *—Kahlil Gibran*

Home Alone Have-To's!

Some of you have to take care of yourself and younger sisters/brothers during the period after you get home from school until your parents get home from work. If this is one of your responsibilities, there are several basic Home-Alone things to do.

Call your parent as soon as you come home. This is, of course, so they will not worry! After placing the call immediately look around to be sure everything is locked and secure. Take a moment to review the "plan" for what to do in case of an emergency.

> **Tip**: A good place to have this plan would be on the refrigerator or somewhere close to the telephone!)

This emergency plan would include what to do about medical emergencies, fire, strangers or disturbing telephone calls. Your next step would be to start following the items on the schedule or checklist that you and your parents have discussed. Are you responsible for making a snack for your sisters/brothers? What are you supposed to do before starting your homework? Do you have special chores to handle? Is it your night to start dinner?

Responsible Home-Aloners keep all of these details in mind, handle them and feel good about themselves for being someone their family can depend on!

Face Family Problems

Your family is not the only family that has problems! Many families have to face such problems as: alcoholism, child/spouse abuse, teenage pregnancies, drugs, divorce, suicides, imprisonment or the age-old problem of money matters! If you find this to be a "scary" thought—it is. It is also a reality in far too many homes. Listed below are some tips to help you face whatever problems exist in your home.

- If you feel there is a family situation that bothers you, make a note to yourself describing the situation in detail. Re-read your note so that you will be able to think a little clearer about it. After looking at your note for a couple of minutes, you may discover that it really isn't a "problem" after all. (This is also a good way to calm down before taking any unnecessary action!)

- Discuss your feelings with your parents. Be open and honest. Ask for their help.

- If they can't help you or you'd rather not talk to them, ask for help from your school counselor, a favorite teacher, minister, neighbor, an adult you feel comfortable talking with or go to one of the many "free" clinics in your area and ask to speak with a physician that can help you with a non-physical problem. Try calling one of the many "hot-line" numbers advertised on television. (They usually do not require you to give your name, are quite helpful and won't make you feel embarrassed for calling).

"Family problems can be resolved
quicker with open discussion!"

- Once you have found a way to handle the problem, your next step would be to "share" with your parents. (Unless it is your parents who are abusing you. If that's the case, talk to your school counselor, minister or an adult that you can trust.) Let them know your concerns. Tell them what you have done in order to handle the problem. *Ask* for their advice. (Discussion is very important!)

- Be responsible enough to act on your decision. Understand, however, that you might experience feelings of guilt about your opinion, the decision you make or the subsequent actions you take. Strive to look at as many sides of a troublesome situation as you can—*before* taking action.

Facing family problems will **not** be easy! It will take strength, patience and a real understanding of right versus wrong conduct. But, remember, it is *almost always* worth the effort you put into it!

Pet Care

Pets are living creatures who can bring quite a bit of enjoyment to all members of the family. Pets are also special. They always seem to love you regardless of your moods, can make you laugh and are there when you just need the company. Take time to care for them by making sure they are comfortable, fed, clean, loved and happy. You can do this by sticking to a schedule. Depending on the kind of pet you have, of course, know when it is time to feed your pets, give them fresh water, refresh litter boxes, provide exercise or fresh air, and what day of the week (or time of day) to do what has to be done. Pets are family, too!

Getting Closer

In lots and lots of homes, *getting closer* to family members seems like an almost impossible task. Everyone is just too busy! Some are cooking, watching television (in separate rooms, of course!), talking on the telephone, attending meetings, working on school projects or on travel for their jobs. Being too busy to be together, however, does not have to be a problem!

With proper planning there are several ways to bring everyone together. Simply **plan a family activity**! Here are a few suggestions to get you started:

Family Meeting Night
Schedule weekly (or monthly) meetings for discussion purposes. It need only last for about an hour. You might even want to make a list of the questions to be discussed. Don't forget to include the younger members of the family! You might want to ask them: "What kind of exciting things happened at school this week?"

Family Fun Night
Plan an activity that is suitable for all the members of the family. Your list might include: going to a movie, bowling, dinner, bike riding, hiking, an indoor or outdoor picnic, playing games or a talent show where everyone has to perform!

Story Night

Have each member of the family "make up a story" and present it to the rest of the group. Set a time limit of about 10 minutes. (Remember to allow more time for the younger family members and be sure to applaud!)

Puzzle Night

Work on the completion of a jigsaw puzzle together. This could take several weeks depending upon the number of pieces. Limit this time to one hour a week. When it is completely assembled, plan time to glue the pieces in place, and prepare it for display on a wall in a particular room. (This makes a nice reminder of time spent together!)

Repair Night

Join forces and repair minor household fixtures, toys, bookshelves and other furnishings. Don't forget to include cleaning marks off the walls!

House Night

Plan to organize kitchen/bedroom drawers, or linen and coat closets. (This is also a good time to clean out those "packed" bedroom closets. Remember, it will certainly be easier to do with extra help!)

Cook Night

Make plans for a smorgasbord where everyone has to prepare a dish. For the younger ones, the idea of putting different breads on a special plate could be considered their contribution. Be responsible for planning the menu, setting the table and acting as host or hostess.

Awareness Night

Pick a "serious" topic that needs to be discussed and shared with the rest of the family. (For example: home safety, drugs, curfews, telephone call limitations, allowances, dating or use of the car.)

"Me" Night   This night would require that each of the family members get up to talk about themselves. They would get a chance to discuss their likes, dislikes, favorite subjects, future goals, or upcoming school/work events.

Newspaper Night   Select different sections of the newspaper and pass them out to each family member. Everyone should be asked to look through their section for about 15 minutes. They should then be prepared to discuss **one** article with the group. The little ones can pick out something from the comic section, but their assignment will be to **color** what they select and tell why they picked certain colors or just allow them the honor of sharing what they have done!

*"Proper planning allows you to
make a point about your purpose!"*

These suggestions will require a bit of *advance* planning:

Sightseeing Trip   Plan a sightseeing tour to one of the local places of interest. The more unusual the better! Look in the Yellow Page Directory to get some ideas.

Weekend Away   Gather location information and costs for a short distance weekend trip that the entire family might enjoy. (Be sure to plan ahead— at least 3 to 6 months in advance!) Contact a travel agency. Tell them you would like to plan an inexpensive family trip and ask them for their help. Many agents will gladly assist you.

Tip: For trips, be sure to include in your plans a "things to pack" list. This is especially important for younger sisters/ brothers because they will need to be kept occupied on a fairly regular basis!

Some "togetherness" time activities are more a matter of *doing* than planning. Here are three very special activities!

Do Not Disturb   Treat your parents to an evening with no interruptions. Take charge of the younger children. Politely tell visitors and callers your parents cannot be disturbed and assure them that you will deliver their messages. This will only work if you make sure to keep your promise to provide some "quiet" time for your parents!

Personal Notes   Write personal notes to members of your family. Do this once a week or a few times during the month. Put them in places they couldn't possibly miss! Your notes could say for example: "Good luck on your spelling test tomorrow"; "Thanks for cooking my favorite meal"; "I thought about you today"; or even, "I'm sorry I upset you yesterday." The nicest note that any member of your family would adore getting would be a note that simply said: "Hi! I love you!"

Kiss, Kiss!   Get into the habit of ending the day by giving each family member a hug, kiss or simple handshake. "Touching" is healthy and makes everyone feel good!

There are hundreds of other ideas. Be creative! Allow your imagination to take hold and plan activities that everyone will enjoy — together.

> *"Family time can create pleasant memories **now** for the future!"*

Caring for Physically Challenged/Elderly Family Members

Do you have a parent who is physically challenged, grandparents or other elderly family members who live with you? If so, then, you have first-hand knowledge that they need special care. It will not be easy sharing care-giving responsibilities with the rest of your family members. In fact, there will be times when you feel resentment about changing your plans to accommodate theirs. As a responsible and caring family member, however, you need to be willing to do what you can so no "one" family member has to do it all!

Give some thought to comfort, convenience and safety. Have "grab bars" been installed around the bathtub/shower and toilet? Does this family member need a special shower chair or bench?

▌**Tip**: Consider installing a hand-held shower attachment.

Make sure there are non-slip strips in the tub. Provide a mirror that is at a comfortable level.

Since some of your physically challenged or elderly family members will be alone, while you are at school and parents are at work, the kitchen should be a major consideration. Appliances like the toaster, can opener, coffee maker and microwave oven need to be located at a comfortable level. They also need to be able to reach can goods, spices and "unbreakable" dishes. Consider the purchase of a "reacher" device so they can easily get to what they need. In the bedroom, it is very important that they are able to get in and out without a lot of help. Search for an appropriate mattress, an attachment to be used for eating, writing letters or playing solitaire, and make sure the telephone is located in easy reach and programmed with "emergency" telephone numbers. It is also a good idea to keep a plastic pitcher of water nearby and have night lights positioned through the room. You might also want to be sure that all "remote-control" items are readily available. In order to feel and be independent, these family members need to be able to function as "normally" as possible. Having access, by remote control, of the television, radio, and security system will do just that.

Following are a few more tips.

- Always tell your family member what you are getting ready to do. This will allow them to "mentally" prepare themselves for what is about to happen.

  - *"I'm going to help you take your clothes off so we can get ready for your bath."*

  - *"It looks like its time for your medication, do you want a cool glass of water or juice, instead?"*

  - *"Okay, it's time for my exercise! So, help me help you out of that wheelchair and onto the bed!"*

- When "lifting" remember to balance your weight, keep a straight back and to bend your knees. Bending forward from the waist and lifting with your back muscles could injure—you! Don't try to actually, lift! Instead, attempt to either push, pull or roll.

- If help is needed with bathing or other personal care, know and believe, that you can be helpful! For bath time, assemble all of the supplies that will be needed (wash cloth/sponge, soap, towel, shampoo/conditioner). Did you remember to clean her/his ears, comb his/her hair and apply body powder? Have you observed that he/she needs to see a professional about foot care?

  > **Tip**: Ask a nurse or home care expert how to give a bath, how to transfer someone from a wheelchair to the bed and how to give a back rub to relieve discomfort.

- Don't forget to put her/his dentures in a cup to soak over night.

- Cut food in small portions. Can she/he eat solid foods?

- If necessary, limit fluids a couple of hours before bedtime.

- Should she/he have problems swallowing large pills ask the doctor which pills can be crushed with a spoon.

- Take a look at a "medical supply" store catalog to find helpful items that will make your job a bit easier and the life of a family member who is either physically challenged or elderly a lot more comfortable.

By keeping their needs and wishes in mind, design a plan-of-action. In the end, they will be comfortable, elevate their level of self-esteem, and reap the rewards of having a sense of independence and gratitude for the amount of caregiving you provide.

Okay...this is it! You now know what to do to become a more responsible family member and, you know what the experts are telling your parents. It is now up to you to do *whatever* it takes to ensure that your personal growth plan succeeds in this all-important area!

Chapter 5
Associate With "Positive" Friends

Having friends is important for your personal growth. Everyone needs to have at least **one**! A friend is a person who you know, respect and trust. You can almost always count on her/him for support, companionship and to give advice they feel will keep you from doing harm to yourself or others. Friends do all of this because they think you are important enough to "care" about.

Friendships

There are no set timeframes about how long it will take to become friends with someone. Friendships simply happen. You could become friends from first sight. Perhaps you and the other person "felt" a special connection. And, one of you took the first step to introduce yourself to the other. It is also possible to meet someone and "instantly" dislike them. After a matter of days or even weeks, however, you suddenly become **best friends**. This can happen! When it does, you wonder, later on, *how in the world the two of you became friends*! Consider, also that there is no set length of time about how long a friendship can go on. Will you still be a "best" friend to someone who has moved away? Suppose they have **not** stayed in touch with you for over a month? Believe it or not...the friendship can, and often does, go on!

Friendships come in many forms. At the top of the list are those you consider to be your "best" friends. They keep your secrets and readily defend you when necessary. They are usually your constant companions. Then, there are your "distant" friends. These friends have moved away (across town or to another city) but continue to keep in touch as often as possible. You exchange letters, greeting cards and telephone calls. You both feel excitement making plans to get together on holidays or to spend time during school breaks.

Another group of friends would be the relationships you establish with a classmate or co-worker. You see each other every day. You share school or work-related interests and activities. Since association with this group is *restricted* to a particular area (school or a work environment), the friendships which develop usually are *not* of a personal nature. On the other hand, however, you might just find a "best" friend in this group. It certainly isn't impossible.

Parents can also be added to this list. Some parents have a remarkable ability to change from the role of "parent" to the role of "friend." This role change allows them to give you a sense of freedom to discuss certain things in both an honest and sincere manner. When talking to a parent, who has agreed to *change-hats* and be your friend, you get a chance to feel more *open and comfortable* in your discussions with them. You will also be able to go places together, enjoy *mutual* interests and share secrets.

> Tip: If you do not ask your parent to "change hats" expect them to simply react as a parent. It will be up to you to say: "please put on the hat of friend so we can talk about something that I want to share with you!

Making, having and keeping friends allows you to experience the positive side of getting along with others. You will also gain a better understanding about someone else's feelings and become more caring for someone other than yourself.

Being a Friend

Being a friend means remembering to keep your word. There will be several occasions when you will find it is quite easy to do this. For example, if you agree to meet someone at a specific time and place, be sure to arrive on time. Being late gives others a negative impression about you.

Another way in which you can show others that you keep your word is to do whatever you have promised to do. Make a promise only when you intend to keep it. This is a sign to others that you are dependable. Naturally, there will be times when you just cannot keep that promise because something unexpected might have happened. But, knowing you usually keep your word, your friends will forgive you.

"Friendship is always a sweet responsibility never an opportunity."
—Kahlil Gibran

I'm "Ear" for You!

Like you, your friends will from time to time, need to have a friend who can sit still and merely—listen! They would, for example, listen, make no comments, allow you to talk about whatever is bothering you and **not attempt to offer advice** during your venting (let-me-just get this out) period!

As a friend, this will **not** be easy. You will be tempted to interrupt them in the middle of their venting to interject (give) your personal opinion. You might even feel a need to say to your friend: "If it were **me** I would do..." By offering advice about what you would do, might cause harm to your friend. Keep in mind that the way in which you would handle the same type of situation, **might not** be the more comfortable way in which your friend should handle it! So, be aware of giving advice—too quickly—without, **first**, looking at both your side as well as your friends'.

Being a positive "ear" means that you:

- Willingly accept the responsibility to listen

- Make a special effort **not** to infuse (offer) what you would do if placed in the same situation

- Keep **quiet**, making sure that your posture reflects that you are **only** "listening".

> **Tip**: Your body language can easily let others know you are either for or against them. So, be very careful to at least appear to be neutral!

Enriching Experiences

While lots of people like to talk about themselves, many do not because no one seems to take the time to ask what they are all about, nor does it seem they're actually listening.

Everyone leads an interesting life. What you might consider to be dull, others see as valuable and sometimes exciting. Having a friend who is a bit different from you can be a source of enrichment for the friendship. It can also enhance your life experiences. Do you have a friend who is different because of their ethnic culture? Is this friend physically challenged, older, living a lifestyle that **feels** uncomfortable to you? Does this friend have a religious belief that is **not** within the teachings of your church? Were they raised in a different city? Have they shared a "secret" with you that they are living with a terminal illness and do not know how long they have to live? All of these individuals can give an added dimension to your friendship. Differences can be good.

Cliques Can Be Cumbersome

Cliques are a group of friends who share many of the same interests. For some it might be that everyone in the group is especially popular. For others it could be their style of dress. Then there are those who are typically referred to as **"The Jocks"**. Their common interest is, of course, all of them are athletes! Be careful about cliques. You will find cliques in almost every area of your life. They are formed in school, college and on jobs. In order to be included you will usually have to change something about yourself. Some of these changes might be the way you walk, talk or dress.

To "fit in" you might have to alter your views about any number of beliefs you have. Suppose you are required to give up some of your other friends because they do not fit the profile of the clique you are in? How would that make you feel? Think about it. Do you **really** want to be just like everybody else?

No Friends?

If you often say you don't have any friends, you probably don't! This is especially true if most of your time is spent on activities that only require **one** person—you. Is your leisure time filled with watching television, reading books or playing video games? When you do decide to venture out, is it to shop alone, go to a play or pickup a fast food meal and eat it in the park—alone? If this is your lifestyle and you are comfortable, fine. But, if you want to start having friends in your life, you are going to have to change!

As a first step, consider that people will only be interested in you if you show an interest in them. Remember who you are and be willing to let others know, by your actions, that being your friend would be a **good thing**! Volunteer to work at a community center. Take a course to learn how to do something fun. Something different. Karate, tennis and golf would be great. What about skiing, white water rafting or learning to sign? Couldn't you add to the list taking instructions to become an aerobics instructor or coach to the little-ones on a neighborhood team?

> **Tip**: Be careful about golf, it **can** be a one-person activity, but is really no fun unless you are with others!) Any of these suggestions will almost assuredly open the door to you making friends. Try one!

Positive Friends

Would you prefer to be around a person who makes you feel *unhappy*? What about a person who constantly talks to you about your faults? How about a person who expects you to do something you (secretly) feel is wrong?

Wouldn't you rather have a friend who made you feel good about yourself? A person who was proud of your accomplishments and always made sure to congratulate you? Wouldn't it be nice to have a friend who *shared* your views on right versus wrong conduct?

If this is the kind of person you wish to have as a friend, then you need to choose people who can have a "positive" influence in your life.

> *"Healthy friendships*
> *enhance positive experiences!"*

Pause for a moment to review some of the typical characteristics of a person who could be considered a "positive" friend.

- ❑ Friends do not ask friends to do something wrong which might be harmful to you or others.

- ❑ Friends are not jealous of your accomplishments. (They are proud of you and say so!)

- ❑ Friends compliment you on your achievements no matter how "small."

- ❑ Friends tell you the truth about yourself in a manner that is not offensive or hurtful because they "care" about you.

- ❑ Friends do not concern themselves with how you look, dress or how "popular" you are. (They like you for yourself!)

- ❑ Friends are loyal and can be trusted with secrets.

- ❑ Friends do not make sarcastic or humiliating remarks about you to others.

- ❑ Friends respect you when you are not afraid to say "no."

- ❑ Friends respect your rights, opinions, political and religious choices even when they do not agree with you!

- ❑ Friends are supportive and dependable.

- ❑ Friends cheer you "up" when you are "down."

Are your friends **really** friends? Are you? Make a special effort to be the kind of friend who has many of these positive characteristics. Then, decide to "only" associate with those you feel truly qualify to be called—your friend.

Dating

When dating be sure to demand respect, give respect, know where you are going ahead of time, carry emergency travel money and, leave a note (or tell someone) about your possible whereabouts—just in case.

▌ **Hint**: Your personal safety should always be a first priority!

Dating is a matter of personal choice. **Your** personal choice! Do not feel obligated to engage in inappropriate activity for any reason. Do not try to go overboard for the sake of impressing your date. Keep in mind that in probably 95% of the time, the person you are dating really **wants** you as her/his date because they like, appreciate and respect you. What about the other 5%? Don't worry about this figure. You will more than likely find out within the first hour or so what their real motives are and be able to plan your strategy for going home early!

If you have a set time to be home, make sure your date knows in advance. And, be sure not to come in **after** that time.

▌ Tip: Parents set a specific time for your safety and protection, as well as for their own peace of mind!

Interracial Relationships

There are many people who still judge others based on their skin color, race or religion. Family members, friends and even perfect strangers can try to make you feel uncomfortable if you are dating someone they view as different.

But, don't let them!

If you really care about this person, and she/he cares about you, too...take the time to discuss ways of handling others around you. Be honest with yourself. Are you sensing negativity from others because you are secretly uncomfortable? Think about it carefully. You just might be missing out on a very good friendship!

Online Dating

Be careful with this one! How do you know that the other person has not exaggerated or lied about themselves? Can you really be sure about her/his age or emotional stability? Is it possible that the other person has a private agenda that could be harmful to you physically or members of your family? These are serious questions to consider, especially since these are days filled with so many weird people with only the absolute worst intentions in mind! And, if you absolutely "have" to meet this person face to face, keep your personal safety in mind.

Troublesome Times

All friendships go through stages of ups and downs. There will be times when you irritate your friend, or your friend irritates you. You disagree about something, so you stop speaking. You promise yourself that you will never include that friend in anything, ever again! Guess what? This is normal and occurs between most friends. In fact, even adults go through troublesome times with their friends, too.

Troublesome times will require an adjustment. In order to make adjustments, however, both of you will need to sit down and *calmly* discuss your differences. There are a couple of suggested adjustment activities you might wish to try.

Adjustment Activity #1: "We Had an Argument"

This activity is designed to help you sort out your feelings.

Yes	No	Comment
❏	❏	She/he is one of my best friends.
❏	❏	She/he is a nice person and someone I can trust with many of my secrets.
❏	❏	She/he makes me feel good about myself.
❏	❏	I can depend on her/him when I am feeling unhappy or depressed.
❏	❏	Our argument makes me feel just awful!
❏	❏	I don't want to ever be friends with her/him ever again.
❏	❏	We have never had this kind of argument before.
❏	❏	We have argued about this before and I am surprised that it is happening again!
❏	❏	I want to talk about this disagreement so we can go on with our friendship.

If you have more "yes" than "no" answers this is a good sign that you and your friend can come to a mutual agreement about your disagreement!

Adjustment Activity #2: "Can We Talk?"

Materials needed for this activity are: a watch, (2) pencils, (2) pieces of paper

Step 1:   Locate a quiet place where you and your friend can be alone. Make sure to agree on a mutual place and be sure you will have at least 45 minutes of uninterrupted time. Toss a coin to see who will be Person A and who will be Person B.

Step 2:   Person A is to be given 2 minutes to talk about how she/he is feeling and why. Person B is to listen, not interrupt and keep track of the time. At the end of this 2 minutes, Person A takes the watch and allows Person B to talk. As before, Person A is only to listen, not interrupt and keep track of the time.

Step 3:   Person A and Person B then need to write on a piece of paper 5 questions to ask each other based on what has been said. Take about a minute or so to do this. When both of you have finished writing your questions, proceed to the next step.

Step 4:   Person A is to ask each of the 5 questions listed one at a time. Pause and allow Person B to answer before going to the next question. Listen closely to the responses given and do not ask additional questions at this time.

Person B then gets her/his turn. Following the same process as Person A.

Step 5:   Person A must now ask Person B this question: "Do you want to remain friends?"

Person B must now ask Person A this question: "Do you think we can work this out?"

Once you complete these 5 steps, it is now up to the two of you to decide what to do next. Do you want to continue to talk about your disagreement? Have you decided that you would rather not continue? Or, did you discover that simply listening to the other person's side gave you more insight into how she/he was feeling and all of this was simply a misunderstanding?

When attempting to repair a friendship never be afraid to agree to talk about it. Always make a special effort to be a serious and courteous listener. Remember to remain calm and do not disrespect the other person (or yourself) by using inappropriate language, yelling or constantly interrupting the other person.

Keep these tips in mind and use them. Chances are *very* good that the friendship will pick up where it left off. You might also find that your friendship will become even *stronger*!

Role Models

People you admire, respect and want to be like, are called "role models." That person could be a parent, classmate, best friend, teacher, politician, attorney, sports figure or an entertainer. It is the level of respect and desire you have (to be like that person) that creates another form of friendship.

It does not matter if you have actually met the person. In your mind, it is a matter of wanting to be as accomplished as they are in a particular sport, as popular as they are in school, or as successful as they are in the business or political world. For those you know personally, it is your observation of how they handle themselves, that is so impressive to you. In many cases, you become aware of accomplishments through television/radio, newspapers, magazines and books. Or, you might choose these individuals on the basis of the positive comments made by others.

"Role models are people, do not expect perfection!"

Role models are good to have. They can inspire you to want to achieve similar goals or give you the necessary encouragement to reach even higher!

Chapter 6
Avoid "Negative" Activities

You are engaging in negative activities if you drink, take drugs, join a gang, smoke, make bombs, carry a gun, frequently run away from home, have sex or think suicide is the answer. Many people consider some of these activities to be an alternative to problems they have to handle. This is definitely not the way to cope!

Some Straight Talk!

Negative activities can be especially harmful to your physical, mental and emotional fitness. In many instances both your social fitness and sense of spirituality will suffer, as well. Do not expect any of these activities to be an alternative in order to cope. This is strictly negative thinking and will eventually harm you. Negative activities block your valuable time and prevent positive actions that are good for you. And, while you are the one who is actually engaging in negative activities, severe harm can be caused to others around you.

"Negative activities are never a protective shield!"

Negative activities can also be deadly! Some of these activities could result in your own death. Can you imagine how you would feel knowing that something you did caused the death of someone else? These things do happen. So, think more than twice before deciding to engage in negative activities of any kind.

Depression

A key element for those who decide to participate in negative activities is probably because they are going through feelings of depression. Feeling depressed is not an uncommon emotion for your age group. You have a lot of life-related adjustments to handle—completely on your own. You might have concerns that your weight, height, sex, race, political, sexual orientation, economic status (where you live or how much money your parents make), student status (whether you are a gifted student or viewed by others as being a bit "slow"), are keeping you from "fitting-in". This can be uncomfortable, a bit scary, and make you feel so uncertain about yourself, you will begin to wonder which way is up!

A person can become depressed for any number of reasons. For example: disliking your physical appearance, being rejected by others (not fitting in), having to handle a death in the family, finding out they have a major illness, or having a reaction to some medications they are taking could very easily alter (change) their moods. Added to this list would be the death of a friend or chronic (frequent periods) of unemployment.

Everyone copes with depression differently. Some simply sleep a lot. Some become so stressed they are not able to think clearly. Some throw their hands up and say: "okay, I'll do this just because!" Then, there are those who may even act-out in the form of violent behavior.

There are signs that indicate you or someone you know might be depressed. Some of the signs to look for are:

- ❑ Feeling sad, uneasy or desperate
- ❑ Feeling guilty, worthless or helpless
- ❑ Having problems sleeping too long or not enough
- ❑ Experiencing a lack of interest in activities that are usually pleasurable
- ❑ Noticing a drastic change in appetite and/or weight loss or gain

- ❑ Feeling "tired" too often

- ❑ Feeling restless or frequently irritated

- ❑ Having constant backaches, headaches or stomach problems that do not seem to disappear with over-the-counter medications

- ❑ Having serious thoughts, too often, about death or suicide

> **Hint**: If any of these symptoms have been going on for more than a few days or, especially, a couple of weeks, professional help might be needed!

Do you know someone who is depressed? Are you? To help get over feelings of depression, it is a good idea to find something to do that will take your mind off whatever is making you feel this way. Get active doing something positive, talk to someone you trust, have a good cry, exercise or read a book of "stupid" jokes!

Negative Activities

Each of the negative activities discussed below can be dangerous and harmful to both you and others around you. As a special note, since **all** of these activities are "negative" and one is **not more** negative than the other, each activity is presented below in alphabetical order.

> **Tip**: read for full understanding, give serious thought to each one and remember that **you** are the most **important** person in your life!

Alcohol

If drinking alcohol hinders your health or daily activities, you might have an alcohol problem. Alcoholism is a disease. It is a chronic (long lasting) disease. It is also considered to be a progressive disease (instead of getting better over time, it quite often seems to get worse!)

Drinking alcohol on a long-term basis *can* cause liver, nerve, heart and brain damage and lead to high blood pressure, stomach problems and sexual problems. It can also be the basis of violent behavior, accidents, social isolation, and difficulties at school, work and in the home.

What to do instead: If you (or someone you know) has a drinking problem, consider getting help, immediately! Get involved with an Alcoholics Anonymous group. Encourage family members to get involved and as part of your support group. Understand, trust your feelings and seek the strength you need to work on you!

Bombs

Thinking about or actually making a bomb could result in the death of others or even *you*! Re-think the "why" that you are considering making a bomb. Re-think the "why" of how you intend to use it. If your reason is to fulfill a class project assignment, what are the chances that it will accidently go off? Would you be prepared to handle the deaths or injuries to your classmates? Should someone else have the same idea, would you readily try to talk them out of it? Is your anger getting in the way of your positive coping skills? Will this bomb be used as a coping tool to resolve a problem you (or someone you know) is going through?

What to do instead: Quite simply, don't make a bomb. Look for an alternative coping tool that will not endanger others or you!

> **Hint:** More and more schools are paying very close attention to those who show an interest in bombs, destruction, and overall hate-related behavior. They have to...there are a lot of lives at stake!

Drugs

Don't use drugs! Say "no" to drugs! Drugs can kill you! Using or selling drugs is illegal! You have seen and heard these messages over and over again. These messages are everywhere; on television, radio, posters plastered on billboards, buses and flyers handed out on the streets. You constantly receive these messages from family members, friends, neighbors, teachers, counselors and pastors.

Are you *really* listening? If not, you should!

Many use drugs as a coping tool to handle everyday life experiences that are stressful, uncomfortable or to be able to fit-in socially. While you might think others do not know you are a drug user or abuser, they know. Some of the signs include: an obvious change in sleeping or eating habits, moodiness or negative behavior, school problems or frequently being absent, a lack of interaction with friends or completely ignoring a favorite hobby or activity, stealing, lying or damaging what once was a good family relationship.

Drug misuse or abuse can be extremely harmful. On the list are: marijuana, cocaine, heroin, an assortment of different street drugs and prescription drugs. Added to the list are tranquilizers, sedatives, painkillers and amphetamines. You will know you are misusing or are a drug abuser if you suddenly start to feel either a physical or emotional "need" for a particular drug. You may not even realize the level of your need until you try to "stop" using it!

Do you think you *might* have a problem with drugs? See how many "yes" answers you have after completing the following set of questions.

Am I Misusing Drugs?

Yes	No	Comment
❏	❏	Have you tried to stop taking drugs completely and discovered, after a few days, you could not?
❏	❏	Do you get irritated, upset or angry with others when they discuss or suggest that you stop using drugs?
❏	❏	Are you jealous of people who use drugs and appear to remain pretty much in control?
❏	❏	Has using drugs caused problems with family relationships, problems at school, when driving or making and keeping friends?
❏	❏	Have you missed an unusual amount of time from school or work over the past 6 months?
❏	❏	Do you believe that you can stop whenever you want?
❏	❏	Do you frequently go on binges with drugs when you are alone and for no particular reason?

❑	❑	Have you experienced "blackouts" (when you cannot remember what you did, where you were or who you were with the day/night before or on a number of occasions)?
❑	❑	Have you had thoughts about what your life would be like if you were **not** using drugs?

If you answered "yes" to three or more of these questions, you might have a drug misuse or abuse problem. Get **immediate** help from a professional!

What to do instead: *Really listen!* Decide, today, to stop using drugs. Keep your plans for future enrichment and success a major priority. Look, listen and learn about the hazards of using drugs. Become an expert about using "positive" coping skills and use them. Ignore peer pressure from those who promote or encourage the use or selling of drugs. Keep always in mind, that *you* are the most important person in *your* life!

> **Special Note:** Taking drugs is definitely dangerous because these narcotics dull the senses, are expensive and ultimately, can ruin your life. While there are many reasons for **not** taking drugs in the first place, one of the main reasons is because a person who begins to use them may find that she/he cannot **stop** using them. You might, for example, find that you have formed a **habit** of using drugs and **cannot** live without them! This could then lead to improper or unacceptable behavior such as committing crimes to obtain money to buy the drugs your body (and mind) are craving.
>
> It is your responsibility to make the decision to avoid taking drugs. It is your responsibility to make the decision **not** to experiment with drugs. It is also your respon- sibility to avoid listening to or being encouraged by others to take drugs. And, if drugs are being sold in your community or in your school, avoid them—"just say no"—and as soon as you get a chance, report the activity to the proper authorities. (You should do this anony- mously.)
>
> *"Saying **no** today paves the way to a positive tomorrow!"*

Eating Problems

Are you or someone you know, so obsessed with being "thin" that a priority in your life is to avoid, at all costs, gaining weight? Do you know someone who is addicted to food? These questions concern eating-disorders. Below is information about three of the more common eating disorders to look at carefully and definitely avoid.

Anorexia Nervosa

Anorexia is an eating disorder where there is significant weight loss resulting from excessive dieting. Anorexics are so obsessed with being thin that no matter how much they really weigh, they still consider themselves to be fat. Their bathroom scale has the final word. If they have lost weight, they feel successful; gaining even one pound is a sure sign of failure. Anorexics often become withdrawn, engage in excessive exercise, experience fatigue, fainting spells and headaches. It is not uncommon for them to frequently use laxatives or diet pills to control their weight. Many tend to only eat diet foods, have feelings of guilt or shame about eating, have difficulty eating in public and while they will happily cook for others, they will not eat. They look, to others around them, as individuals who have lost far too much weight. In their minds, however, the mirror vision they see is a reflection of someone who is at (or continuously working on being) at the perfect weight! Yes, they do this, on purpose, to be and remain thin! Did you know that many Anorexics do not even think they have a problem?

Bulimia Nervosa

This eating disorder is when someone will eat anything they want and *immediately* take whatever action is necessary to get rid of what they just ate. Sometimes the immediate action taken will happen **before** the end of the meal! It is not unusual for them to force themselves to vomit, abuse the use of laxatives, diet pills and enemas, engage in excessive exercise and use fasting as forms of *immediate* action. Bulimics are typically "secret eaters", make frequent bathroom visits and constantly complain about having a sore throat. They avoid eating at restaurants or planned social events that include eating. Bulimics experience depression, mood swings, very low self-esteem and fatigue on far too frequent a basis.

Bulimics, unlike Anorexics, do not *look* starved. Their goal is usually to maintain a normal weight and continue to *look* healthy. While they may *know* and *accept* the fact that they have a problem (an eating disorder) it is their perception of how their *outward* appearance is, that counts. In fact, to them, how others see them is so important that they will do almost anything to keep their secret—a secret!

Compulsive Overeating

Overeating can and does lead to obesity. Compulsive overeaters use food as a coping tool to deal with stress, emotional and uncomfortable life situations. They binge on food but do not purge. They are often depressed, avoid activities because of embarrassment about their weight, go on many different diets and typically eat very little in public. It is not uncommon for Compulsive Overeaters to feel that their weight is the reason they either succeed or fail in personal relationships, at school, on the job and in their social life. Very much like Bulimics, weight is their central focus—even though they *know* they have a problem.

What to do instead: Tell someone you have a problem and ask them for help. That person could be a friend, school counselor or a doctor. By telling someone you have a problem, you have taken the first step. You have admitted that there really is a problem and you want help and support to be able to stop! Concentrate on physical activity for enjoyment and healthful reasons. Be more proud of *who* you are than how you *look*! Forget about having the ideal body size and weight you see in movies, on television (do not forget about those weight-loss commercials that come in between!) and your favorite magazines. Do not be surprised when you (or someone you know) suddenly discovers that it is not your physical appearance that is attractive and draws others to *want* to be around you, it is—you!

Gangs

Joining a gang **can** mean flushing your morals down the toilet! Gangs promote a *false sense* of love, discipline, belonging, recognition, power, companionship, excitement, self worth, physical safety and protection. Belonging to a gang also encourages violent behavior. Gang members use violence to show how much power or authority they have over others. They use guns, knives, bombs and an assortment of implements to harm, maim or kill others. Being in a gang has, for many years, been made to appear to be very exciting and an escape from family or social pressures through movies, television programs and some rap performers' music, videos and style of dress.

> **Hint**: Lyrics coupled with the right music **can** be quite inviting. So, enjoy the music **but** really listen to the words— you might not like what is being said!

Gangs advocate (support) violence as a tool toward leadership. They use violence for survival purposes when they feel threatened by anyone for practically any reason.

Gangs are a community within themselves. The survival and well-being of their community, is, unfortunately, based on the level of control they have using violence as a coping tool. Since many gang members are school-age youth who have very low self-esteem, you or someone you know, could be at risk of being approached to join. Many join gangs for a number of reasons. Some of these reasons include:

- The need to feel a sense of belonging
- The need for personal recognition and power
- The need to have friends and a sense of excitement in their lives
- The need for physical protection from others.

Would you really want to join a group of people whose main activities are based on using violence? Would you, or someone you know, really want to be responsible for harming or killing somone just to feel a sense of belonging or a sense of (false) love?

What to do instead: Work on improving your level of self-esteem and coping skills. Become a more involved family member. Try to get more active in school activities so there is no room to include participation in negative activities. Make sure to give serious consideration and take positive action to protect your personal safety. If you feel uneasy, uncomfortable or threatened by a gang member, **tell someone immediately**. Gang members can be very persistent when recruiting new members. So, simply remember to just say "no" when approached to join!

Graffiti

Defacing private property on purpose is a sure sign of immaturity. It tells others that you do not respect public or private property. Many paint, scratch and generally mark-up walls, statues, sides of buildings, private homes, park benches and even subway cars. They sometimes write profanity, racial slogans or signs. This kind of negative activity often costs several thousand dollars for clean-up or replacement. Along with this negative activity is the possibility of facing criminal charges.

What to do instead: Don't do it at all. Find a positive alternative activity!

Guns and Firearms

The Children's Defense Fund's latest information released in 2000 showed that in a single year: 3,761 children and teens were killed by gunfire, 2,184 were murdered by gunfire, 1,241 committed suicide using a firearm, 262 died from an accidental shooting, 2,197 were European-American, and 1,416 were African-American.

If you do not receive a "safety-chat" about using guns or firearms, then do not use them! Having a gun or firearm in your possession can make you experience a sense of power over others. It can also be such a curiosity that you might even want to share the fact that you have one with your friends. This is **not** a good idea because guns and firearms **can** be very dangerous for you and others around you! A firearm could be a gun, rifle, machine gun, shotgun or a pistol. The size of the firearm makes no difference because all are dangerous.

Never handle a firearm unless you have your parent's permission. When you do, a responsible adult should always be with you. If you find a firearm, it is never a good idea to touch it. Inform an adult or call the police and let them know where to find it. Playing games with firearms can be extremely dangerous. These are not toys!

Never point a firearm of any kind at others, pets, birds or other animals (including BB guns, toy guns, water pistols, darts, bow and arrows, etc.). And, do not allow anyone to point a firearm at you. If this should happen, immediately leave their presence for your personal safety.

Safety Concerns

While gun laws, rules and regulations differ from state-to-state, there are a few basic safety tips to keep in mind if a firearm is in the home.

- Always keep firearms out of the reach of children!
- Firearms should never be left loaded and unattended.
- Never assume that the firearm is "unloaded". Make it a habit to **always** handle a firearm as if it is **loaded**. Do not squeeze the trigger to test it!
- Be careful not to accidentally point the firearm at others. When handling a firearm—stay alert!
- Handling firearms while under the influence of drugs or alcohol (including some over-the-counter medications like cough, cold or allergy medicines) can be very dangerous because you may not be as fully-alert as you need to be.
- Store firearms and ammunition separately. Ammunition should be stored in a metal container such as an ammo box.

Be protection-minded. Do what you can to protect children, family members and friends. Avoid taking any form of firearms, knives, or other implements to school (or anywhere else). Disassociate yourself from those individuals who do! It is against the law and you could get into a lot of legal trouble, damage your future and/or bring an end to someone's life—or your own! Also remember, to never let *anger* be the force that directs your actions.

"Fury and firearms can be a deadly mixture!"

Playing Jokes

Playing jokes on others is **only** funny if there will be no physical or emotional harm caused. Remember, everyone **cannot** take a joke! Defacing personal property, as a joke, is inappropriate. Threatening to assault someone, as a joke, is not funny. Performing dangerous stunts, as a joke, is not funny. It is also considered inappropriate to purposely insult, embarrass, or publicly make fun of someone in the presence of others. Can you take what you give to others?

What to do instead: Be sure the person you pick **can** take-a-joke! Never make jokes about a person's weight, height, religion, ethnic background, where they grew-up, eating habits, their physical appearance, how they walk, talk, or smell. Do not make threatening remarks, write a threatening list about who you intend to assault (attack) or make-up an impending (forthcoming) life-threatening activity you are planning, call 911 to report a crime, fool around with fire hydrants, make-up stories about a kidnapping, or, say you saw a robbery, a child being rapped or a wife-beating happening—as a joke!

You could endanger others by your actions. Remember that, depending upon the level of your joke, you **can** face some legal stuff like:

- Being fined a particular amount of money
- Criminal charges
- Having to serve time in jail.

Profanity

Using profanity (cussing) can paint an ugly picture about you! Profanity goes by many names. Among them are: cursing, swearing, use of vulgar (ugly, bad or offensive) words. Profanity is probably constantly around you. You hear it at home. Your friends use it. You hear it in many of the movies you watch. But, that does not mean using profanity is okay or an acceptable form of communication. Some people use profanity when they are angry, to get attention or to gain control over others. Some use profanity, so often in their conversations with others, that at some point, it becomes a habit. Can you imagine talking to a teacher, someone who is interviewing you for a job or your pastor and "slipping" by using one of those 4-letter words?

This form of communication is both inappropriate and can be extremely offensive to others. And, when used during those times when you are angry, can be viewed as a form of verbal abuse.

What to do instead: Work on improving your communication skills so you will not have to use profanity when talking to others. Find some other words! Bad words can be insulting, harmful, hurtful and very inappropriate. Break the habit—now—so you will not continue to be viewed as an "offensive" person to talk to!

Railroad Trespassing

Depending on where you live, of course, playing a game of "beat the train" with on-coming trains is a definite negative activity! According to the Federal Railroad Administration (FRA) "nearly all trespassing fatalities (deaths) are preventable by staying off railroad tracks and property".

Playing with trains is only all right if the trains, tracks and landscape are toys—model trains, miniature trees, grounds and houses. In real-life, however, you can endanger your life by playing games with real trains or being on railroad property **without** permission. The FRA defines a trespasser as "a person who is on that part of railroad property used in railroad operations whose presence is prohibited, forbidden or unlawful." Railroad tracks, tunnels, trestles, bridges and yards (the grounds) are private property and should not be used for recreational purposes. Did you know that as a trespasser you could be arrested and fined by the railroad or local police?

What to do instead: Never play "train" games with a **real** train. Look for and observe all train property signs, rules and flashing red lights. Avoid walking on the tracks!

"Smart pedestrians live longer!"

Running Away from Home/Homeless Youth

Running away from home is only **one** alternative to handling personal problems. And, running away as a means of coping can lead to even more problems! Did you know that there are several categories of runaway and/or homeless youth? In a brochure published by The National Network of Runaway and Youth Services, the following definitions are offered to describe these different categories.

- **Runaway youth** refers to a young person under the age of 18 who is away from home at least one night. Governmental definitions add that this is "without parental permission," because many leave home to find a safer environment.

- **Homeless youth** lack parental, foster, or institutional care. These youth have left home often with the knowledge of their parents or legal guardians.

- **Throwaway youth** are young people left to fend for themselves because parents or legal guardians have thrown them out of the home without concern for their welfare.

- **Street youth** are long-term runaway, homeless, or throwaway youth who have become adept at fending for themselves on the street.

- **System youth** have been or are in custody of the state due to child abuse, neglect, or other serious family problems. Some are placed in a series of foster homes and may eventually leave the system of their own volition (because they feel a need to protect themselves on a personal, mental or physical level!).

This brochure goes on to include a few facts about what happens to a young person who runs away from home. Here is what they had to say:

> "A youth who runs away or is thrown out often has no choice but life on the streets. The need for shelter, food, clothing, and protection becomes a matter of survival that can lead to drug use or abuse, sexual exploitation, and crime. Unless an emergency shelter or specially designed outreach and transitional living services are available to help, chances for survival are questionable."

What to do instead: Of course...don't run away from home! Do whatever is needed in order to be able to cope. Seek a professional if you feel (or a friend suggests that you need one). **Never** feel that you are alone in your misery or have to handle uncomfortable situations—totally alone! Do not be afraid to talk. Talk to your school counselor, pastor, a neighbor you truly trust, a medical professional or your parents (**only** if they are not the "involved" parties that are causing your discomfort!) Never be too proud to seek help! Too many run-away youth end up homeless! Is this what you *really* want?

Sex

There is not a whole lot of new advice that can be shared about becoming sexually active during your teen years. To be or not to be sexually active is a decision that only *you* can make. It is personal. It is important enough to be given lots of serious consideration and much thought. Your decision should not be guided by the pressures of your peers, as a form of rebellion against parental controls, to satisfy your curiosity, as a tool to either impress or keep that "special someone" in your life or in response to a dare (challenge).

Experts at the American Academy of Child and Adolescent Psychiatry had this to say about getting pregnant:

Teen pregnancy is usually a crisis for the pregnant girl and her family. Common reactions include anger, guilt, and denial. If the father is young and involved, similar reactions can occur in his family. Babies born to teenagers are at risk for neglect and abuse because their young mothers are uncertain about their roles and may be frustrated by the constant demands of caretaking. Some teenage girls drop out of school to have their babies and don't return. In this way, pregnant teens lose the opportunity to learn skills necessary for employment and survival as adults.

Becoming sexually active during your pre-teen or teen years **could** result in:

- Becoming pregnant

- Having to drop out of school

- Being a teen parent and having to cope with an enormous amount of responsibilities that will be both emotional and financial

- Getting a sexually transmitted disease (venereal disease) like genital herpes, genital warts, gonorrhea, hepatitis B, syphilis and even—the absolute worst—AIDS

- Having to cope with emotional/stressful periods because your decision was to say "no" (for whatever reasons)

- Tarnishing your reputation by being viewed by others as someone who is always *available* to have sex, regardless of the consequences.

Let's take a moment to look a bit closer.

Expect to feel afraid about the day you have to tell your parents.

Expect to have to consider the possibility that you might have to drop out of school.

Expect to be required to think about the "financial" aspects of having a child (hospital bills, food, clothes, babysitters, daycare, etc.)

Expect to have *thoughts* about abortion or adoption (even though these ideas are really not the ideas you grew up believing were acceptable alternatives!)

Expect to go through a number of physical discomforts during your pregnancy because your body has not, necessarily, reached the maturity level required for childbearing. What you might have to endure would include, for example, morning sickness, feeling tired and having the urge (need) to sleep more often than usual, experiencing heartburn, backaches, swollen feet and hands, leg cramps and unusual eating habits that may tend to cause excessive weight gain (aside from the baby's weight)!

Expect to think the way that many teen moms think, that since you are the exception, and feel fine, pre-natal care (going to the doctor while pregnant) is really not necessary! This is a wrong and dangerous assumption. Every pregnancy is different. And, even a doctor cannot predict that you will have a normal or uncomplicated pregnancy and/or delivery. Your responsibility for the well-being of your child is to seek medical attention, immediately; follow the doctor's orders and take care of yourself and your baby by eating healthy, exercising and taking your doctor-prescribed medications. You should also avoid alcohol, cigarettes and drugs.

Expect to experience a number of changes in your life. Your time will no longer be totally your own. You will have to share time with your child. This will mean no dating, going and coming when you want to, no attending parties or being with your friends. Where dating is concerned, whether you are the "mom" or "dad", you will have to face *rejection*, on some level, from others who prefer **not** to become involved with you because you have a child. Particular concern will also have to be given to scheduling practically all of your time around your child's needs—first!

Expect a number of teen fathers to: (1) place the blame for the pregnancy on you because you did not **insist** they use protection; (2) decide **not** to help out financially; (3) ask you to marry them so they can make everything "right"; or, (4) say that their pride was hurt because you (probably due to their reaction of anger) said something like: "You said you loved me! This **is** your baby! I can't believe that you are acting this way and saying what you are saying!"

What to do instead: Get in touch with your true feelings and be sure your decision to become sexually active is based on what *you* consider to be appropriate for *you*. Do not allow your peers or that "special someone" to influence you to do anything that does not feel comfortable to you. Should you feel an absolute "need" to become sexually active, **please remember to use protection!**

Smoking

Yes...you have seen most of the commercials. You have read the Surgeon General's warning on each and every pack of cigarettes you purchase. You have also been able to observe the many adults who are trying, with a **lot** of difficulty, to break the habit. Smoking and use of "smokeless" tobacco like snuff or chewing tobacco is a definite health hazard, can be addictive and really is *not* all that attractive.

Interested in a few scary facts about tobacco in the African-American community?

- The money African-Americans spend on cigarettes in just one day would be enough to send nearly 2,000 youths to college for an entire year.

- African-Americans tend to smoke cigarette brands that have higher levels of tar and nicotine.

- Three out of four African-American smokers buy Menthol cigarettes. These types of cigarettes have added chemicals that make it easier to inhale smoke deep into the lungs.

A couple of reasons that many teenagers begin smoking or using "smokeless" tobacco is probably because their peers do. Many want to fit-in or be included. Let's keep in mind that this is a personal choice, in spite of the fact that your parents have given numerous lectures on the hazards of smoking or using "smokeless" tobacco. Have you decided to smoke (or use "smokeless" tobacco) to *get back* at your parents? If so, keep in mind that you will be the one who suffers on a physical level and **not** them!

Smoking **can** lead to heart disease, lung cancer (and even death), a yellowing of your teeth and fingernails, addiction to nicotine, a *real* drain in your wallet and, there are laws that say if you are under-age, it is illegal for you to make a purchase.

If you are a smoker, then at least be a safe and courteous smoker. Here are a few **musts** for smokers:

❑ Never lay a cigarette on the edge of a table, counter or other piece of furniture;

❑ Never toss a lighted cigarette out of a car window;

❑ If you are in a setting where there are **no** ashtrays available, chances are it is a "non-smoking" area, so wait to light-up or leave the area;

❑ Do not blow smoke in someone's face or allow smoke to drift in their direction;

❑ Always ask others for *permission* to smoke in their car, home or in their presence. If they say "no," it is courteous behavior to honor their wishes.

Non-smokers know who they are and how they feel about others smoking around them. It is either "okay" or it is not. In any case, at least be honest and courteous to those who smoke around you. Do not be afraid to ask the smoker **not** to smoke in your presence, your car or in your home. Simply say: "I really prefer that you **not** smoke when we are together." You will probably only have to say this a couple of times. If you have to say it several more times, do not worry, the smoker will eventually get the message and either honor your request or avoid you for a short time—until they get over being a bit upset with you—and eventually get over it! In either case, you will have done what you felt was best for *you!*

What to do instead: If you do not *start* smoking (or using smoke-less tobacco) then you will not have to learn how to *stop!*

Suicide

As a pre-teen, teenager or young adult, the kinds of life-adjust-ments you find yourself facing can be extremely new, uncomfort-able and oftentimes—frustrating. But, please know that you **can** cope. Know also, that thinking about suicide is a definite sign of depression. And, suicide is absolutely the *worst* coping tool to consider!

Suicidal thoughts or actions are often linked to several elements. On the list are drug and alcohol abuse to seek some sort of *relief* in order to *escape* from uncomfortable situations for a "short" (tem-porary) period of time. If a person's family support system is unsta-ble, bound by negative emotional threads, or is obviously unsupportive, the chances of using "positive" coping skills for sur-vival can often trigger this person to ask her/himself the question: "Why bother?". Death and divorce, feeling unloved, going through periods of self-doubt or feelings of inferiority have a way of fueling thoughts of suicide as an alternative. There is also the ele-ment of feeling helplessness or hopelessness. In fact, these feelings can be so over-powering (stressful) that common sense alterna-tives simply do not exist in the minds of those considering suicide.

What to do instead: Learn and use positive coping skills. *You* are, after all, the most important person in your life!

Should a friend or relative mention suicide, view and treat their dis-cussion—*seriously!* Considering what they are saying as harmless chit-chat or making jokes—is **not** a good idea. As a **first** action, ask the person if they "think" they are depressed. Then ask them to tell you **why**. This will promote a discussion which just might allow them to "vent" (talk about what is bothering them). Taking the time to "listen" and knowing how to respond could make the difference between an attempted suicide and a successful one!

What to do instead: Be mentally and emotionally prepared to be a "shoulder" to someone who needs to simply talk. Be cautious, however, to just be a listener. Do not be judgmental about their problem or situation. Do not offer advice except to gently suggest that perhaps they also need talk to the school counselor, a favorite teacher, the pastor at their church or a medical professional. Solving their problem is not your responsibility. Saying what you would do in the same situation is inappropriate because your job, at the moment, is to simply listen! While it might not be easy, always attempt to remain calm. Give your full attention. And, remember, both your body language and facial expressions can induce (bring on) either a calming affect for this person or make her/him feel that you are not really being sincere.

Violent Behavior

Using violence to cope with any situation is never appropriate behavior! Many people use this form of behavior to: settle a disagreement, gain control over others, show how "brave" they are, or to fulfill a "dare." Some even participate in violent activities so they can be accepted by a particular group.

This is unhealthy behavior. It includes physical, verbal and sexual abuse in the form of hitting, hurting, shooting, stabbing, poisoning, sending "hate" letters, making threatening telephone calls, defacing (damaging) personal property, or stalking (following someone in order to make them afraid). These are only a few examples. Unfortunately, there are many, many other types of violent behaviors. What you need to keep in mind, however, is that the end result could lead to criminal charges being filed against you, the death of others, or even your death!

What to do instead: Look for non-violent ways to cope with problem situations. Talk to a person you trust, a counselor or your pastor. Contact an organization (Hot-Line) that can give you guidance.

*"Violent behavior **never** leads to an acceptable resolve!"*

$a\gamma in9$ No!

Since you or someone you know might be approached to engage in negative activities, it is important to remember that you can choose **not** to. All it will take is for you say: "no!" Having the ability to say "no" is often difficult for some people. You might even discover that this word plays an important part in your plan for personal growth.

Here are some examples of how to say "no" and get your point across **without** insulting, feeding into someone else's anger or causing physical/emotional encounters for yourself.

Saying No!

"Thanks, but no thanks!"
"I'd rather not!"
"I'm not interested, so let's not talk about it any more!"
"Nope!"
"Absolutely not!"
"I'll pass!"
"I just can't!"
"Forget it!"
"I really don't think so!"
"I don't want to!"
"I think, not!"
"If you are being serious, just scratch me off your list!"

About Being Arrested/Incarcerated

Should you be arrested, you need to be prepared to understand what the police officer says and does. Like many of the movies you watch, the police officer says something to the person who has been arrested. Have you really heard the words?

By law, everyone who is arrested is told their "Miranda" rights. It is something like: *"You have the right to remain silent and not say anything which might incriminate yourself. Anything you say can and will be used against you in a court of law. You can stop answering questions I ask you at anytime. You have the right to have a lawyer with you when you go to court or during questioning. If you cannot afford a lawyer, one will be appointed for you."*

Without going any further, should you be arrested, call a family member or friend, immediately. Ask them to find you a lawyer so that whatever legal actions need to be taken, can be taken, as soon as possible.

The Words

Being arrested means hearing legal terminology (words/phrases) that will sound like a foreign language to you. This terminology will be used by police officers, lawyers and judges. *Not* knowing what they are talking about can be very scary! So, below is a short list to help you become more aware of what is being said.

Definitions

Word/Phrase **What It Means**

Arraign   To bring a defendant before a judge to hear the charges and to enter a plea (guilty, not guilty).

Arrest   The official taking of a person to answer criminal charges. This involves at least temporarily depriving the person of liberty (their personal rights) and may involve the use of force.

Assault	An intentional show of force or a movement that could reasonably make the person approached feel in danger of physical attack or harmful physical contact.
Attest	Swear to; act as a witness to; certify formally usually in writing.
Bail	Money or property deposited with the court to allow the release of a person in jail until time of trial.
Battery	Any intentional, unwanted, unprovoked, harmful physical contact by one person (or an object controlled by that person) with another person.
Bench Warrant	A paper issued directly by a judge to the sheriff or other peace officer to permit the arrest of a person.
Bond	A sum of money, securities, or an agreement given in good faith to insure that the parties or party in an action are protected and will comply (agree) with the orders of the court.
Case	Lawsuit; a dispute that goes to court; can be civil or criminal.
Civil Action	Every lawsuit other than a criminal proceeding; a lawsuit that is brought to enforce a right or gain payment for a wrong, rather than a court action involving the government trying to punish a crime.
Coercion	Compulsion or force; making a person act against their free will.
Collateral	Money or property put up to back a person's word.
Complainant	Person who starts a lawsuit.

Contempt	An act designed to obstruct (block) a court's work or lessen the dignity of the court. A willful disobeying of judge's command or official order.
Decree	A judgement of a court that announces the legal consequences of the facts found in a case and orders that the court's decision be carried out.
Defendant	The person against whom a legal action is brought.
Detainer	A document filed with a criminal justice agency to hold a person while awaiting the receipt of an arrest warrant.
Due Process	The Due Process Clause of the U.S. Constitution requires that no person shall be deprived of life, liberty or property without due process of law.
Eviction	A landlord putting a tenant out of property by taking direct action through the courts.
Felony	A serious crime. A crime with a sentence of one year or more.
Forthwith	To take action or respond immediately, or as soon as possible.
Fraud	Any kind of trickery used by one person to cheat another.
Garnishment	Attachment of debtor's property or wages to satisfy a debt.
Habeas Corpus	A judicial order to someone holding a person to bring that person to court.
Impound	Take into the custody of the law until a legal question is decided.
In Lieu Of	Instead of; in place of.
Incarceration	Confinement in a jail or prison.

Indictment   A formal accusation of a crime, made against a person by a grand jury upon the request of a prosecutor.

Injunction   A judge's order to a person to do or to refrain from doing a particular thing.

Jurisdiction   The geographical area within which a court (or public official) has the right and power to operate,

Lawsuit   A civil action; a court proceeding to enforce a right (rather than to convict a criminal).

Levy   To assess, raise, collect or seize.

Liable   Responsible for something.

Mandate   Judicial command to act.

Negligence   The failure to exercise a reasonable or ordinary amount of care in a situation(s) that causes harm to someone or something. It can involve doing something carelessly or failing to do something that should have been done.

Non-support   Failure to provide financial support.

Notice to Quit   Written notice from a landlord to a tenant that the tenant will have to move.

Obstructing Justice   Interfering by words and actions with the proper working of courts or court officials.

Opinion   A judge's statement of the decision she or he has reached in a case.

Paternity Suit   A court action to prove a person is the father of an illegitimate child and to enforce (financial) support obligations.

Plaintiff   Person who brings a lawsuit against another person.

Preventive Detention	Holding persons against their will because they are likely to commit a crime.
Processing	Involves completing arrest reports, fingerprinting, photographing and presenting the prisoner to appropriate authorities for the service of the charging document and the determination of eligibility for bail, bond or incarceration.
Repossession	Taking back something sold because payments have not been made.
Reprieve	Holding off on enforcing a criminal sentence for a period of time after the sentence has been handed down.
Respondent	In civil law, the one who answers the charge.
Restitution	Giving something back; making good for something.
Revoke	Wipe out the legal effect of something by taking it back, canceling, rescinding, etc.
Search Warrant	Written permission from a judge or magistrate for a sheriff or other peace officer to search a particular place for evidence, stolen property, a wanted person, etc.
Seizure	The act of a public official taking property because of a violation of the law.
Sequester	To isolate or hold aside; for example, to sequester a jury is to keep it from having any contacts with the outside world during a trial, and to sequester property is to have it put aside and held by an independent person during a lawsuit.
Service	The delivery of a legal paper, such as a writ, by an officially authorized person in a way that meets all formal requirements.

Show Cause	A court order to a person to show up in court and explain why the court should not take a proposed action.
Subpoena	A subpoena by which a person is commanded to bring certain documents to court.
Summons	A writ informing a person of a lawsuit against her or him. It tells the person to show up in court at a certain time and place. A summons can also be directed to anyone in a civil or criminal case who is needed to testify in that case.
Temporary Restraining Order	A judge's order to a person to keep from taking certain action before a hearing can be held on the question.
Trespass	A wrongful entry onto another person's property.
Vacate	Annul, set aside; take back; for example, when a judge vacates a judgement, it is wiped out completely.
Warrant	Authorization by a judge or commissioner.
Writ	A judge's order requiring that something be done outside the courtroom or authorizing it to be done.

Hint: Where is your dictionary? The definitions provided here are very basic. So, to really be more aware and knowledgeable, look them up for further clarification!

Reminder

Engaging in negative activities can be harmful to your physical, emotional, social and spiritual well-being. All negative activities need to be avoided. As a substitute, look carefully for and engage in **only** those activities that are positive, will allow you raise your level of self-esteem to the point that you become a firm believer in the importance and worth of taking care of you—first!

"Consequences are always available as a reminder!"

Chapter 7
Think "Safety"

When it comes to safety, there are a lot of important things to think about. Your plan, therefore, really needs to include ways you intend to protect yourself from harm. You are, after all, responsible for you—first! It should also include paying particular attention to potential dangers at home, at school and where you work. Plus, you should be concerned about safe travel from riding a bus to skateboarding.

"You can never learn too many safety tips!"

At Home

Anything and everything you can do to make the place where you live "safer" will be good for everyone who lives there! How safe is your home? Do a "walk-through" to check on various areas in your home. Following is a check list to get you started.

My Safety Check List

Yes	No	Comment
❏	❏	Are all of the smoke detectors working properly?
❏	❏	Is it time to change the batteries in the smoke detectors?
❏	❏	Are there designated places to safely store books, games and toys so the floors in each room can remain clear?
❏	❏	Are the stairs (with or without carpet) in good condition?
❏	❏	Do you see any loose tiles, missing screws in electrical outlets or cracked window panes that need to be replaced?
❏	❏	Are non-skid mats available in the bathtub and showers?
❏	❏	Is there a stepladder available to stand on when reaching for things on high shelves?
❏	❏	Do you have a fire extinguisher located in a convenient place in case of an emergency? **Hint**: An "extra" extinguisher on another floor or in another part of the home can provide even more protection!
❏	❏	Does everyone know where the fire extinguisher is and how to use it?
❏	❏	Are all electrical cords in good condition?
❏	❏	Are there any rugs that need to be replaced because they are unraveling or lifting at the corners?
❏	❏	If there is a gun in the house, are the gun and ammunition stored in separate places and out of children's reach?

❑	❑	Are electrical appliances unplugged after use (so younger family members will not turn them on by accident)?
❑	❑	Is there a designated place to store all cleaning supplies?
❑	❑	Are electrical cords (and extension cords) taped along the floor and behind furniture to keep someone from either playing with them or tripping over them?
❑	❑	Are paints, paint thinners and other flammable materials stored in an appropriate place (away from fire sources)?
❑	❑	Are the banisters and handrails in good, strong condition?
❑	❑	Is there an escape plan that everyone knows about, in case of an emergency?
❑	❑	Is "911" for emergencies printed clearly on each telephone?
❑	❑	Does the hot water heater (or furnace) have storage around it that is closer than 18 inches?
❑	❑	Does the furnace filter need to be cleaned or replaced?

"Safety plans are only good if they are used!"

Review this list, once again. What do you plan to do to correct any of these safety hazards? Here is a **"Make Sure"** list to use as a guide.

My "Make Sure" List

❑ **Make sure** stove and vents are clean of grease build-up.

❑ **Make sure** flammable liquids are not stored near a heat source.

❑ **Make sure** to test smoke detectors on a regular basis (at least once a month).

❑ **Make sure** trees near entrances to the house are well-trimmed.

❑ **Make sure** that outlets (in all rooms) are not overloaded.

❑ **Make sure** matches and lighters are out reach of young children.

❑ **Make sure** the clothes dryer is always free of lint.

❑ **Make sure** all entrances are well-lighted.

❑ **Make sure** sharp knives are kept out of reach of young children.

❑ **Make sure** to wipe up spills—immediately to prevent slipping.

❑ **Make sure** to have home fire drills at least every three months.

Fire! Fire!

Do you know what to do in case of a fire? One set of experts (Knox) suggests the following tips:

For a Major Fire Get everyone out of the building. Don't stop to gather up possessions. Immediately call the fire department from a neighbor's home or a telephone booth.

If Trapped On An Upper Floor Go into a room, close the door, and stuff the gap (or, that one inch of space from the floor) at the bottom of the door, with clothing, bedding, or rugs to stop smoke from entering. Open a window and shout for help! If the room fills with smoke, lean out of the window or lie down on the floor to get below the level of the smoke. If possible, tie a wet rag around your mouth and nose to keep some of the smoke fumes out. Make a rope of sheets, towels, belts, etc., to use only as a *very* last resort.

**For A
Small Fire**

Get out of the room and close the door so that drafts cannot fan the flames (or make them more intense!).

> **Hint**: A fire can take half an hour to burn through a solid door!

If upholstery is burned by a cigarette falling on it and is just beginning to smolder (to burn without a flame but with a lot of smoke), pour water over it. If the fire is smoldering seriously or is already burning, get out of the room and the house; the foam used in some upholstered furniture gives off lethal or poisonous fumes. Then, call 911!

**Clothes
on Fire**

Get the person on the ground to stop the flames from rising up toward their face; wet the flames with water; or wrap her/him with a blanket or coat to smother the flames—the heavier the material the better! **Do not** roll her/him on the ground because the hot clothes could burn her/him, or the flames could spread to other areas of the body. **Make sure** you do not grab a plastic material to smother the flames; it will melt and could cause severe burns.

Grease Fire

Turn off the heat under the pan or turn off the main power supply. Smother (extinguish) the flames with a lid, a large plate, a baking pan, or a damp (not wet) dish towel. **Do not** move the pan or pour water over it; you'll fan the flames (make them bigger!).

An Oven Fire Turn off the heat and let the fire burn itself out. **Do not** open the oven door; air will feed the fire.

Electrical Fire Turn off the main power supply at the circuit breaker or fuse box. Extinguish the fire with an *all-purpose fire extinguisher* or one that is designed for use on electrical fires. If you don't have a suitable fire extinguisher, smother a burning appliance with a heavy rug or blanket. The heavier the better! **Do not use water** unless you know that the main power supply is turned **off.**

If you can't control the fire quickly, shut the door to the affected room, get everyone out of the house, and call the fire department from a neighbor's home. **Never use water** to put out a fire in a television, stereo or computer, even if it is turned off, because there may be residual (extra electrical power left over after it has been turned off) in the equipment and you could get an electric shock!

Gas Leaks A word of caution about gas leaks: **never try to repair a gas leak yourself**; you could cause an explosion!

For small gas leaks, search for the leak by checking all knobs on a gas stove, the gas taps, and pipes, and make sure that the pilot lights have not gone out. Put out any open flames and cigarettes **before** searching for the leak. If in the dark, **use a flashlight** and **not** a match, lighter or candle to search for the leak. **Do not** turn on an electric light—the spark could ignite the gas. If the smell lingers and you can't find the source, call your gas company right away! If there is a very strong smell of gas, open doors and windows, put out all open flames. Leave, find a telephone and call the gas company, immediately!

Poison "Precautions" at Home

All homes need to be "poison-proofed" for safety. This is especially true if you have younger sisters and brothers, children of your own or children who visit. To "poison-proof" your home follow the precautions listed below.

Kitchen Area Household products such as detergents, drain cleaner, and dishwashing liquids should **not** be stored under the sink. All cleaners, household products and medications should be out of reach for children. Harmful products need to be stored away from foods.

Bathroom Area Medicine chests should be cleaned out regularly. Old medicines should be flushed down the toilet. All medicines, sprays, powders, cosmetics, fingernail supplies, hair care products, mouthwash, etc. need to be placed out of reach.

Laundry Area All bleaches, soaps, detergents, fabric softeners and sprays need to be placed out of reach. Make sure that all products are kept in their original containers.

Basement/ Garage Insect spray, weed killers, gasoline, car products, turpentine, paints and paint products should be stored in a locked area.

Did you know that thousands of children are *accidentally* poisoned each year? The six rules given below will help you to do your part in preventing accidental poisonings in your home.

❑ Make sure that "safety-lock" tops are on all prescription drugs.

❑ Never transfer a product to another container that would attract a child (or an elderly person with failing eyesight or episodes of loss-of-memory).

❑ Younger children should be taught never to put leaves, stems, bark, seeds or berries from any plant into their mouths. And, keep poisonous house plants out of reach of young children.

❑ When using sprays, insecticides and pesticides, make sure children are not in the area because breathing the fumes could be very harmful.

Special Note: It is a good idea to put the telephone number of your local Poison Control Center somewhere near that other important number—**9-1-1**!

Think "Safety" at School

Thinking about safety at school means you are giving serious thought about what you can do to be safe outside/inside of the school building and during after-school activity time.

Here is another important checklist to use.

My "Safety" at School Personal Survey

Yes	No	I am careful to try to do the following for my safety and the safety of others!
❑	❑	Always pick-up articles that have been dropped on the floor.
❑	❑	Make a special effort to sit properly and keep my feet under my desk so that others will not harm themselves by "tripping" over my feet in the aisle.
❑	❑	Avoid leaning against glass doors or windows.
❑	❑	Give special attention to the carrying of sharp, pointed objects such as pencils, pens, scissors, and tools.
❑	❑	Avoid putting certain objects in my mouth (for example: pencils, paper clips, chalk, paper, etc.)
❑	❑	Resist the temptation to "push" or "shove" other students.
❑	❑	Avoid the urge to "run" instead of "walk" on the stairs or along hallways.

❑	❑	Give "extra" attention to watching *where* I am walking.
❑	❑	Make sure I am following school rules concerning "safety practices.

While this is a very short list, the more "yes" answers you have the better. And, congratulations for taking such good care of yourself at school!

Safety at Work

To be safe at work stay prepared to avoid having accidents. Many experts say every year thousands of people are injured on the job. Some are injured so severely they can't work any more! In order to minimize your chances of being hurt on the job, there are some basic rules that might help.

Always, actively **think** about your safety at work. Never use a machine without, first, being given instructions. Does your job require you to wear protective equipment? Find out. Are there a set of safety rules and guidelines for you to follow? Find out. Ask your supervisor to provide you with information or booklets about avoiding slips, trips and falls, proper lifting and moving, use of chemicals and machinery (where appropriate for the type of job you have). After finding out, be sure to keep these safety "musts" in mind as you perform your job tasks.

My Personal Safety

When you start thinking about your personal safety begin with the three C's! **C**are about being personally safe by avoiding situations, people or places that could cause you harm. Take **C**ontrol of any potential dangerous situation by being alert and prepared. Protect yourself. Use **C**ommon sense as the basis for any decisions you make.

Step-By-Step

Did you know there are rules available to help keep pedestrians safe? Before crossing a street, for example, always stop, look left-right and left again before proceeding. Then, do another left-right-left **while** you are crossing. Use these same rules even where there are traffic lights that indicate "walk" or "don't walk". It is a good idea to try to make eye contact with the drivers so you can be assured that they **see** you. These are such busy days that many drivers are often so preoccupied with other things, they do not always focus on what they are doing (driving) and forget about making pedestrians crossing the street, a priority!

> **Hint:** Remember, lots of people these days drive and talk on the telephone. Keep this in mind for your own safety!

Here's another tidbit of information suggested by the Federal Highway Administration: "...At intersections where 'Right Turn On Red' is permitted, the pedestrian must always be looking for turning vehicles before stepping off the curb. As they attempt to merge with moving traffic on the crossing street, drivers will usually be looking **away** from the corner and toward oncoming traffic. It's up to you in this case to be absolutely sure that any driver wishing to make a right turn sees you. If you're uncertain, just wait until the vehicle passes, then look again, and cross safely."

They also say: "Don't take those 'No Right Turn On Red' signs for granted. Even when an intersection has these signs posted, you, as the pedestrian, should still make certain that motorists (drivers) in the right turn lane see you. Don't step off the curb without checking! Motorists make mistakes too; don't compound their error by stepping out in front of a moving vehicle. Be patient."

Rape

Rapists are people who feel a need to harm and embarrass another human being. No one is safe from rape! Rape happens to children, mothers, grandmothers, wives and any ethnic group. It can happen to anyone regardless of their income, type of job, religion, lifestyle or physical attractiveness. It can also happen to people who are physically challenged and even to men. A rapist cannot be automatically picked out of a crowd. They do not walk, talk or act strangely. In fact, rapists are usually known to their victims as an acquaintance, friend, neighbor or relative.

A pamphlet prepared and distributed by the Community Relations Division of the Metropolitan Police Department (Washington, DC), offers some sound advice. Here are a few highlights.

Taking Precautions

Most rapes occur outside, on the street, in a park, playground or school-yard. Be alert to your surroundings and the people around you when you're outside...particularly if you're alone or it's dark.

- Stay in well-lighted areas as much as possible.

- Walk confidently, directly, at a steady pace. A rapist looks for someone who appears vulnerable.

- Walk on the side of the street facing traffic.

- Walk close to the curb. Avoid doorways, bushes, and alleys where rapists can hide.

- Wear clothes and shoes that give you freedom of movement. Don't burden yourself with too many packages.

Many rapes occur in the victim's home, in a garage, elevator or an apartment laundry room. In some cases, the rapist may be a burglar who breaks into a house and unexpectedly finds someone home. In others, an attacker purposely looks for women home alone. Do you live alone? Are you a single parent or a college student? If so, one of the best ways to prevent sexual assault is to protect your home!

- Have your locks changed or re-keyed when you move into a new house or apartment.

- If strangers ask to use your telephone in an emergency, offer to make the call yourself. Ask them to wait outside while you make the call.

- Install good exterior lighting around your house or ask that this be taken care of at your apartment building.

- If you think someone may be following you, or if you see a gang of kids hanging around your door, don't go in, especially if no one else is home. They may force their way into your apartment, once you put the key in the door. Always have an alternative plan to go quickly to a neighbor's house, if necessary.

- If you come home and find a door or window open or signs of forced entry, don't go in. Go to the nearest telephone call the police (**9-1-1**).

Be aware that rapes also happen in cars and other vehicles. Most take place in the rapist's car, so be very careful about accepting rides from strangers. It's a good idea **never** to hitch-hike! When driving:

- Always lock your car.
- Check the back seat and under the car before you get in.
- Keep the doors locked while you drive.
- Park in well-lighted areas.
- Never go to an ATM when there is no security around.

What Should You Do If You're a Victim?

If you prefer not to call the police right away, get help from a friend, your doctor, a hospital emergency room, or contact a rape or other crisis service that may be available in your community.

The most important thing to remember after an attack is that you should not touch anything, change your clothes, wash, or douche until you have contacted the police and been taken to the hospital. If you do, you may accidentally destroy valuable evidence that the police and prosecutor might need to arrest and convict your attacker.

The Child Victim

Each year more than 100,000 children suffer some type of sexual abuse. In many cases, the victim is female and the offender is male. Who is the typical offender? In over one-third of the sexual abuse cases involving children, the offender is known to the child and the child's family. In other words, the abuser is often a parent, relative, or close family friend. Because children are so trusting and defenseless, they are especially vulnerable to sexual assault.

How to Respond

Children often make up stories, but they rarely lie about being victims of sexual assault. If a child tells you about being touched or assaulted, take it *seriously*. Your response helps determine how the child will react to the abuse. Stay calm. Explain that you are concerned about what happened, but not angry with the child. Many children feel guilty, as if they had provoked the assault. Children need to be reassured that they are not to blame, and that they are right to tell you what happened.

Sometimes, a child may be too frightened or confused to talk directly about the abuse. Be alert for any changes in behavior that might hint that the child has suffered a disturbing experience.

> **Tip**: In the case of children, take whatever steps you feel are necessary. Contact the police, seek assistance from a friend, pastor, hospital emergency staff or a crisis center in your community. Don't forget to give serious consideration to consulting an attorney, as well!

Apartment Living

Living in an apartment building means you are sharing space with strangers! Do you know at least one-third of the people in your building? You might, if you happen to be president of your building's Tenant Association. But, just how well can you actually know them? They, like you, want to protect their privacy and have peace of mind about their safety.

Whether you live alone or with others, respect the privacy of others. Do not be a "Peeping Teresa/Tom" because it is impolite, can cause discomfort to others and could be considered a criminal offense. Be polite and cordial to **all** of your neighbors.

If you live alone with your mother, grandmother, or perhaps an older sister, remember that you do not have to share this fact with everyone in the building, nor, do you have to offer that you have a dog for protection! Be cautious. Aim to protect your privacy for your personal safety!

Living alone also means taking special precautions for safety. It is never a good idea to give your name or specific whereabouts on your answering machine. This just might be the "invitation" that a burglar is counting on! Instead, record a "we" statement. Your message could, for example be: "We are probably on the phone, so please leave a quick message and we will call you back!", or, "**Fred** and I are doing whatever, but we promise to call you back right away!" Be creative. But, remember to make your message a "we" and not an "I" statement. Another suggestion is that you remember **not** to label your keys. If lost, they could end up in the wrong hands. Going away for a few days? Great! Have a terrific time, but do not leave your door keys under a mat, in the mailbox or anywhere near the door. If you can think of creative places to hide your keys, so can a *burglar*! Consider giving your keys to a neighbor you trust or a friend who lives nearby.

Here is an **extra** thought to consider. Make sure that your mailbox does not show that you live alone with another female. Rather than have your full name or first initial and last name, simply put a **fictitious** first initial for your "husband" and your real first initial and last name. It would read: "L. & J. Smith". This notation does not say who is the **husband** or who is the **wife**! You might also think about only using your last name. Try **not** to be "too" creative. You might confuse your mail carrier to the point that you will **not** receive your mail! While burglars will eventually catch on to this system, or whatever creative system you come up with, you will at least have peace of mind about your personal safety—for a period of time!

"Peeping is against the law!"

Going Out!

Whether you are going out on a date, attending a business meeting or lunch with someone you do not know that well, stay alert! Regardless of the situation, if you are being talked to or touched in an inappropriate manner, you do not have to stay! In fact, when you feel "uncomfortable" for any reason with the person you are out with, simply make up an excuse and leave. It's just that simple! Remember, *you* are *your* first priority!

Safe Travel

To travel safely you need to be prepared and organized. Your safety and that of others will require you to be alert about possible hazards. You need to educate yourself about the kinds of accidents that occur frequently. You need to be aware of the many precautions experts suggest. You also need to, frequently, share this information with others.

Here are some travel tips for your "personal" safety.

Bus Riding "Musts"

The National School Transportation Association provides suggestions about school bus riding. If you look closely, however, many of these suggestions might also apply when riding on a public bus.

The Ride

Be quiet. The driver needs your help and she/he may have trouble concentrating if there is too much commotion in the bus. Stay in your seat.

Keep the aisles clear. Nothing...books, bags, legs, arms or bodies...should block the aisle. Do not stand in the aisle. If the driver is forced to make a quick stop, you could be thrown around and hurt yourself and others.

No pets allowed. Animals, including pets on leashes, in boxes or in cages are not allowed on the bus.

Share your seat. Don't save a spot for friend, but keep the seat open for anyone who wants to sit down. (You'll have plenty of time to talk to your friends once you get to school)!

Getting Off

Be organized. Be ready to leave when you reach your stop. Don't keep the driver and the other bus riders waiting while you gather your books and other belongings.

Stay put. Wait until the bus has stopped completely before you get up from your seat. And, always let the people in the front of the bus get off first.

Don't push. You'll get out faster if no one shoves or pushes. Also, chances are better no one will trip and fall, causing delays.

Leave immediately. After you get off the bus, leave the area quickly so that you are out of the way of other buses bringing more children to school.

Stay clear. Keep away from the side of the bus. If you must cross the street, cross in front of the bus. But, wait for an "all clear" signal from the driver before you leave the curb. Look both ways before crossing.

As an added tip, remember: If an emergency situation arises, you can help by staying calm. Listen to the driver and follow instructions. Help the driver by getting the smaller children off safely!

Driving

Quite simply...follow the rules and regulations presented in the driver's guide. Be an alert driver. Be a courteous driver (and rider!) Observe all signs, street markings and speed limits. Go to the nearest Department of Motor Vehicles for a booklet.

"Drinking and driving cause dangerous dilemmas!

Taking a Taxicab

In every city, state and county you will find that rates vary. Did you know that you can simply call the taxicab company and ask what it will cost for them to take you to a certain place? Give them the location where you will be picked-up and where you need to go. If for any reason you feel uncomfortable with the driver, discretely write down his name and cab number. (Don't forget to put the cab company name.) Tell the driver you have changed your mind and would like to be let out at the next corner. Pay the fare, exit the cab and when you can (that same day) contact the cab company and report the driver. Remember, your personal safety **always** comes first!

Train Travel

Traveling by train is great. You only need to remember to follow all rules. Many will be posted, some can be found in pamphlets at the station and if you really have questions, ask a train agent. Don't forget to purchase your tickets in advance!

Rail Crossings

This may seem like an odd topic to include, but it is very important. Did you know that according to the Federal Railroad Administration, someone in Ameria is hit by a train nearly every 100 minutes? So, for your safety, whether you are walking, biking, skating or driving, be sure to: (1) always slow down and look both ways; and, (2) obey the warning signs and devices (gates, lights and bells) at all highway-rail crossings.

Flying

Afraid to fly? Lots of people are, but you don't have to be! Flying is considered to be one of the safest ways to travel. And, like traveling by train, you just need to remember to follow the rules and get your tickets in advance!

Here are a few more tips for your personal safety (Savage):

- Don't tempt-a-thief! While you are at the ticket counter keep your luggage in sight. This is especially important if you are checking luggage outside. Be sure that your luggage has baggage tickets which have been attached and that the stubs have been stapled to your ticket **cover.**

  > **Tip:** Make sure that all of your luggage has identification tags on them. And, put some form of identification "inside" each piece. This includes any carry-on luggage you might have! Don't forget to "lock" each piece of luggage.

- Once aboard, listen carefully to the flight attendant's safety instructions, and memorize the routes to the exits near you.

- Take as few "carry-on" items as possible onto the plane. There simply will not be enough space to stow them!

■ To get answers about **anything** concerning flying, call air-
line and ask to speak with one of their Public Relations
representatives.

> Tip: If you are a first-time flyer or really have a fear of
> flying, ask if the airline offers special seminars!

Elevators and Escalators

When riding an elevator watch your step. Leave closing doors
alone. If the doors do not open, ring the alarm button and wait for
help. If there is a fire in the building, use the stairs. Escalators and
moving walks can be a little tricky! Step on and off carefully. Be
sure to hold the handrail, face forward and be alert. Escalators and
moving walks are made for people, not strollers. Give special
attention to the protection of younger children by holding their
hand and helping them to step on and off carefully. Stand so that
you do not touch the sides below the handrail.

Peddle Safely

First things first—always wear a helmet! Remember to observe all
traffic laws and signals. Avoid riding double or doing stunts. Try to
always ride near the curb and in the same direction as traffic. Look
for alternate routes, rather than ride through busy intersections
and heavy or high-speed traffic. It is always a good idea to **walk,
not ride** your bicycle across busy intersections and left turn corners. Be cautious about riding in wet weather. If you must ride in
the dark, make sure your bike has a headlight, taillight and reflec-
tors. It is also a good idea to wear clothing with reflective-trim
applied. Be especially careful **not** to wear loose clothing or long
coats. There is always the possibility of clothing being tangled in
the chains!

Skateboard Safety

Yes, skateboarding can be fun, but can also be very dangerous!
There are, however, a few tips to keep you safe and allow you to
have a lot of fun. According to the Consumer Product Safety Commission, the following suggestions will help make your skateboarding time safer.

❑ Never ride in the street.

❑ Don't take chances. Complicated tricks require careful practice and a specially designed area. There should only be **one** person per skateboard. Never hitch a ride from a car, bus, truck, bicycle, etc.

❑ Learning how to fall in case of an accident may help reduce your chances of being seriously injured.

❑ If you are losing your balance, crouch down on the skateboard so that you will not have so far to fall.

❑ In a fall, try to land on the fleshy parts of your body.

❑ If you fall, try to roll rather than absorb the force with your arms.

❑ Even though it may be difficult, during a fall try to relax your body, rather than stiffen.

Now that you know about some of the do's and do not's, here are a few tips about protective gear! These experts say:

> "Protective gear, such as closed, slip-resistant shoes, helmets, and specially designed padding, may not fully protect skateboarders from fractures, but its use is recommended as such gear that can reduce the number and severity (seriousness) of injuries. Padded jackets and shorts are available, as well as padding for hips, knees, elbows, wrist braces and special skateboarding gloves. All of this protective gear will help absorb the impact of a fall. With protective gear, it is important to look for comfort, design, and function. The gear should not interfere with (your) movement, vision or hearing."

Basic "First Aid" Hints

First Aid is the help given to an injured person immediately following an accident. First aid helps to keep the injured person comfortable, reduces suffering and may even save her/his life. In minor injuries first aid may be all the help that needs to be given.

However, in most cases, the injured person also needs the care which only a doctor can give.

When an accident or sudden illness strikes, keep as calm as you can. An excited person does not think clearly. Unless you know *exactly* what to do to help the injured person, do not touch her/him. If she/he is conscious let her/him know that you will get help as quickly as possible. Then go for help at once or get someone to do it for you.

If the accident occurs in the school building or on the school grounds, notify a teacher or the principal. They will know what to do, as most schools have a plan to follow when accidents occur.

If a person is seriously injured at home or elsewhere, and no adult is nearby, get to a telephone as quickly as possible. If you know the name of the injured person's doctor, call her/his doctor. If you don't know the doctor's name, you can get help by calling either the police or the fire department.

There are a few things you can do while waiting for help to arrive. If the person is conscious, suggest that she/he lie down. Whether she/he is conscious or not, you can cover her/him with a blanket, sheet, coat, sweater, or any other satisfactory covering that will keep her/him warm. If the person can hear you, try to keep her/him cheerful (tell a "dumb" joke!) Try to make her/him feel that everything will be all right. Let her/him know that help is on the way!

As a final note, remember that a seriously injured person is not to be moved except by a person who knows what she/he is doing. You may do more harm than good if you try to move an injured person. Learn first aid. Ask your school nurse, counselor, hospital, police/fire department or call the local chapter of the Red Cross to find out where you can take a course.

First Aid Kits

Without exception, every home should have a First Aid Kit and everyone should know where it is in case of emergencies! Listed below are some of the basic items you need to have in your First Aid Kit at home.

- Absorbent bandages—medium-size, large, and one extra large
- A box of individually wrapped adhesive bandages
- Open-weave bandages
- Elastic bandages for strains and sprains
- Gauze dressings
- A triangular bandage to make a sling
- Roll of sterile cotton
- Hydrogen peroxide

Added to this list are:

- Pair of scissors
- Selection of safety pins in different sizes
- Pair of round-ended tweezers
- Thermometer
- Aspirin **and** an aspirin substitute (to help reduce fevers)
- Calamine lotion (for soothing sunburn, bites, stings, rashes)
- Mild antiseptic cream for minor wounds
- Ipecac syrup to induce vomiting in case of poisoning
- Petroleum jelly.

Reminder: Be sure to carefully read and follow the instructions written on all of the items you include in your home First Aid Kit!

Start thinking "safety" today!

Chapter 8
Study "Seriously"

If you would rather see more strong B's than shaky C's on your report card, then you need to get "serious" about studying! Available help is all around you. There are certain areas where your parents' involvement will be a help. Don't forget about school counselors, neighbors, friends, community/church groups, and especially, yourself!

How Parents Help

Let's face it, school work is really **your responsibility**—not your parent's! Their job is to make sure you have a comfortable and quiet place to study, enough supplies and encouragement when you need it. To do this, they enforce certain restrictions on anything that might interfere with your study time. For example, you are often required to turn off the television (and your music), not allowed to make or take telephone calls and not permitted to have visitors.

Their goal is to see that you are properly prepared to study. Parents do what they can because they are concerned about your future. And, afterall, aren't you concerned, too?

How much do your parents do to help you get better grades? See how many times you have a "yes" answer to the statements listed below.

How My Parent's Help Me

Yes	No	Comment
❏	❏	My parents know how much homework I have each night because they ask me.
❏	❏	My parents help me organize my assignments and answer any questions I have.
❏	❏	My parents attend PTA meetings, pre-college orientation seminars or join school committees.
❏	❏	My parents know who I hang out with after school and monitor my time.
❏	❏	My parents spend time with me discussing not only school work but how my day went.
❏	❏	My parents like for me to teach them what I have learned.
❏	❏	My parents attend my school activities, band performances and games.
❏	❏	My parents discuss current events with me, take me to museums or concerts and new places.
❏	❏	My parents encourage me to write by having me send thank-you notes and cards or making sure I keep a journal.
❏	❏	My parents make sure we have reference books, maps, dictionaries, etc., at home for me to use. Or, make sure I have library time.
❏	❏	My parents meet regularly with my counselors or advisors to be sure I am on target with my classes.
❏	❏	My parents try their best to be sure I get enough sleep and exercise.

If you do not get a lot of "yes" answers, perhaps you can discuss some of these points with your parents.

> **Tip**: Make an appointment with your parents to talk about this list! Sometimes just having their involvement can make the difference between those strong B's and shaky C's. Think about it!

How Teachers Help

Your teachers can do more than just teach! While they always offer to help, it is up to you to at least ask! If you do not, how will they know you actually **want** their help? Consider the following suggestions.

- ❑ Be a "listening" student even if you do not always speak-up and get involved in classroom discussions.

- ❑ Teachers are like parents. They almost always know when you are not telling the truth! If you do not have your assignment completed, say so! And, be willing to accept the consequences **without** a fuss!

- ❑ **Always**, at least attempt to do your assignments. Teachers will be looking for those students who are honestly "trying"! They are professionals, so if there are personal or family problems that you have shared with her/him, this will be taken into consideration. And, they might even offer help before you ask for it!

- ❑ Be a "courteous" student. Respect what the teacher is teaching and provide her/him with a product that reflects your very best.

- ❑ Be "prepared" for each class. Do your homework. And, do not forget lots of teachers **look** for those students who show an "interest" in class and will readily offer them help—if they think it is needed.

- ❑ Do not forget to ask questions! Teachers *want* to answer. It will single you out from several others. And, it will make it a bit easier for you to ask for help, should you need it!

The School Counselor

School or Guidance Counselors are available to help you—help yourself! They monitor your attendance, the amount of credits you earn and keep track of whether or not you will be able to graduate with the appropriate amount of class credits to get into college. They are also available to give advice. During those times when you have more than school-related problems to handle or a need to talk, your School Counselor is the one to turn to!

As trained professionals, their job is to help you do whatever will protect your well-being, remain focused on your responsibility as a student and help you with you when it comes to personal problems. They sometimes sponsor seminars on topics about preparing for college, entrance exams, financial aid, what life will be like with **and** without a college degree, career decision-making, or the parent involvement concerning a variety of areas.

Motivating "Me"

You **can** be a person who takes her/his studies "seriously." All it takes is for you to sincerely *want* to get better grades and *look* for ways to get motivated.

Motivation is something that comes from *within* you. It is a special feeling that only you will be able to recognize in yourself. *How will you know you are motivated?* You'll know when you can say to yourself: "I want to do better in school and get higher grades because it is really important to *me*"—and, *honestly* mean it!

Think "Positively"!

A good portion of self-motivation is being able to think (and act) positively. Having bad grades, now, does not mean you will have them later. If your goal is to study to learn, better grades will suddenly begin to surface. Only settle for grades that make you feel comfortable. Be proud of successfully earning a better grade. Remember, you worked hard to get it.

Negative Thinking

Negative thoughts can actually keep you from doing good things for yourself!

Are there moments when you seem to be having more and more negative thoughts while you are working to achieve your study goal? If so, simply "stop" for a moment. Take a quick 15-minute break. During this break, try to figure out what the problem is and "put it on-hold" until **after** your study time! Stay focused. Your study time is supposed to be **only** for study purposes.

By the way, this happens, from time to time, with everyone. Many people go through periods when their thoughts drift to something negative. You might suddenly start thinking about problems with family members, money, friendships or your job. These thoughts are **never** planned. They simply **pop-up**. Shake them off and move forward!

Less Social Time

Once you become actively-involved in getting better grades, there is another area of discomfort you might face. It is perfectly okay if you start getting fewer and fewer invites! Some of your classmates (co-workers, too) may not understand or be able to appreciate that you are working on achieving a specific goal and simply cannot "hang out" like you did before. True friends, however, will understand, help you as much as they can and "wait" until you are ready to rejoin many of the regular group activities.

> **Hint**: Don't be surprised to find that some of your friends begin to follow your lead. They just might be interested in improving their own grades and you could be the example that makes them give serious thought about—setting their own priorities!

Motivating Suggestions

Getting motivated will involve a five-step process:

Step 1:   ***Want* to get better grades**—Only *you* know how important it is to *you* to get higher grades in a particular subject.

Step 2:   ***Set* goals**—Making a workable plan is sure to help you meet the goals you want to achieve.

> **Tip**: On your plan or schedule be sure to target the more troublesome subjects—first!

Step 3:   ***Be* ready to work toward better grades.** Do not be afraid of failure. Look forward to doing what has to be done to reach your goals. If success means putting in extra hours and giving extra effort, do it!

Step 4:   ***Use* creative ways to achieve your goals.** Look for a classmate (or someone in a higher grade) to tutor you. Purchase or borrow self-help books (from a bookstore or the library) that give *clearer* explanations, practice exercises and answer keys so you can *test* yourself. You might even consider **being** a tutor. Helping someone else with a subject that is especially difficult for them, will give you **added** review for the same subject that you happen to be more comfortable with. Consider joining (or starting) a "study group!"

Step 5:   ***Plan* a reward for yourself.** Decide on a specific reward for your hard work and the better grade you have earned.

> **Hint**: Remember, when choosing a reward, use both your imagination and common sense. Make sure the reward is one that will be more "pleasing" to you than "harmful!"

"Failure can often fuel success!"

Study Tools

A number of supplies and bookshelf items need to be included on your bookshelf. By making sure these items are readily available, you will be able to save time and be more "efficient" in the use of your "study" time. A basic set of supplies should consist of:

- Pens, pencils, highlighters, pencil sharpener
- Spiral notebooks (several), notebook paper, 3-ring binders, plain paper (for typewriter or computer)
- Wall calendar, appointment book calendar
- Ruler, compass, "metric" measurements guide, calculator
- Tape, stapler, staplers, paperclips several sets of notebook dividers (8 ½ x 11)
- Index cards (3" x 5", white with lines)
- Report covers, folders with pockets (in assorted colors)
- Glue stick, correction fluid
- Scissors, a three-hole punch

Added to this list and depending on what courses you are taking, be sure to incude: a small tape recorder, tapes, watch/clock, graph paper, slide rule and perhaps—a protractor!

Now, let's concentrate on your bookshelf. It should contain:

- Dictionary and Thesaurus
- Set of Encyclopedia
- Crossword Puzzle Books (great for a 10 minute break and even better for improving your spelling!)
- Self-help books
- A *World Atlas* (can be quite helpful for information identifying capitals, living environments and tidbits about economic status levels!)
- A Grammar Handbook (to be used as a double-check for your peace of mind—that you have written it right!)

"Tools are only useful if used!"

Storage Areas

No room in your room for storing these supplies? Try storing them in a gift box (large enough for a man-size bulky sweater) that is flat enough to slide under your bed. Make it a habit to remember to return supply items to their proper place as soon as possible. Can you imagine how frustrated you will feel when you have to take valuable time to "look" for one of these items—especially when you have a deadline to meet?

Since there is no law which says a bookshelf **has** to be "attached" to a wall or **has** to be part of a bookcase, then you can be as creative as you wish. You might, for example, purchase a set of sturdy bookends (metal, if possible) to prop your reference books up—in a convenient corner of your room—on the floor—along a convenient wall! The key to storing them is to be sure they are easily available, yet out of the way.

Here is another suggestion: cover with fabric or contact paper at least six old telephone directory books to use as book-ends. Make sure the "height" is equal on both the left and right side (you will need to stack 3 books on each side). Place your books in the middle. Consider also: cinder blocks or painted bricks (these might be too heavy for your room—so check with your parents to be sure). Take a walk through an office supply store for more ideas! Use your imagination!

Special "Notes" Notebook

The last item on the bookshelf would be a three-ring binder containing study notes, articles, lists of self-help tips, etc., which would be grouped by subject. This special "Notes" notebook would be used as a **review** source.

Divide the notebook into sections that correspond with the subjects you are taking now (or those you will be taking next semester). Collect any "tips" or "short-cuts" you happen to see in magazines, books or on television that you can use to help with your study time. Don't forget to surf the web! You might, for example see an article or a small booklet in the grocery store that has tips on reading more rapidly (and retaining more). There might also be a commercial that tells you where to get more information on a topic you happen to be interested in for an upcoming project. These are the kind of items that would go in your "Notes" notebook for future reference.

Ready to get started? If so, decide today to get really good at knowing the meaning and appropriate use of prefixes, roots, stems and suffixes.

> **Tip**: Check your English books for a a reminder about the definition of prefixes, roots, stems and suffixes!

You will need to make-up separate sheets that only list a mixture of ten.

> **Hint**: With short lists, you can easily make it a goal to complete only one list at a time. It will be easier to absorb!

Here is a short list to get you started.

Prefix	Meaning
ab, abs	from, away from
ad, ac, af, ag, an, ap, ar, as, at	to, forward
an, a	without
be	over, thoroughly
bi	two
cata	down
circum	around
com, co, col, con, cor	with, together
contra	control, against
de	down, away
di	two
dis, dif	not, apart
ex, e	out
extra, extro	beyond, outside
hyper	above, excessively
in, il, im, ir	in, on, upon
inter	between, among
intra, intro	within
mega	great, million
mis	bad, improper

multi	many
neo	new
non	not
ob, oc, of, op	against
para	beyond, related
per	through, completely
peri	around, near
poly	many
post	after
pre	before
pro	forward, in favor of
proto	first
re	again, back
retro	backward
se	away, aside
semi	half, partly
sub, suc, suf, sug, sup, sus	under, less
tele	far
trans	across
un	not
uni	one
vice	in place of
with	away, against

Root/Stem	**Meaning**
ac, acr	sharp
ag, act	do
ali	another
alter	other
anthrop	man
apt	fit
aqua	water
aud, audit	hear
ben, bon	good
biblio	book
bio	life
breve	short
cap, capt, cept, cip	to take
capit, capt	head
carn	flesh

celer	swift
chron	time
civi	citizen
compl	to fill
cord	heart
cred, credit	to believe
da, dat	to give
dem	people
di, diurn	day
dic, dict	to say
doc, doct	to teach
ego	I
erg, urg	work
err	to wander
fall, fals	to deceive
fid	belief, faith
flect, flex	bond
fort	strong
frag, fract	break
fug	flee
gen, gener	class, race
grad, gress	go, step
greg	flock, herd
helio	sun
it, itiner	journey, road
jur, jurat	to swear
labor, laborat	to work
leg, lect, lig	to choose, to read
liber, libr	book
log	word, study
magn	great
mal	bad
mar	sea
mater, matr	mother
mori, mort	to die
morph	shape, Form
nav	ship
neg	deny
nev	new
omni	all

oper	to work
pass	feel
pater, patr	father
path	disease, feeling
ped	foot
port, portat	to carry
quer, ques, quir, quis	to ask
rid, ris	to laugh
rupt	to break
sci	to know
sect	cut
sent, sens	to think, to feel
solv, solut	to loosen
string, strict	bind
tempor	time
ten, tent	to hold
terr	land
tract	drag, pull
urb	city
vac	empty
ver	tru

Suffix	Meaning
able, ible	capable of (adjective suffix)
ac, ic	like, pertaining to (adjective suffix)
ary	like, connected with (adjective or noun suffix)
action	that which is (noun suffix)
cy	state of being (noun suffix)
escent	becoming (adjective suffix)
fy	to make (verb suffix)
ive	like (adjective suffix)
old	resembling, like (adjective suffix)
osis	condition (noun suffix)
tude	state of (noun suffix)

Make up notebook sheets that list ten of the words that most people frequently misspell! Here is a list.

ability	absence	abundance
acceptable	accommodate	accumulation
achievement	acknowledge	addressed
advertise	advice	affect
aggravate	aggressive	aisle
all right	already	altogether
amateur	angel	antiseptic
apologize	apparent	appreciation
approximate	arrangement	assistance
audience	August	auxiliary
balloon	benefitted	bored
borrow	boundary	breathe
bulletin	bureau	burial
cafeteria	calendar	campaign
capital	capitol	careless
category	ceiling	cemetery
choose	chose	circumstance
citizen	column	congratulate
commitment	committed	comparative
competent	competition	compliment
conference	conscience	conscientious
continual	controlled	convenience
corroborate	council	counsel
daybreak	deceive	December
deception	decision	dependent
descent	describe	desert
desirable	develop	development
device	difference	dilemma
dissatisfied	dissipate	dissipate
distinction	disappoint	disastrous
ecstatic	effect	efficiency
efficient	eight	eligibility
eliminate	embarrassment	emergency
envelope	environment	equipped
essential	exaggerate	examine
exhausted	exhilaration	experience
familiar	fascinating	fatigue

February	flourish	friend
government	grievance	guarantee
handkerchief	happiness	hideous
innocence	intercede	interpreted
irritable	jealous	judgment
kindergarten	knowledge	leisure
library	likelihood	livelihood
mischievous	misspelled	neighbor
noticeable	occasion	occurred
pamphlet	parallelism	particular
pastime	patience	peaceable
perceive	perseverance	persistent
personality	personal	personnel
pleasant	please	potatoes
practical	precede	preceding
predictable	preferential	preferred
prejudice	principal	principle
privilege	procedure	propeller
quarreling	quiet	quite
realize	receipt	recipe
recognize	relieve	remedy
repetition	resemblance	resistance
resource	respectability	responsibility
restaurant	rhythm	ridiculous
sandwich	Saturday	schedule
severely	shepherd	significance
similar	sincerely	sophomore
souvenir	stationary	sympathy
temperature	tendency	therefore
thorough	through	together
unnecessary	unusual	vacuum
vegetable	vicinity	waist
weather	Wednesday	weight

More Tips About the "Notes" Notebook!

Why not switch from your favorite television program, turn to one of the educational programs on cable and take notes that are related to some of the subjects you are taking in school this semester? Try to spend at least 10 minutes a day to add material to your notebook, and another 15 minutes to review a particular section. Make it a practice to read the entire "Notes" notebook once a week. (Sunday evening, perhaps?)

Do not attempt to memorize the material. Simply read everything you have included in the notebook that week starting from page 1 and going to the end of your notebook. Only review this material once. Monday through Saturday you would begin, again, inserting any new material you feel needs to be included. And, the process would start all over again the following Sunday.

Once you get into the habit of regularly using this special notebook and system for review, you will probably be surprised at the amount of information you have been able to not only collect, but retain as well!

By the way, make sure that your notebook is not only informative, but entertaining as well. Sprinkle a few positive quotations throughout. And, don't forget to add a couple of jokes. It will make your weekly reading and review time even more interesting. Here is a good one to include:

> "You're looking well, Gloria," said the visitor heartily. "Yes, I am, aren't I?" agreed the young woman. "Especially since I've just had angina, arteriosclerosis, tuberculosis, pneumonia, aphasia, hypertrophic cirrhosis, and eczema!" "That's terrible!" exclaimed the visitor in concern, "to have had all those things at your tender age!" "Yes," the young woman agreed. "It was the hardest spelling test I've ever had!"
>
> —Anonymous

Study Tips

In order to study "seriously" you need to form solid study habits. Below are a few study tips to get you started.

- ❑ Avoid interruptions (television, music, telephone, visitors, etc.)

- ❑ Take at least a 10 minute break between assignments until you have completed all of them.

- ❑ Take a few moments to re-read completed assignments before going on to the next subject.

- ❑ Make it a habit to finish all of your assignments the day the assignments are given. Try not to wait until the last minute!

- ❑ For projects that are assigned weeks or months in advance (science fair projects, research reports, book reports, etc.), make a special effort to begin gathering reference materials, pre-planning activities and art supplies, as soon as possible. Develop a schedule of when to get what; when to have part of the assignment ready; and, when to have the entire project completed.

- ❑ Make a list of questions you feel you need to ask your teacher when you go to class the next day. If necessary, request a brief conference after school so that your questions can be answered.

- ❑ If you are better in a particular subject than your friend or classmate, offer to "tutor" them. The repetition will be good practice for you, and your friend will profit by the "extra" help.

- ❑ Set aside at least one day a month to visit the library for a few hours. Use this time to "leisurely" read books for enjoyment. You might also want to read books that are of special interest to you or those subjects related to a particular project. Give special attention to the suggested readings that the authors have listed at the end of the book. Make it a point to locate these sources for further reading.

❑ Make your own set of "study" tapes. Tape notes, passages from your school books, and any "short-cuts" you may have read about in other books, magazine articles or the newspaper. Add this information to your "study" tape on a weekly basis. Listen to it as often as possible so you will be prepared for upcoming tests.

❑ Make up a special set of "study" cards. Use 3"x 5" index cards. Write the question on one side and the answer on the back. Ask a family member or friend to quiz you.

"Rushing through assignments can result in rapid failure."

Taking Notes

Taking notes is time-consuming but a necessary ingredient for getting better grades. Many people like to rely on tape recorders. While they are a definite time-saver, tape recorders can also cause many unexpected inconveniences. Many teachers do not allow their students to bring tape recorders into the classroom. What happens if the battery goes dead before you even realize it? Suppose it malfunctions right in the middle of a lecture? Is your plan of action to take notes **and** tape a session? If so, isn't this double time being used?

Before trusting your tape recorder, try instead, to trust yourself! Look for a self-help book on "note-taking", "shorthand" or develop your own set of note-taking abbreviations. You can use **absolutely any abbreviation** you want. These are, afterall, **your** notes. And, the bottom line is: saving time!

When taking notes, never worry about complete sentences or correct punctuation. You have a limited amount of time, you cannot write as fast as the speaker is talking, and expect to feel frustrated when you cannot write **everything** you hear. You **want to**, but can't! What you **can** do, however, is learn to use a few signs, symbols and abbreviations to save time. Practice using some of these note-taking shortcuts.

Signs, Symbols and Abbreviations

Use	For Word(s) or Phrases
s	is
f	for, from, forever
c	can, could, consider, can cause
cn	cannot, could not possibly be, cannot cause
	the (*raised slightly above the line = the; on the line = a period*)
l	will, well
e	we
r	are, our, hour
	and
+	also, in addition to
z	was, were
b	be, being, by
i	if
v	have
o	on, only
S	she, should
u	you, your, yourself
H	he, him
y	why
=	equals, is the same thing, is defined as
≠	is not the same thing, is different, unequal
eg	for example
ie	that is, in other words
@	at, about, approximately
↑	increases (*arrow pointed up*)
↓	decreases (*arrow pointed down*)
?!	(I need to get more information for this section)**********

This is a very short list, but should give you some idea of how to save time taking notes. Be creative! Add a few of your own.

(**Hint**: u c i u try!)

Skimming a Text

You will have numerous opportunities when it is essential that you skim a text. Skimming simply means that you will be selecting *specific* areas of a reading assignment to *review*. It does not mean you will be reading faster than normal! To be a successful skimmer, do the following:

- Read the introduction, conclusion and summary sections
- Give particular attention to the beginning and last lines of paragraphs
- Look closely at any illustrations
- Realize that any words, phrases or sentences that are in **bold** or *italics* must be important—so be sure to read these as well!

As a reminder, do not forget that at some point you will absolutely have to read the entire text, so set aside a planned amount of time to do just that!

Test Taking Suggestions

Taking a test can be a fairly frightening experience! This is usually the case for most people. What most do not realize, however, is that with proper planning, a sufficient amount of sleep, a good breakfast the day of the test, and an ample supply of #2 lead pencils, taking a test will be a cinch! Try the following tips.

- ❑ Avoid "cramming" the night before a test. Get a good night's sleep so you will be fresh, relaxed and ready to do your best.

- ❑ If you have a lot of brothers and sisters, explain to them that you are going to be taking an important test. Encourage them to play quiet games the night before so that you can study and rest; or make arrangements to go to the library to study with a friend.

- ❑ Think positively. Have confidence in the fact that you have adequately prepared for the test and cannot help but do well!

❑ Be as relaxed as possible! If you are tense, you will not be able to understand the directions, absorb the questions or remember what you studied.

❑ Avoid watching the clock. Seeing the time go by will only **waste** time and make you nervous. Keep in mind that since it is absolutely "impossible" for you to stop the passing of time, all you can do about it is to **use** it—wisely.

❑ Answer as many of the questions you can, first! Then, go back to those that were more difficult.

❑ Be sure to read the directions—carefully. Or, make certain you understand the directions given by the test-giver. Do not be afraid to ask the test giver to repeat the instructions. (Often, after instructions are given, the test-giver will simply ask if there are any questions—don't hesitate, ask right away. You might not get another chance before the test begins!)

Test Taking Tips for Different Types of Exams

True-False   If any part of a true-false statement is false, the answer is false. Look for keywords or qualifiers such as all, most, sometimes, never, or rarely. Questions containing absolute qualifiers such as always or never often are false.

Open Book   When studying for this type of test, write down any formulas you will need on a separate sheet. Place tabs on important pages of the book so you don't have to waste time looking for tables or other critical information. If you plan to use your notes, number them and make a table of contents. Prepare thoroughly for open-book tests. They are often the most difficult.

> **Tip:** For machine-graded, multiple choice tests, be certain that the answer you mark corresponds to the question you are answering. Check the test booklet against the answer sheet whenever you start a new section and again at the top of each column.

"Negative thoughts negate positive actions."

Chapter 9
Expand Your "College" Consciousness

For the purposes of this book, "College" is defined as an institution of higher learning that is above the high school level. This includes two-year and four-year colleges, universities and technical/trade schools. If you are thinking about going to college, or have already started making plans, here are a number of tidbits you may find helpful.

"Why" I Want to Go!

The decision to go to college is really yours to make. It is a serious one. And, it will mean that you have to make a commitment of 2-4 years of your life. Think about some of the "why's" you have about wanting to go to college—seriously!

Do you want to go because your best friend is going? Are your parents so insistent that you feel uncomfortable saying "no"? Does it matter that you might be able to get a better paying job if you obtain a degree? Is your main goal to become a professional in a particular profession (nurse, doctor, teacher, etc.) where a degree is an absolute essential? Or, do you simply want to go to college just to have something to do **before** deciding on a specific career?

Look at your reasons for wanting to go to college. By doing so, your decision-making and planning activities are sure to be a little easier!

> **Hint**: The best time to start thinking about doing a college-search is when you are in the tenth grade. If you start later (for example, in your senior year) that's okay, too! It just means you have less time to devote to serious college-search activities.

Getting Guidance

Aside from your parents, the **one** person to consult who would be more knowledgeable about college concerns, is your school counselor. Many of the questions you have can be readily answered by her/him. Some of the questions you need to ask are:

- Am I taking the proper courses to meet college entrance requirements?
- How do I choose a college?
- How do I apply?
- What kind of questions are usually found on applications?
- At a college interview, do they want to know what my favorite subjects are, how I spend my summers, what my hobbies are, or why I want to go to their college?
- Could I be rejected because my SAT scores are low?
- Do colleges consider my personality, extra-curricular activities or my volunteer work in their decision to accept me?
- If I play a sport, will I have a better chance of getting a scholarship?
- Where can I get information on financial assistance?
- Which historically black colleges should I look at first?

These questions will probably prompt you to ask still others. So, set-up an appointment to speak with your counselor. Take a list of questions with you and be sure to make a copy that you can give to your counselor. By doing so, the two of you will be able to talk in an orderly and time-saving manner. You might also want to think about setting up an appointment for once a week—three weeks in a row. Remember, other students will probably be doing the same thing, so be "fair" with the amount of time you request with the counselor!

Planning

Once you begin to entertain the idea of going to college, a good first step to take, is to get your parent's viewpoint. Ask them how they feel about the idea. Share your thoughts and goals with them. You may be the first member of your family to go to college. If so, be sure to let your parents know how important it is to you and ask them to participate in the application process. Ask if going to college will cause a financial burden for them. Would they prefer that you attend a local college? What are their feelings about you living on campus?

Discuss whether or not you will have to work part-time. Do you think you could juggle studies and a job at the same time?

Next, do a bit of research on your own. Purchase (or borrow from the Library) a college guide book. There are several on the market. Among them are: *ARCO: The Right College, Barron's Profile of American Colleges,* and *Cass & Birnbaum's Guide to American Colleges.* You will be able to get information on admission criteria, expenses, financial aid, faculty specifics, the campus environment, facilities, student activities and much more for hundreds of colleges and universities.

Partial Listing of Historically Black Colleges

Alabama A & M University
Alcorn State University
Bennett College
Bethune-Cookman College
Bowie State University
Clark Atlanta University
Coppin State College
Dillard University

Elizabeth City State Universities
Fayetteville State University
Fisk University
Florida A & M University
Grambling State University
Hampton University
Howard University
Jackson State University
Johnson C. Smith University
Langston University
LeMoyne-Owen College
Meharry Medical College
Morehouse College
Morgan State University
Norfolk State University
North Carolina A & T State University
North Carolina Central University
Prairie View A & M University
South Carolina State University
Southern University—Baton Rouuge
Spelman College
Stillman College
Talladega College
Tennessee State University
Texas Southern University
Tuskegee University
University of Arkansas at Pine Bluff
University of Maryland Eastern Shore
Virginia State University
Winston-Salem State University

If you have specific colleges in mind, send a letter to the college requesting information.

> **Tip**: Typing is always better than writing—it looks more professional!

Following is an example of a letter you might want to send:

Letter Requesting Information
About A Particular College

Starting at the left margin, type:

(Your) Address
(Your) City, State, Zip Code
Today's Date

Go down on the page about (3) spaces and type:

Office of Admissions
(College Name)
(College Address)
(College City, State, Zip Code)

Go down on the page about (2) spaces and type:

Dear Admissions Specialist:

Go down on the page another (2) spaces and type the body of your letter:

I am a student attending (Your High School's Name), which is located in (Your High School's City and State). My goal is to go to college and I think your college would be a good choice. Please send information about the college, entrance requirements and an application.

Go down (2) spaces and type:

I look forward to hearing from you soon!

Go down (2) spaces and type:

Sincerely,

Go down about (3) spaces and type:

(Your name)

(Write your name—do not print—in the space above your typed name.)

The information you receive will help both you and your parents decide which college would best suit your needs and help you reach your goals. Give special attention to the requirements needed for admission; where the college is located; if tuition and on-campus living costs are within your family's reach; and, if the dormitories are co-educational.

Keep a record. List at least 20 different points you (and your parents) feel are most important in making a decision. You might want to *rank* each college on the basis of "yes—maybe—no". Share this chart with your counselor to get her/his comments, suggestions or advice. The format provided below might be helpful.

Possible College Choices

\# _____

College: _____

Address: _____

Comments: _____

_____

_____

_____

Rating: Yes_____ Maybe_____ No_____

Next, review your choices. Really look at the comments you made. Now, select the 5 you want to get serious about. Use index cards. Record the college name and address. After giving each choice a bit more attention, put them in order of preference. These will be the colleges you will be giving your full attention.

> **Tip**: If none of the initial 5 colleges don't quite meet your needs, simply go back to your original list, pick 5 more and start again. There is a college, out there, for everyone!

Visiting the College

Do not let catalogs fool you! All colleges have their own personality. And, so do you. By not visiting the college, you will not know if both personalities can be a comfortable fit. Remember to dress appropriately. It is perfectly all right to wear casual clothes. But, no jeans, shorts or denim jackets. Even the professors dress casually, so it is appropriate for you to do so, too. While the Admissions Officer may be dressed in business clothes, remember she/he has to deal with the public and is, after all, in a business-related work environment. Be on time.

Take a tour of the campus. Try to talk to some of the students. Pay attention to how they speak and dress. Ask about the classes, professors, health care, social stuff and campus security. Try to get a feel for the college to see if you think you will comfortably *fit in*. If possible, see if you can stay overnight in a dorm. Many colleges have special overnight-stay programs for potential freshmen so they can get a closer look at college life. Ask for a copy of the school newspaper to see what issues they find worthy of publishing. When you return home, make a list of both the *good* and *bad* points you have about the college. Should you have further questions, talk to your counselor or write to the Admissions Office of that particular college.

At the interview, take along your set of questions, a copy of your high school transcript, your resume (if you have held several jobs during high school) and a pleasing smile! On your list of questions to ask include:

- Class size

- How much weight is placed on SAT and ACT test scores

- Are there strict dorm rules about playing music, drinking or severe punishments for violating certain rules?

Be careful about what you say. Avoid using the words "like" or "you know" in every other sentence; don't chew gum; watch your posture (sitting erect gives the appearance of confidence!); and, do not use "slang" expressions for any reason! And, you will be on time for your appointment—won't you?!

Things to Pack

Going away to college means living away from home. It also means taking certain items with you for your new home away-from-home. Since this marks the beginning of a new and independent lifestyle, many students (parents, too!) are not quite sure about what to pack.

Pack only the bare essentials! Once you are settled in, you can then decide if there will be sufficient room to store additional items without "crowding" your roommate. Be prepared to get along without certain luxury and convenience items. Make a list of the items you feel you **absolutely** have to pack. In general, you need to list such items as clothing, linen, cooking and eating supplies, cleaning supplies, non-perishable food products, first aid items, sewing/mending supplies, an alarm clock and enough school supplies to last at least one semester. Below is a checklist to get you started.

"My Checklist of Things to Pack"

❑ *Clothes Items*

Keeping in mind that you will be coming home at least twice during each school year, pack only those clothes that you need for specific seasons. Pack everyday wear, underwear (including a few sets of thermal underwear), a rain/shine coat, winter coat, gloves, hat, warm scarf, bathing suit/trunks, shorts, jogging suits and sleep wear.

❑ *Personal Items*

Pack a tooth brush, toothpaste, mouth wash, dental floss, deodorant, soap, hair/shaving supplies, nail and foot supplies, fingernail polish, cotton balls, perfumes or colognes, jewelry items, lotion, hygiene products (sanitary napkins, condoms, etc.), boxes of Kleenex, and Q-Tip swabs.

❑ *Linen Items*

It might be wise to have, at least, three changes of linen. Your linen would consist of: 3 bottom fitted sheets and top sheets (in twin size, only); one light blanket and a comforter (for cooler nights); towels and washcloths.

❑ *Medication Items*

If you are on "special" medication, be sure to pack an ample supply. Include emergency medical items such as: Band-aids, creams for cold sores, antiseptics, alcohol, Vaseline, aspirin, cold tablets and medication for the relief of pain due to cramps.

❑ *Food Items*

Pack non-perishable food items. Your list might include: boxes of spaghetti, macaroni and rice; a five-pound package of flour and sugar; tea, coffee and hot chocolate; a supply of instant soups; cans of your favorite vegetables in single-serve portions; frozen dinners or vegetable side dishes for one; and, your favorite snack foods—popcorn, potato chips, nuts, candy, etc.

❑ *Cooking and Kitchen Items*

Your main meals will be served at the dinning hall. For those snacks and occasional meals you prefer to prepare on your own, be sure to pack a "special" set of supplies. You will need: cooking utensils, a can opener, cookware (for conventional and microwave ovens), cooking oil, seasonings, potholders, dishwashing cloths, scouring pads, dishwashing towels and detergent, plates, cups, eating utensils and a few glasses. (If you can, try to take along an ample supply of **paper** cups, plates, plastic eating utensils and napkins!)

❑ *Equipment and Furnishings*

The packing of those items you consider to be "equipment" or "furnishings" will require that you give extra concern to your choice of what is important and really needs to be packed! Under the heading of "Equipment and Furnishings" you might want to pack a refrigerator and/or microwave oven; a typewriter and/or personal computer; a desk lamp; a calculator, a small television alarm clock, hairdryer, ironing board and iron.

Note: Some campuses will not allow certain electrical appliances. Check before packing!

❏ *School Supplies*

Pens, pencils, notebooks (spiral and several three-ring notebooks), paper (lined and typing paper), paperclips, scissors, tape and dispenser, stapler and staples, report covers, dictionary, thesaurus, pocket-size notebook.

❏ *Miscellaneous Items*

Stamps, envelopes, your address book, a combination lock, a flashlight, umbrella, rolls of change.

Money Matters

Being on your own means handling your own finances. It will be *your* job to keep track of *your* money! Know how much you have at all times. Know where it has to go, and decide how far it will have to be stretched.

To do this effectively, you'll need to become acquainted with the three B's—*budgets, bank accounts and buying power.* Let's take a look at each of these.

"Spend sparingly and spread wisely!"

Budgets

A budget is simply a listing of the how much money you have and how you intend to spend it. It will take a few tries before you are able to set-up a budget that will work without too much penny-pinching. So, keep trying until you find that after paying all of your expenses, you have enough money left over to live "comfortably."

One of the biggest budget problems you will face is not having enough money! And, there will be many, many occasions when you just *have* to have *more.* Buying clothes and dating, for example, can wreck even the best of budgets!

Be honest! Do you really need to purchase that article of clothing? *Be creative!* Plan dates that are both fun and inexpensive. *Be enterprising!* Look for ways to earn extra cash. Offer to provide a service. For instance, offer to tutor, type, rent computer time, make deliveries, run errands, do laundry or handle housekeeping chores.

As a special note, *absolutely avoid* the temptation to engage in **any** forms of *illegal activities* as a means of supplementing your income!

"Money can sometimes cost too much!"

Handling your money will be easier if you set-up a "monthly budget." Don't cheat! List *all* of your expenses.

If your expenses are more than your income, start again. Try to reduce the amount of money you intend to spend for personal or food items. Be careful to always handle those expenses that are absolutely important—first! Make a special effort to budget *all* of your money.

If you find there is money left over after paying for expenses, add a small portion to a particular expense item or add a separate expense item called "Money to my savings account." This could be money set aside for emergency purposes.

Knowing how much money to allow yourself for travel and pocket money will be tricky! Basically, you only need to remember three things: (1) your funds are limited; (2) the cheaper your means of transportation, the more you can save; and, (3) penny-pinching on *this* month's budget, means "extra" cash next month!

> **Hint**: Hitchhiking could cause harm to your personal safety—so, don't do it!

Try the following sample.

My Monthly Budget

For the Month of: _____

Income (List separately and add)
    Check for Books: $_____
    Money from Home: $_____
    Gift from Uncle Charles: $_____
    Secret Money from Aunt Wanda: $_____
                 Total Income = $_____

Expenses (List separately and add)
    Books: $_____
    Personal Items: $_____
    Food Items: $_____
    Travel Money: $_____
    Pocket Money: $_____
              Total Expenses = $_____

Budget Summary
(Subtract total expense amount from total income amount)

    Total Income $ _____
    Total Expenses $ _____
    Budget Balance $ _____

(Budgeting all money equals a "zero" balance !)

Special Note: The real secret to using a budget successfully, is to stick to it! So be patient. It takes practice and lots of self-discipline.

Bank Accounts

Open a checking account (and savings account if you can) as soon as possible. Many colleges have a bank on campus or in walking distance. Ask the "new accounts" bank representaive to explain the different types of accounts available. Ask for their advice. They will also show you how to write a check and fill out a deposit slip. Do not be afraid or embarrassed to ask for help. They are usually more than willing to assist you.

Try to pay-by-check as often as possible. It is not a safe idea to carry large sums of money on you or leave large sums in your room. With a check, you will be able to have a record of where your money was spent.

Most banks have a "money machine" so you should have no problem getting small amounts at a moment's notice. Since it is very easy to forget a trip to the money machine—be careful—keep your receipts and write the amounts in your checkbook as soon as possible!

At the end of the month, the bank will send you a statement that lists all the checks you have written, money machine transactions and other withdrawals, the amount of deposits you've made, bank charges, fees and your balance. On the back of this statement you will find instructions on how to "balance" your bank statement. The purpose of the statement is to make sure that your records and the bank's records match. If not, someone has made a mistake! Lots of people have trouble balancing their monthly statements. Don't you be one of them! If you need help, ask a bank officer.

Buying Power

Finding ways to save money will enable you to buy more for less. Stretch your money as often and as far as you can. Here are a few tips to guide you in the right direction.

- ❑ Buy "used" instead of new books.

- ❑ Use coupons to save on the purchase of shampoo, toothpaste, detergent, food items (pizzas, too!)

- ❑ Set up a "food cooperative" where you and 5 to 10 other students prepare a shopping list and buy the same brands of items in bulk—sharing the expense. (What you save will amaze you!)

- ❑ Make a shopping list and stick to it!

- ❑ Shop in thrift stores for odds and ends.

- ❑ Learn the art of "swapping!" (Swap one bar of soap, for example for a bottle of lotion.)

- ❑ Buy "sale" items only. (Brand name items cost more!)

❑ Swap services for items. (Two hours of tutoring for a large pizza!)

❑ Don't borrow and avoid loaning money.

*"Money borrowed is a debt owed
and another expense in your budget!"*

Odds and Ends

The mini-topics which follow have been included to give you a little more *food for thought!*

Campus Security

Be *security sensible*! At some point during your interview or tour, be sure to ask about the campus security measures which are enforced. Some of the questions you and your parents might want to ask are:

■ How many security officers usually work the day shift? the night shift? How many are female?

■ Can students get an escort to their dormitories during evening hours?

■ Are the security officers required to complete training courses similar to that of a police officer? Are they licensed to carry a weapon?

■ How much protection will you have if you live off-campus?

■ How close is the nearest police station to the campus?

■ Are the dormitories locked at a certain hour?

■ What kind of locks are on the individual rooms?

■ Is there a guard posted in the lobby of the dormitory?

■ How often are the grounds patrolled?

■ Are security seminars given frequently?

Your protection and the safety of your personal belongings are important concerns. Remember, you will be living away from home—and, on your own! Isn't it better to know ahead of time just *how much security you can depend on*?

Letters of Reference

Colleges will ask you to have letters of reference sent from people (not relatives) who can vouch for your good character. Write a short letter to those you wish to use as personal references. Here is a sample you might want to use:

Request for Letters of Reference

Today's Date

(Your address)
(Your city, state, zip)

Mr./Mrs./Ms./Pastor (Person's full name)
(Person's address)
(Person's city, state, zip)

Dear Mr./Mrs./Ms./Pastor (Person's last name):

I hope to attend (name of college) in the Fall. This college requires a letter of reference from people who know me very well and can vouch for my good character. I would like for you to write them a letter.

Please send the letter to me so I can put all of them together. The letter should be addressed to: Office of Admissions, (name of college, address, city, state and zip code). It should include how long you have known me; in what capacity (as a neighbor, member of the church, at school, etc.) and, why you feel I would be a valuable member of their college community.

If you have any questions please call me at (your telephone number). I appreciate your kindness and sincerely thank you!

Cordially,

(Write your name here)
(Print your name here)

Don't forget, "typing" is always best!

Ask a teacher, one of your school counselors, the Pastor at your church, a neighbor or a former employer. You will need at least five references. You probably will not have any problems getting reference letters because those who know you, only want the best for you. They will more then likely be very proud to send a letter on your behalf and appreciate the fact that you thought about them!

Dormitory Living

Be considerate of your roommate's study and sleep habits. Make your habits known to them. Be neat. Remember, your roommate is not a relative and may not be as forgiving about your untidiness as your brother or sister were at home! Don't be afraid to ask for privacy and be sure to extend the same courtesy to not only your roommate but other dormitory residents as well. Try preparing a set of guidelines that both you and your roommate can agree to follow. Abide by the rules set forth by the college and your dorm monitors. Be helpful, cooperative and patient. Respect and preserve dormitory property—its furnishings, the facilities and the grounds. On sharing a kitchen or bathroom, keep in mind that it is selfish to expect others to clean up behind you and a sign of thoughtlessness to take more time than you really need!

> *"Borrow trouble for yourself,*
> *if that's your nature, but don't lend it to your neighbors!"*
> *—Rudyard Kipling*

Coed Dorms and Guests

Some colleges have coed dormitories. These are dormitories that have both male and female students living in the same building. Many of them are housed on different floors, while others allow students to share facilities. If this will be a problem for you, it is suggested that you find out ahead of time before you accept a particular room assignment. Your conduct (whether in a coed dormitory situation or inviting guests to your room) will be a matter of personal choice. Allow your sense of maturity, common sense and self-image to guide your decision to act in a "responsible" manner.

Credit Cards

Credit card companies like to encourage students to apply. Before applying, give serious thought to "how" you intend to pay the monthly charges. Keep track of your charges. Always set aside enough money for two monthly payments ($20–$40) even though you will only be paying for one monthly bill. This is your emergency bill money! Pay your bills on time. You will be establishing credit and in order to open accounts later on, it will be important that your credit record show you are a responsible person who pays on time.

"It's always cheaper to think before you charge!"

Pledging

Deciding to join a sorority or fraternity is a good idea. It promotes sisterhood and brotherhood. You gain a sense of belonging, make new friends, engage in group interaction and have a lot of fun! Use common sense and your feelings of right versus wrong conduct in making the choice to join a particular sorority or fraternity. Do not let the pressure of others influence your decision. Abide by your sense of values, fair play and solid judgment. If you are not selected, do not feel that it is the "end of the world!" Simply, feel bad for about an hour and then go on with your life.

Remember, disappointments are a part of life. And, not being selected will have no bearing on your academic standing nor, will it make a significant change in your life or the goals you have set for yourself.

Keeping In Touch

Try to regularly communicate with family members and friends. Write at least a short note to say hello. Remember to send birthday greetings and anniversary congratulations, in a timely fashion. Purchase a box of all occasion cards so that you will be prepared. Try not to call because telephone bills can become very expensive, very fast and in a very short period of time! Why not purchase stamps, instead?

"Reach out and touch only when you can afford to,
otherwise...write!"

Chapter 10
Search "Carefully" for Work

Getting a job can be harder than the job you **get**! Whether you are searching for summer, part-time or permanent full-time employment, your chances for success depends on the amount of preparation you put into it. Your preparation would include, for example: having a pretty good sense of the kind of problems you will have to face in looking for work; knowing where and how to look for a job; understanding many of do's and don'ts about the interview process; and, knowing how to act once you get hired. To increase your chances of getting a job you need to be prepared.

Give this section some serious thought so you can have a head-start over the competition!

Possible Problems

Here is a bit of sad news. Many experts believe that teens, typically, have a harder time getting a job than an unemployed adult! Below are a few of the reasons they use to justify their beliefs.

- The job market is so tight that there simply are not enough jobs available for either teens or adults, and you need a job that fits your busy schedule, skill level and future goals.

- Wages for your age group are so low, that you really don't feel motivated enough to apply for certain jobs.

- You go from job to job, in a short period of time, simply to be able to earn an additional 50-80 cents per hour in wages. This is called "job shopping." (Many leave one job to go to another after having worked for as little as 3 weeks!)

- By not staying at a job for a significant amount of time (3 months–1 year) you do not get a chance to learn the art of having a positive "work" attitude. You also cannot gain enough work-related skills to allow you to go on to another job which might pay more—depending on your level of skills.

- With little or no training, it can be difficult to function in the workplace.

- You have a lot of competition from your peers and hundreds of unemployed adults. There is additional competition to be concerned about with the many individuals arriving from other countries who are also searching for work.

- Your age group can be unfortunately, easily and seriously attracted to illegal activities for a quick way to earn money.

- For some, there are concerns about your having a child to support or facing the battle of having a criminal record.

- , Even though there are laws against discrimination, some companies may not hire you because you are a person of color. If you are sure this is the case, you can report them to your local Attorney General's office.

These are just a few of the problems which might make it difficult for you to get a job. In spite of these problems, however, and with a little patience and solid planning, you *can* find work.

It's the Law!

Employers have to follow certain federal, state and local Child Labor Laws before they can hire you. This is for your protection and theirs.

Child Labor laws in most states list a number of jobs that are considered "harmful" or "hazardous" to those who are younger than 18 years of age. Some jobs involve using chemicals or dangerous machinery and are considered unsuitable for young workers. Since you attend school, there are restrictions on the number of hours you can work and specific periods of the year when exceptions may be granted. Because it is the law, most employers are more than willing to comply with these rules and regulations. Those who **do not** face the possibility of being fined up to $10,000, put in jail or both!

To make sure you are old enough to work, the employer will ask you for an employment certificate. This is usually called a "work permit." You can get one from your school counselor or by contacting the Department of Labor: Wage and Hour Division. (Look in the White Page telephone directory for the telephone number.)

Do you need a little encouragement at this point? Well, think of your job hunting experience as an "unpleasant" dream that won't last forever! With this thought in mind, go forth and do your absolute best. Remember, knowing what you are up against—ahead of time—will make your job search activities much easier to handle!

"Search with determination to block-out frustration!"

Where to Look

There are a number of ways and places to look for work. You can begin by asking your parents, relatives, friends or the school counselor if they know of any openings. Do you have a friend who will be leaving her/his job? Ask them if they will recommend you as a replacement. By asking those you know, first, your chances of getting a job could be a lot easier. Here are a few more ways:

- Look for "Help Wanted" signs at local stores, fast food establishments and small businesses in your area. These places usually have signs posted in their windows.

- Place notices on bulletin boards in your area. On a three-by-five index card type or neatly print: your name, telephone number, the best time to call and the kind of work you want. Be sure to get permission from store managers before you post your cards.

> **Hint**: It is always a very good idea to get your parent's permission to use the family's telephone number!

- Do not, under any circumstances, put your home address. There are too many weird people who could cause harm to you and your family!

- Look for job openings or announcements on television (some cable stations have one channel that is specifically devoted to job announcements—see your cable channel guide). Listen to radio stations that give job openings on a regular basis. Find a computer and see what the Internet has to offer.

- Government offices have lots and lots of bulletin boards! Visit the government offices in your area and look at the announcements they have posted.

- Let your fingers do the walking. You can find the telephone number of most businesses in the Yellow Pages under, either its business name or kind of business. Make a list of the companies that interest to you.

Call each of the companies and ask for the "Human Resources Office." Tell them you are looking for a job and would like to know if they have any openings. Many companies have "job-lines" so you might want to ask for the job-line telephone number, first. Then ask for the procedures to follow in order to apply.

> **Tip**: Fax numbers are sometimes magical! Be sure to ask for the company's fax number so you can quickly fax your resume. Remember, it will be quicker by fax than by mail! Maybe there is a fax service at school or your local library; or perhaps your parents can use the fax at their job. If not, many office supply stores offer fax service for a small fee.

> **Tip:** The Internet is a great place to find job possibilities, and it might be the easiest. With just a click of the

mouse you can send your resume to several companies at once.

- Visit your state employment office. This office has a com-
puterized listing of several hundred openings, offers job
and career counseling and, can direct you to the nearest
office which handles youth placement referrals for summer
jobs, after school jobs, or adult/teen part-time or permanent full-time employment. Their services are "free"!

- Contact private employment agencies. These agencies
can be found in the Yellow Pages Directory under
"Employment." They are in the business of "placing" or
finding suitable jobs for their clients. These agencies give
you a test, determine what your skills are, and match your
skill-level with the needs of a prospective employer.
Some agencies will charge you a special fee for finding
you a job. This may be costly and if you are just starting
out, not necessarily an expense you may want to occur.

  Hint: If you are looking for a summer or part-time job it
  is not a good idea to consult this type of agency. They
  handle clients (most of the time) who are looking for
  permanent full-time work.

- Contact the offices of state elected officials such as your
congressman, senator, school board officials, county
executives, PTA presidents, etc., and ask for guidance on
where to look for employment.

- Call civic organizations. Many of these organizations
have announcements posted and/or members in need
of summer, part-time or temporary help. Try contacting:
Boy Scouts of America, Boys and Girls Clubs, Camp Fire
Girls, the Chamber of Commerce, Girl Scouts of America, National Federation of Business and Professional
Women's Clubs, the YWCA/YMCA and any others you
can locate. When looking for a job, consider your interests and try to find something that would enhance your
future career goals.

"Persistence can bring a profitable payoff!"

Here is another suggestion. How "daring" are you? Try putting an ad in your local newspaper under the section called "Positions Wanted." (Remember to get your parent's permission, first, of course.)

Let the ad run in the Sunday issue for three weeks in a row. This will allow you to get the most exposure and save you several dollars. Should you need money to run the ad and have to ask your parents to pay for it, be prepared to reimburse them for the cost of the ad. In fact, make a special effort to repay them as quickly as possible—preferably out of your first paycheck!

Avoid going on interviews or taking a job in an area that is unfamiliar, unsafe or too far from home. Don't work late hours during school season. If you should get an interview based on an ad that you've placed, ask for references and have your parents check out the prospective employer's credentials, and possibly go with you to meet them.

Sample: "Position Wanted Ad"

"Teen seeks job as math tutor. Grades 3-6. In-house services, reasonable rates. Call (evenings) (000) 000-0000".

"High school student seeks responsible job in law firm for the summer. Call evenings, (000) 000-0000".

"New graduate majoring in chemistry seeks responsible full-time position in small lab. Call (000) 000-0000".

"Baby-sitter: my home, Happy County area, ages 5-9. Experienced. Call (000) 000-0000".

Telephone Talk

In many instances, your initial way to search for work will begin with making telephone calls. These conversations give the listener a mental picture about you. Your voice tone, choice of words and level of courtesy, therefore, are very important. This will be your first chance to make a good impression.

Before going any further, complete the following short quiz on "First Calls."

First Calls

Each of the questions listed below are either true or false.

True	False	Question
❑	❑	The manner in which I speak to the telephone operator or receptionist is not really important.
❑	❑	If the person who answers the phone is rude to me, I have the right to be rude to them.
❑	❑	Keeping a telephone log of the calls can be a valuable tool for the future.
❑	❑	It is not necessary to give my name when calling to see if there are any openings.
❑	❑	Being courteous and brief will make a positive first impression.
❑	❑	Sounding desperate for a job is a sure way to get an interview.
❑	❑	It is better to call between the hours of 10:00 a.m. and 4:00 p.m.

Statements 3, 5 and 7 are true. So, feel comfortable knowing you are a courteous individual, have a business manner and are a person who is organized. If you chose "true" for statements 1, 2, 4 and 6, some improvement might be in order!

In general, making the initial call to a company to see if a position is available, requires that you: (1) use a pleasant tone of voice; (2) speak clearly; (3) use manners (whether they do or not!); and, (4) be brief, yet, informative about the purpose of your call.

Your sample conversation (once you get someone in the Human Resources Department) might be as follows:

"Good morning. My name is _____. I am calling to ask three quick questions. First, if you have a "job-line", second, if you have any positions currently available? and third, how can I apply?

▌ **Tip**: Be sure to write whatever information you can get!

End your conversation with: Thank you for being so helpful and have a delightful day!"

If you remember to sound confident, comfortable and professional you should have no problem getting a pleasant response. Do not forget to practice using a tape recorder! What you hear will, of course, be what they hear. So, be prepared.

Answering the telephone and keeping track of possible interviews is your responsibility. Try not to burden other family members. Try not to schedule interview times too close to each other. If you do, there is a strong chance you will be late for one or more interviews that day. Always include travel time on your schedule. You can expect to be at an interview for about 1-2 hours.

▌ **Hint**: Some companies give written or computer tests after you have completed the application. This is their way to get a better picture of your skills and qualifications!

If you are lucky, you might be interviewed the same day!

Use an "Interview Log" to keep your dates and times straight. By doing so, you will save a lot of time and be more organized. Only do one sheet for each interview. Assemble the sheets by date and time. As a quick reference, be sure to put these dates and times on your pocket calendar or schedule. Below is a sample log sheet.

"Promptness is always a plus!"

Interview Log Sheet

Appointment Date:_____

Appointment Time:_____

Interview With: _____

Position Title: _____

Company Name: _____

Company Address: _____

Company Telephone: _____

Company Fax Number: _____

Mode of Travel: ❑ Drive ❑ Bus ❑ Cab ❑ Subway

Directions: _____

_____

Special Notes: _____

_____

The day **before** any interview, always review your log sheet! You will find these sheets very helpful as both an organizing and a confidence-promoting tool.

Your Resume

Always take time the night before (or, an at least an hour before) to review your resume. By doing so you will be better prepared to answer any questions the interviewer might ask. It won't make a very good impression if you have to keep looking at your resume in order to answer a question!

Your resume gives the interviewer more information about you than the application form you will be required to fill out. It should be no more than two pages (one is usually best). It should be neatly typed, and not have white-out or misspelled words. If you cannot type, ask someone who can! A good resume includes all or some of the following elements:

❑ Name, address, city, state, zip code and telephone number (don't forget to put your area code and a fax number.)

❑ Education (school names and addresses, major subject areas, degrees earned)

❑ Work experience (list your current job first, then any past employment.)

❑ Extra-curricular activities (school clubs and community organizations that you belong to let the employer know you can get along with people.)

❑ References (name, address, telephone number. Be sure to get their permission in advance; and, remember that your references should be non-relatives, only)

There are many books in the library that can give you more details concerning the kind of resume you need, along with sample formats. Always do a draft first and have someone look it over. It is very easy to miss your own mistakes.

Application Forms

When applying for a job, the first task you will have is to fill out a job application. Quite a bit of the information will already be on your resume. But, when filling out the form, you need to give particular attention to providing the same information in a shorter version. Besides, most applications do not give you enough space to write a whole lot, anyway!

Like your resume, the job application is also a reflection of you. If you turn in an application that has "scratch-outs" and generally does not look neat, you could be perceived as a potential employee who will not do "neat" work. If you **write** instead of **print**, this could mean you are a person who will not be able to follow directions. Here are some points to keep in mind about filling out job applications.

- ❑ Quickly review the entire form **before** filling-in your answers and be sure you understand **all** of the directions.

- ❑ Follow all directions as carefully as you can.

- ❑ Remember to print as neatly as possible.

- ❑ If you make a mistake (no erasers, please! Simply draw a neat line through it and beside or above the mistake write the correction. By all means, however, try **not** to do this more than twice!)

- ❑ Be sure your responses are short but to the point.

- ❑ If there are questions that do not apply to you, write-in: N/A.

- ❑ When you come across the section that asks what salary you want or are expecting, write-in "open". If you already know what the salary is, fill it in.

- ❑ For those sections that ask about criminal records—tell the truth. You might be surprised at how many potential employers are willing to extend a second chance!

- ❑ Immediately after completing the application, take a few deep breaths (get up and drink some water) then review it (line-by-line) before turning it in.

> **Tip**: Take along 2-3 "black" ballpoint pens. They are neater and clearer than using pencils. Avoid pencils, unless you are asked to use one!

Miscellaneous Letters

A number of different letters will be needed for your job search activities. Each of the letters should have the following elements and format. And, once again, typing is best!

Basic Letter Writing Format

Your Last Name *(centered)*
Your Address *(centered)*
Your City, State, Zip *(centered)*
Your Telephone Number *(centered)*

Today's Date

Ms. or Mr.
Her or His Title
Company Name
Address
City, State, Zip

Dear Ms. or Mr. :

(Main portion of your letter goes here)

Sincerely,

(Your handwritten signature goes above your typed name, here)

Olivia M. Johnson

Enclosure: Resume

Now that you have a sample format, let's work on the body of the letters.

Letter of Interest

This is a general letter to be sent to practically any company you are interested in.

Main Portion:

> I am interested in being considered for the position of _____ that is currently available at Company Name . Enclosed is my resume for your review.
>
> I believe my educational background and work experience qualify me for consideration. It is my hope that you share this belief and will grant me an interview. I can be contacted by telephone during the hours of _____ to _____. You can also contact me by fax at _____.
>
> I am looking forward to becoming a member of this organization's *(agency, firm, etc.)* team. I hope to hear from you soon!

Letter Responding to an Ad

Use this letter for the ads you see in the newspaper, on bulletin boards or circulars passed out on parking lots!

Main Portion:

> I am interested in being considered for the position of _____ which appeared in the classified section of _____*Name of Newspaper*_____ on date it appeared. Enclosed is my resume for your review.
>
> I trust you will find that my educational background and work experience fit the profile of the individual you are seeking for this position. I can be contacted by telephone during the hours of _____ to _____ . You can also contact me by fax at _____.
> Please know that I look forward to hearing from you soon!

Letters of Reference

This is the letter you would send to people you want to use as a reference.

> **Hint**: When you send this letter do not forget to enclose a copy of your resume!

Main Portion:

Can you help me? I am currently looking for a job and want to list you as a reference. You have known me for years, so my thought was that you would be an excellent person to verify my character, honesty and dependability.

> To Whom It May Concern:
>
> This letter of reference is written to verify that I have known _____(my name)_____ for the past (number of years). Over these years, she/he has been a person who is of good character, can be trusted, is dependable and is a friendly. Her/his personality, coupled with, work experience and educational growth go a long way in my opinion of her/him. She/he has always been able to handle challenges and competition. These are the kind of traits that are rare for most people.
>
> Please do not hesitate to hire her/him. You would be making a mistake if you did not! (My Name) is a person that any company would be pleased to have on staff for any position.

Please consider doing this for me and know how very much I appreciate your support!

Presentation on Paper!

Use "nice" paper. It looks better. Make sure you use the same paper for your resume so everything looks like a set. Even better, can you get matching envelopes? If not, white paper is always appropriate as long as everything else is in order!

Thank You Card

It is always an ideal professional practice to send a "thank you" card after an interview. Not too many people really understand how important sending a card can be! By doing so you give the interviewer a "reminder" that you were there! This gives them an opportunity to "remember" you by name and for the fact that you took the time to say "thanks!"

Purchase some plain and very "unfancy" thank-you cards. DO NOT TYPE!!! Instead, use your best penmanship and write:

> Thank you for the interview on (date of interview). It was a pleasure meeting you. I look forward to a positive response, soon!

Sign your name, address the envelope and mail the card!

> **Tip:** It is always a good idea to write the card the same day. If you can, mail it either the same day or at least by the next day. Once, again, promptness counts!

The Interview

A number of preparations have to be in place before the interview, during the interview and after the interview. These tips should help.

Things to Do Before the Interview

Be "mentally" prepared to answer questions about yourself. Your response will let the interviewer know that you are confident you can handle the job. Some of the kinds of questions you might be asked are:

- Do you follow directions easily?
- Why do you want to work for this company?
- What are some of your strengths? weaknesses?
- Which of your courses do/did you like best? least?
- Do you have some special skills you feel this company would find valuable?
- Do you get along well with others?

Decide on answers to these questions. Practice what you will say a few days **before** the interview. Practice the night before will not hurt, either! Ask someone to give you a "practice" interview so you can feel more comfortable when the "real" time comes.

> **Hint**: Expect to feel nervous or uneasy at the **first** interview. It's perfectly normal. Learning from the first interview prepares you for all the rest!

Assemble an "interview folder". Take this handy folder with you to the interview. It should contain the following items:

- Your resume
- List of references
- List of questions you want to ask about the company
- Your practice notes on how to answer certain questions.

This folder will make the interview process go much smoother, help you be more prepared and might just impress the interviewer.

> **Tip**: The best times to schedule an appointment for an interview are before 11:30 a.m. or no later than 4:00 p.m. Many offices are very busy just before lunch (11:30 a.m.–1:30 p.m.). There is also a lot of activity before closing times (5:00 p.m.–6:00 p.m.).

Always go to an interview alone! Never take a friend, parent or relative. This is something that you must do completely on your own. People who take others with them **could** make the interviewer think they are insecure or lack self-confidence.

As a final suggestion, do not forget to dress for success! Check your wardrobe. Have you decided what you will wear? Pull your interview-outfit together one or two days before!

*"First interviews are intimidating **and** informative!*

Things to Do During the Interview

Plan to be alert and attentive. Interviewers will be looking for signs that you are not only interested in getting the job, but that you are excited about working for their company. Always think before answering questions. Make sure you sit using good posture. It is a good idea to keep constant eye-contact with the interviewer. This is usually considered a sign of confidence.

> **Tip**: If you feel a bit uncomfortable looking someone in the eye, they really won't know if you're not if you pick a *focal point*. Look at the interviewer **slightly above their eye-level and centered between their eyes!** Believe it or not, you will give the appearance of eye contact, without even looking into their eyes! Try practicing this with a friend or family member.

When you are called into the interviewer's office, extend your hand for a handshake as a professional form of greeting. Say: "Good morning/afternoon! Thank you for seeing me today. **Do not** sit down until you are offered a chair.

> **Tip**: Naturally, no gum-chewing, eating candy or smoking during the interview!

Smile and be pleasant, yet, professional. Watch your speaking skills! Using slang, inappropriate conversational words or phrases **could** end your chances of getting the job. Listen carefully. Answer in complete sentences and just loud enough for them to hear. Speaking too loudly or too softly could make the interviewer think you would be either an uncooperative worker or one who is too timid for the position! Never interrupt the interviewer. Never place your personal belongings on her/his desk. Avoid giving the interviewer the impression that you only want the job for the money! Instead, aim to leave her/him with the thought that, while salary is an important factor, you are looking for a company that will provide you with a level of learning you can share with the company, and will also help you to accomplish your personal goals.

Avoid talking a lot. Remember, you are not in-charge! So, do not attempt to be the **lead speaker**. Listen, very carefully, to all questions. Take your time answering questions. Answer questions that only require a "yes" or "no" with a simple "yes or "no". There will be many opportunities when you will have a chance to answer questions in more detail. It is never appropriate to interject (throw-in) personal problems at home or school during the interview. This is a time-waster for both you and the interviewer. And, it usually has no bearing on whether or not you are qualified to handle the job for which you are applying. Allow the interviewer to do her/his job—interview you.

At the end of the interview, say: "This was a very comfortable interview. I enjoyed meeting you and thank you for seeing me." Offer to shake hands and leave. That's it!

Things to Do After the Interview

Okay, it is finally over! Now you need to:

- Send a "thank you" card
- Accept that you **may not** get the job
- Expect to receive a "congratulations you-have-been-accepted letter" and be happy, or a "thanks-but-no-thanks" letter in the mail.
- Move forward and prepare for the next interview!

Behavior On-the-Job!

You got the job! Congratulations!!

It is time to discuss a few job etiquette things to ensure that you will be able to keep the job by acting in an appropriate manner.

- ❑ Never be afraid to ask questions.
- ❑ Take notes on instructions given to you by your supervisor.
- ❑ Should you make a mistake, **always** admit it. After all, your supervisor knows that **everyone** is not perfect and will usually give you another chance. Remember that by making mistakes, you also learn how **not to** make them, again!
- ❑ Make sure you keep your work area neat, work in an organized manner, and fully understand the instructions given by your supervisor.
- ❑ Be on time for work everyday. If an emergency comes up, remember to call-in and say that you will either be late or will not be coming-in at all. Watch the clock! Be sure you are calling-in within the appropriate timeframe.

❑ Accept criticism willingly. Look at criticism as a learning experience.

❑ If given added responsibilities, accept them. Look upon added responsibilities as another learning experience that **could** lead to future promotions.

❑ Always attempt to get along with your supervisor. They are, after all, in their official capacity, the individuals who can make the decision to keep or terminate you from the position!

> **Hint**: Even though your supervisor has this level of authority, you **do not** have to endure **any form of harrassment** while under their supervision. As an employee, no matter where you work, you **do** have rights that **must be** honored. Understand this, clearly. Understand, further, that you do not have to continue to stay in a position that makes you feel your constitutional rights are (have been) abused, or, that you feel your personal safety/well-being is in jeopardy (danger). Employers **cannot** do or cause you to feel such things in the workplace. It is the law!

❑ Keep a "positive" attitude. It can make your job less stressful. It could get you promoted. Letting go of a positive attitude can hurt you physically, emotionally and cause you to lose your job!

❑ Never be a "gossip spreader"! Avoid sharing comments or entering into conversations where co-workers are, obviously, spreading rumors. If it makes you uncomfortable to "listen" to, imagine how the person being talked about will feel once she/he hears what is being said. Remember, **you** could be the topic of the day!

As a final note, be mindful that organization and preparations are important in your attempts to get a job. You might not get the first, second or even fifth job for which you apply, but do not become frustrated. Let each of your interviews be a "learning" experience from which you can gain strength and confidence. With proper planning and a little patience, you **will** become employed!

Chapter 11
Consider "Hiring" Yourself

You want to work but can't find a job. You have applied at the usual places that typically hire teens or new college graduates and found that all the positions were filled. You even tried to sign up for the summer youth employment programs, contacted employment agencies, put an ad in the paper and called those companies that were of interest to you. Did you discover that all of your efforts—still—did not lead to your getting a job? Where can you go from here? Try *creating* a job by starting your own small business!

Self-employment **can** be one alternative to unemployment. It will allow you to be independent, to gain practical business experience that will enhance your studies, and help you to earn money.

The Self-Employed Person

Being self-employed means you are in business for yourself. You are the owner of the business. In fact, you are the *employer*, not the *employee*, for a change! It also means that you make all the decisions, sometimes supervise a small staff and are responsible for the well-being of the company, whether it succeeds or fails.

Self-employed persons also have another name which is a little fancier. That name is "entrepreneur." By definition, an entrepreneur is a person who organizes and manages a business, assuming the risks involved for the sake of profit. While both the self-employed and the entrepreneur handle the same kinds of mechanics associated with operating a business, the only real twist is that entrepreneurs tend to rely on their instincts (or inner feelings) a little more. There is just something within them that has a way of driving them to go on, stay focused and when failure happens, they immediately regroup, refocus and move forward. Failure is just another challenge!

Traits of Self-Employeds

People who are (or wish to be) self-employeds tend to have the same traits (characteristics).

- They are usually leaders and enjoy being independent.
- They set goals and work toward completion.
- Their health is usually good and they have lots of energy.
- Getting along with others is not a problem for them.
- Handling responsibility, evaluating situations and making "quick" decisions to resolve problems is the kind of challenge that pushes them to go further.
- They are detailed-oriented.
- They almost always have a business-like manner and appearance.
- Budget, to them, means finding the best bargains so they can make the most profits!
- They are honest, respectful and caring about the well-being of their company and their staff.

Having What It Takes

As a first step toward making the decision to be the **employer** (your own boss), you will need to find out if you have the kind of personality, sincerity and stamina that will be required. By answering the following questions—honestly—you will be able to determine if being self-employed is really for you!

Am I Really Ready?

❏ Am I physically and emotionally prepared to be self-employed?

❏ Do I look at problem-solving as a challenge and **want** to be the one to find a resolve?

❏ Am I a people-person or someone who can get along with others very well?

❏ Do I work better alone?

❏ Do I want to be self-employed just for the money?

❏ Am I uncomfortable with the idea of having this level of responsibility?

❏ Am I creative enough to integrate new ideas into the company?

❏ Will it bother me to have to work long hours?

❏ Do I have enough self-confidence to do this?

Were most of your answers more positive than negative. Look closely! Do you really feel you have what it will take to be self-employed?

Fighting Back!

Use self-employment as a way to fight-back at unemployment! Review the many reasons that experts feel are problem areas for "why" you are not able to get a job. With a little effort, you can easily turn these negative reasons for "why" into positive actions that will help you succeed as a business owner.

Problem Area: **The lack of available jobs**

Develop your own job; one that fits your particular time schedule. Ask yourself two questions. What do I do well? How much time can I spare per week? Then, schedule your hours around school responsibilities, household chores, leisure activity time, etc.

Problem Area: **Low minimum wages**

Decide how much money you would like to make on a weekly or monthly basis. Set "realistic" goals. Work toward meeting those goals. Remember, that no matter what kind of business you have, there will always be competition. So strive to be as unique as possible by offering a service or product that will cause your competitors to consider **you**—the competition!

Problem Area: **Job shopping**

Changing jobs on a frequent basis does not look good to someone who is considering hiring you. If you are doing this, there is a good side to be considered, only if you are giving "active" thought to becoming self-employed! By job-shopping, on purpose, you need to make sure that you acquire as many skills as you can from each job. It is quite possible that one or more of these skills will be of value when you decide to take the big step and become the *employer*—not, the *employee*!

Here is an example: on job #1, you were hired as a car wash attendant; job #2 was a cashier position at a retail store; and, at job #3, you were a messenger for a courier service. Each of these positions were different. The one element that is to your advantage, however, is that they all required interaction with the "public." This means that you have the potential to work with others and the ability to deal with the public—who will, more than likely be your customers. The cashier position gives you an added skill—handling money!

Problem Area: **Negative attitudes**

To gain work experience in the kind of business you intend to start, volunteer to work at a similar company in exchange for informal training. Being in a work environment will help you understand "how" to act on a job and help you to operate your business in a professional manner and become a "fair" supervisor.

Problem Area: **No training**

Once you have decided on the kind of business you will start, make it a point to improve your skills through extra courses, reading materials, tips from professionals, and viewing business-related programs on television. Volunteer work is also, good! In fact, many companies really look at the kind of volunteer time you engage in and give consideration along **with** your work "experience"!

Problem Area: **Competition**

If there are a large number of teens in your area, join forces and start a business together. If this is not possible, make sure your business has something a little bit different to offer. Competition is healthy and oftentimes heavy! Always try to be fair. Using unfair tactics in business dealings with your competition, will hurt you—eventually!

Problem Area: **Illegal activities**

It is easier to do wrong than right! You may discover too late that this kind of self-employment can be **very** harmful. By allowing your common sense to lead you, making the decision to enter into activities for "quick and easy money" will, in fact, not be worth the pain, pressure or inconvenience in the end. Put these energies to work by promoting a small business that is completely—legitimate—instead!

The Good, Bad and Ugly!

Some of the good things you will get as the *employer* and not the *employee* include the following:

- You work for yourself, not others.
- You will gain confidence, positive self-esteem, practical work experience, and have the opportunity to decide on "self-employment" as a career choice.
- You can attend school and have a successful business.
- Your hours are your own.
- You will be able to plan your own work, organize your time and be instrumental in the success of the business.

■ You will probably be working out of your home so there will be no worries about commuting costs, handling chores or caring for other family members.

■ You will make money depending on the goals you set for how much you want to make on a weekly, monthly or annual basis.

■ You will get a chance to enjoy working because it is a part of you.

Like everything else in life, there are also some disadvantages to being the *employer* and not the *employee*.

■ You will have less time for leisure activities, especially when you first start the business. As time goes on, however, you will be able to make some time for fun! You will also find that there will be periods when you have more work than you can handle alone—and periods when you wish you had any work at all!

■ In the beginning there will be a lot of paperwork and recordkeeping to handle (for example: writing letters, making flyers, keeping customer records, filling out tax forms, writing checks, etc.).

■ There will be times when your customers don't pay on time. This will be hard for you because you might have to purchase additional supplies or have employees to pay.

■ If something goes wrong or one of your employees makes a mistake, you as the employer will have to take the "heat"! This can be a very serious responsibility.

■ You will have both nice customers and some who are rude and nasty-tempered. It will be hard, but necessary, however to remain polite and courteous for the sake of your business. And, instead of screaming just smile and try to work out any disagreements that surface.

■ Be *really* aware and do some homework! For many businesses, you will be required to adhere to (follow) state/ federal laws concerning self-employment which may include: (a) operating a business that is legally within Child Labor Law restrictions; (b) being "officially" incorporated as a small business; and/or, charging state taxes on a product being sold.

> **Tip**: Call the Small Business Administration in your area to make sure your plans to start a business are within the guidelines based on your age, where you live, the service you intend to market or the product you intend to sell!

"It is better to work for yourself than not at all!"

Choofe an Idea

The kind of business to start is completely up to you. By using your imagination, creativity and doing some research, you can turn a favorite hobby, skill or interest into a successful business. And, by putting a new "twist" on an old idea, you might be able to make your competition look at you—a whole lot differently! To get your creative juices flowing, give some thought to the ideas listed below. See if any of these ideas seem appealing. Suggested company names have also been provided. Use this list only as a guide while you are deciding on the type of business you want to start.

Business Venture Ideas

Company: Pen-to-Paper　　　　**Type: Service**

Offer to provide hand-lettering of invitations, greeting cards, thank you notes, flyers and envelopes.

Company: Pet Sit　　　　**Type: Service/Product**

Provide a 24-hour (taped) message of area boarding facilities for pets ranging from rabbits, turtles and baby chicks to cats, dogs and horses. Develop a special directory that lists these facilities, its address, telephone number, contact person, rates the kind of pets which may be boarded and **sell** the directory.

Company: Apart-From-Home   **Type: Service**

Offer to apartment-sit while owners are away for the night, weekend or the summer. As an added plus, include in your service (depending on how long they will be away) to organize a particular closet, bookcase, kitchen/bathroom cabinet(s), etc.

Company: Apron Appeal   **Type: Product**

Design and sell novelty aprons to flea market vendors, church, social and civic clubs as a fundraising item; or, sell them to small restaurants and carry-out establishments.

Company: Artificially Yours   **Type: Product**

Sell artificial floral arrangements to gardeners who can't grow anything—real!

Tip: A craft store has numerous selections that can be planted outdoors and be strong enough for winter temperatures!

Company: Baby Stuff   **Type: Service/Product**

Offer to accompany "new moms" or make purchases for them of the many infant items they will need before the baby arrives. Develop a "Handy Checklist" booklet that list the items and sell the booklet.

Company: Bike-a-Mat   **Type: Service**

Provide a washing and repairing of bikes service.

Tip: Contact a local bike shop to see if they would handle repairs and be willing to use your service as one of their added services!

Company: Bike Chauffeurs   **Type: Service**

Offer to chauffeur children to and from the library, choir practice girl/boy scout meetings or just for fun on a double-bike.

Tip: Rent one until you have made enough money to buy one!

Company: Party Pic-ins   **Type: Service**

Offer to make all the arrangements, purchase supplies, equipment, handle entertainment, design the menu and purchase the food for children's parties.

Company: Board Work   **Type: Service**

Offer to give chess and checker game lessons to children, only.

Tip: You might also want to include computer games!

Company: Sani-Camps   **Type: Service**

Provide general housekeeping tasks for owners of recreational vehicles at camp sites. As a plus to your service, offer to baby-sit the little-ones so their parents can have a break!

Tip: Keep in mind that some household cleaning materials can only be used if you are 18 or over!

Company: Purr-for-Show   **Type: Service**

Offer to be the organizer of neighborhood or area cat shows put on for fundraising purposes. Change the name to "Bark-for-Show" and you can provide the same service for dog owners.

Tip: The fee you charge will be a tax-deductible item for the organization or group, so don't feel guilty!

Company: Catalog Consultant   **Type: Service**

Handle catalog purchasing for others. Your service, for example, would be able to do comparative shopping to find the best prices, complete the order form and handle the irritating details to correct and make okay, anything that could be an inconvenience to your customers.

Company: Clippers   **Type: Service**

Offer to clip newspaper and magazine articles for students, freelance writers, researchers, teachers and homemakers.

Tip: Many homemakers would simply love to have someone else do the clipping of coupons for them!

Company: Cookbook Finders   **Type: Service**

Become an expert at locating cookbooks with recipes for all tastes and all occasions. Offer your expertise as a service.

Tip: You will need to become more than familiar with cookbooks and recipes that are focused on low sodium, vegetarian dishes, quick meals, what can or cannot be microwaved, etc. So, a trip to the library and looking in specialized magazines will be a must!

Company: Tutor   **Type: Service**

Provide tutoring for academic subjects. As a plus, offer to provide help with sports activities to students who want to feel confident enough to, at least, try out for the team!

Company: Lead On   **Type: Service**

Offer to take pets to and from scheduled vet appointments, for a simple walk or to the pet salon.

Company: Plate Date   **Type: Service**

Offer to provide after-party clean-up services to home owners, schools and offices.

Hint: Special insurance may be needed in case personal belongings are broken, so check on this first!

Company: First Aid, Firsts   **Type: Product**

Sell a specialized first aid kit to homeowners, students and small businesses. Develop a booklet about first aid tips and sell the booklet.

Company: Funny Face   **Type: Service**

Hire yourself out as a clown for advertising purposes. You could contact shopping mall stores, vendors, convention headquarters, car dealerships, food markets or neighborhood stores!

Company: Bread and Butter   **Type: Service**

Offer to handle "emergency" grocery shopping for others. This could also include handling the weekly grocery shopping for area senior citizens, or simply offer to accompany them and give whatever assistance you can.

Company: You Forgot?   **Type: Service/Product**

Offer to "remind" others of family/friend birthdays, anniversaries, etc. Your service would send not only a reminder notice, but an appropriate card to be signed and mailed. If you and a friend are good with words and can draw—design your own cards and sell them!

Company: All Occasions   **Type: Service/Product**

Offer to handle decorating homes for the holidays. Some families like to have their homes decorated for more than just Christmas. You might want to try to interest others in decorating their homes for Thanksgiving,

Easter, the Fourth of July and Halloween. As a plus, design your own decorations and sell them!

Company: A-Plus   Type: Service

Offer to assist teachers with the correction of assign-ments. Remember, teachers have families, too! So, helping them have more time can be very important!

Company: One Up, Two Down   Type: Service/Product

Offer to repair, design or instruct others about kites. Sell your designs and try to get street vendors, specialty stores or grocery stores interested in your business for advertising purposes!

Company: Return-a-Book   Type: Service

Offer to return library books for others. You might also offer to handle research for specific subjects related to your customer's interests and needs. Include reminder calls for video returns!

Company: Bags to Go   Type: Service/Product

Offer to rent luggage for those who travel occasionally. Make arrangements with a luggage store to give you a commission on any purchases your customers might make, as a result of your referral. Design a "How to Pack" booklet and sell it!

Company: Plant Sit   Type: Service

Offer to take care of plants when the owners have to be away for an extended amount of time. Be sure you really know "how" to care for plants!

Company: In-Line   Type: Service/Product

Offer to purchase tickets for others for concerts, games and special events. Develop a monthly "Events Sheet" that lists upcoming events and sell the sheets. As a plus for you, contact promoters to see if they will give you a commission for ticket sales you make!

Company: File Experts   **Type: Service**

Offer to organize homeowner's important papers and records in a systematic manner. (Develop a booklet on "Filing Tips for the Homeowner" and sell it!)

Company: Time Out   **Type: Service**

Offer to "entertain" customer's children with activities that are educational and fun, so that parents will have a breather for a few hours. (This might include a visit to the library, storytelling time, a walk in the park, teaching them how to play chess or simply coloring book activities!)

Company: Packers Before   **Type: Service**

Offer to help people packing for a move with their pre-packing activities **before** the movers arrive!

Company: Memories   **Type: Service/Product**

Offer to organize and prepare photograph albums for others. Your plus might include offering to enlarge certain photos and have them framed!

While many of these ideas might seem "silly" or "un-workable" give them a close look. All are services and products that most people need.

Be sure to consult the "Child Labor Laws" in your state so you can be absolutely sure that you are old enough to engage in any of these business ventures. Also, depending on your age, of course, remember to get your parent's permission in advance because many business venture ideas could cause an inconvenience for other family members.

What you need to remember is that "nothing is impossible!" Once you figure it out on paper, start doing some research. Begin thinking in a positive manner. Then get started. Give your idea a try. By doing so, understand and be prepared to accept, the business succeeding or failing. Should you succeed, look at yourself in a mirror and say: "Terrific!" If you fail, look in the mirror and say: "This wasn't quite right. Tomorrow will be the first day to make it better!"

The Plan

Let's do a quick review. You want to work but can't find a job. To remedy this situation you have decided to start your own business. You feel you have what it will take to operate and manage your own small business. You have selected a business venture idea and really feel it will work. You are excited and ready to put your energies into motion.

Now, let's pull your plan together!

Money Matters

How much will I need. The amount of money you will need to get started depends on the kind of business you have in mind. If you decided to provide a service such as "typing letters" and you already have a computer, then you would only need enough money to purchase paper and diskettes. Or, suppose you intend to sell a product. If the product is a ready-made item, you would need enough funds to purchase a very small stock of that item for resale.

Should your product be a craft item (something that you made), then your costs would have to include the purchase of all supplies needed to make a minimum of one dozen right away so that you could recoup (get back) enough money from your sales to make a profit and purchase additional supplies for the next dozen items.

In order to determine how much money you will need for start-up costs, consider the following suggestions.

- ❑ Think small! Try to keep your initial start-up costs **under** $100.00.

- ❑ If you can, try to get advance requests for services or orders for the product you will be selling. Be honest. Tell people you are just getting started but you need to get

12-24 requests/orders in advance. Promise to call once you meet your quota of 12-24. Make sure to call within 5 days. When you call, tell them: "I am calling to let you know that I am officially in business thanks to your support! You will begin receiving the service/product by (date) . Thank you very much for your patience!"

Now, order your initial inventory of supplies based on the advanced 12-24 requests/orders.

❑ Use what you have. Do not make any unnecessary purchases. List the materials, supplies and equipment you already have and then list those items you need to purchase or rent.

❑ Be a "bargain" shopper. The less you have to pay for initial supplies (without giving up quality) the better!

❑ List your projected expenses. Do not forget to include items such as postage, copying, faxing, travel (by car or public transportation) and the fee for equipment rentals.

These are important points to keep in mind because the real object of being self-employed is to provide a service, sell a product and make a profit. Why spend **more** than you have to and risk losing money—instead, of making it?

Where Will It Come From?

Stay focused on keeping your start-up costs **extremely** low. You might try:

❑ Asking parents, relatives or friends for a "small" loan. The loan you request could be as little as $10.00 or as much as $50.00. What is really important, however is to make arrangements for a "quick" repayment of the loan. Be sure to put your agreement in writing. Below is a sample of a "Small Loan Agreement" you might wish to use.

Hint: Remember, this is only a sample so adjust it to your needs!

Small Loan Agreement Statement

On (date you receive the loan), I received $ .00 from (Name of Person) as a small loan to help me start my own business. By this "Small Loan Agreement Statement" I promise to repay the entire amount in (1, 2, 3 or 4) number of payments. Each payment will be given in the amount of ($ .00) , on a weekly basis every (day of the week). Repayment of this loan will begin on (date of first repayment). The last payment will be given on (date of last payment).

_____   _____
(Your signature here)   (Person's signature here)

_____   _____
(Print your name here)   (Print person's name here)

_____   _____
(Today's date)   (Today's date)

"Having lots of loans can quickly reduce your profits!"

This will assure the person loaning you the money that you are sincere and fully intend to pay back their loan.

> **Hint**: Always keep in mind that whenever you put promises on paper, this agreement can be considered/viewed as a "legal document" and, could be used against you, in court, should you not provide what you promised!

❑ Use as much of your lunch money, allowance and birthday money as you can to cover expenses for your business.

❑ Offer to do a few odd jobs for some of your neighbors or family members, and charge a small fee. Let them know what you are saving the money for and you might be surprised at how cooperative and supportive they are!

❑ Collect paper, newspapers, aluminum and glass items. Take them to the recycling center for extra money. It's hard work, but keep your goal always in mind!

Can you think of some other things you can do to earn the money you need to start your business—that are, of course, **not** associated with illegal activities. Make a list and use them!

"Mental" Organization

Self-employed people are organized people. Being self-employed has a way of making the most **un-organized** person turn into a person, who suddenly starts working in an organized fashion. This is probably because they have a purpose and the business they work for is their own. It just happens! You will find yourself having a place for everything and putting everything in its appropriate place. You will also gain a special appreciation for the importance of managing your time.

Since you will be working at home, there will be a few particulars to keep in mind. First, you will need your parent's permission and support. Will you be allowed to advertise your service/product on flyers, in ads or other promotional material using your home address and telephone number? How inconvenient will it be for family members to have to answer the telephone when you are **not** at home? If you live in a home where everyone goes to bed early, will your working late at night be a disturbance? Strive to be **more** accommodating to family members so that you will **not** inconvenience them, too much!

"A wise home-worker makes consideration a priority!

Setting Up Your Office

Whether you have decided to start a service or product sales business, your **basic** workspace area should include the three "A's":

❑ Ample space so you can work in comfort. This might even be having enough space for you to sit on the floor in your bedroom!

❑ Appropriate lighting, ventilation, privacy and quiet.

❑ Allocation of sufficient storage space for supplies and equipment.

Equipment and Other Stuff!

Again, the kind of equipment and miscellaneous supplies you will need, depends on the type of business you intend to start. Below is a short list of basic supplies to get you started.

- ❑ Computer (or typewriter)

- ❑ Calculator

- ❑ File cabinet or storage containers. Many office supply stores will have just what you need or find a box with a lid that is big enough to hold your files—cutting costs is the main objective!

- ❑ Index cards. Use to record client's name, address, telephone/fax numbers, and email addresses; use the back of the card for special notes about the client.

- ❑ Calendar—both wall and pocket-size.

- ❑ Business cards, letterhead stationery and envelopes. A local printer will be able to help you; or, do your own on the computer!

- ❑ Bookkeeping book. Check at your office supply store; you'll find several choices available so select the one that suits your needs!

- ❑ Regular office supplies. These would include: file folders, envelopes, paperclips, stapler, staples, pencils, ballpoint and felt tip pens, post-it notes (a great timesaver for reminders!), correction fluid, dictionary, typing paper, etc. (You probably already have these items for school purposes so look at how much money you are saving, already!)

Tech-Tips

These are days when there are an assortment of technological tools and toys (depending on your definition, of course!) that can help you be more efficient, effective and successful with your small business. Some of these wonder-tools are already available at home. With these being such busy-days for everyone, your Mom or Dad probably have some kind of software, already installed on their computer to save them some time! Take a moment to ask if you can take advantage of what is already in-house to promote your business!

On the market are numerous "aids" that, depending on your type of business, could be very beneficial. Keep in mind, however, that you **do not "absolutely" have to have them**! On the list are:

Voice mail   Where you would be able to record a special message for your clients or customers.

Call-forwarding   Which would allow you to receive and re-route your calls to a telephone number of your choice from any location.

E-mail (electronic mail)   Gives you the opportunity to send a typed-text to others that they can conveniently download (print-out) off of their printer.

Mobile phones That give you the freedom to call anyone at anytime for any reason.

Pagers   Give you the opportunity to "screen" incoming messages so that you will be the one to "screen and prioritize" those callers who need to be contacted—at once!

Setting Rates

What to charge is your choice! You can either charge a fee or fixed rate for providing a particular service or selling a special product.

Depending on your business venture idea, do a bit of research. By looking in the Yellow Page Directory for a similar service, contact them and ask for a "rate sheet". **Do not tell them that you are in the planning stages of starting a similar business**! If you do, they may be hesitant about providing the information you are requesting!

The basic formulas to follow when considering **what** to charge, for either a service-focused business or the sale of a product are:

Estimating My Rates

(Note: Based on 12 clients or the sale of 12 products)

Service Business

Worksheet: Questions to Answer	Dollar Amount

(a) How much is this service worth per hour? $_____

(b) How many hours will be needed?
(____ hours x (a) will equal what?) $_____

(c) How much will be needed for expenses?
      Postage: $_____
      Printing: $_____
      Supplies: $_____

(d) Total expenses $_____

To Do: Add (b) + (d) and divide by 12. How close is this figure to (a)?

Product Sales

Worksheet: Questions to Answer

(a) What is my selling price for this product? $_____

(b) How much will be needed for expenses?

      My *real* cost: $_____
      Cost of materials: $_____
      Postage/handling: $_____
      Tax amount: $_____

(c) Total expenses: $_____

To Do: Divide (c) by 12. How close is this figure to (a)?

If the amount you have to spend in expenses is **larger** than the amount you are looking for in profits—start again! Look for ways to reduce your expense items. By doing so, you will be able to gain more profits.

This should give you a sense of "what to charge" for your services or the product you are attempting to sell. Don't be surprised to find that you will have to re-work these figures—a couple of times—so you can feel more comfortable about the amount of profit you really want to see. Trial and error are key elements to a successful small business!

"Striving for quality can increase quantity!"

Legal Concerns

As a self-employed—regardless of how "small" the business is—you need to be knowledgeable about your responsibilities as the *employer*, not the *employee*! This will include a fairly clear understanding about Child Labor Laws, self-employment issues and required self-employment taxes.

Seek a professional who can provide you with the necessary information to ensure that you can establish, operate and reap the rewards of being self-employed. Call the Small Business Administration in your area. Also, go the library and do a bit of research. You will find quite a few books on starting a small business and gain more insight about the legal stuff you need to know. Some of the questions you need to find answers to are:

- ❑ Do I need a special license to operate this kind of business?
- ❑ Can I operate this kind of business from home?
- ❑ What kind of business and tax concerns will I have to handle?

Find out what you need to know **before** getting started.

Checking Account

You will need to have a separate checking account for your business. Checks are an excellent tool for recordkeeping purposes. Never put your business-earnings in your personal checking account. It is important to see what you are making and where your money is going. Talk to a bank representative about opening a business checking account. Ask for their suggestions about the kind of checks you should get and how many you should order. Don't forget to let them know you are starting a **small** business!

To Market, To Market

Once you have decided on the kind of business you intend to start, your next step will be to see if there is a need (market) for your idea. Having a market for your business means that there are enough "others" who really need your service or product. If you are creative enough, you can take an old idea and spice it up, just a bit, to make your business more appealing than that of your competitors! Here are a few marketing tools you might want to consider:

❑ **Flyers**—Design and distribute throughout, not only your neighborhood but several others as well.

❑ **Pamphlets**—Write, design, distribute and advertise in local neighborhood papers, businesses and recreation centers; consider hiring a few children to actually pass out your pamphlets (or flyers).

❑ **Telephone Survey**—Call friends, teachers, family members, neighbors, Church members, organizations, etc., to see if your service or product is **needed**. Really look at the answers. You might be surprised to learn that the service or product-for-sale is something that is needed and no one else has thought about providing!

Doing It!

To ensure your success as a small business owner and operator, remember to find out if your service or product is needed, seek the assistance of a professional for those areas you do not have a clear understanding about, observe state and federal laws concerning the kind of business you can or cannot start, and be flexible about re-inventing your business venture idea—if necessary.

You *can* do this! You *can* start your own business, provide quality services or sell a needed product. You *can* do what it takes to be successful as the *employer*, not the *employee*. You *can* earn money!

Chapter 12
Cook "Carefully"

Knowing how to cook is a needed ingredient on your plan for personal growth. You will need to know how to cook because this might be one of the tasks your parent's will assign to you. Of course, if you have Southern roots, your mom probably started teaching you to cook when you were very young! Are you a college student? If so, then you will probably have to cook for yourself to save money. Or, if you are going to be living on your own, pretty soon, chances are there will be more times when you have to cook for yourself...instead of getting prepared-food packages from home!

Shopping

It takes practice and knowing what to look for when doing grocery shopping. And, the more you shop, the better you will become. Shopping for food, in a busy supermarket can be very stressful. The wisest way to be a *successful* shopper is to learn to be a *smart* shopper.

Some Do's and Don'ts!

Make a list and stick to it! Prepare a list that corresponds with the floor plan of the store so you will not have to go down a particular aisle more than once. This can cut your shopping time by almost one-third.

> **Tip**: Do a walk-through so you will know which items are located in aisle one, two, etc., in order to prepare your list!

Try not to put anything in your cart that you do not *absolutely* need. Keep your budget always in mind. Be a comparative shopper. Do not purchase the first item you see without checking prices of the other brands. Try to let refrigerated or frozen items be last in your cart so they will stay cold longer. It is always a good idea (if you can) to shop alone so you can concentrate and not be tempted to make unplanned purchases. And, do not shop when you are *hungry*. This can cause you to make unplanned purchases and almost forget about your list!

Clip Coupons

Using coupons is a *cents-able* way to save money when shopping. You can get coupons a number of ways. Some come with products you have purchased, in magazines, newspapers and even in the mail. You could also ask friends, relatives or neighbors to clip and save them for you.

Set-up a coupon file. There are so many coupon clippers these days, do not be surprised to find a ready-made "coupon organizer" on the shelves of many office supply stores. Many are already set-up with indexes for a number of the categories you need. Others allow you to write-in your own, on the blank section tabs provided. A few of the categories you might want to include are: cereals, baby, dairy, cleaning products, snacks, soups, coffee/tea, paper products. Now, all you need to do is:

- Clip the coupon
- File it in the appropriate category by expiration date
- Use them when you go shopping!

> **Tip**: Try to get a couple of friends interested in clipping coupons. It will only take about an hour a week. Pick one day of the week to clip (Sunday would be a great day, while you are relaxing! Then, agree to meet once every two weeks or every week for about 30 minutes to exchange coupons.

> **Tip:** A lot of community chain supermarkets offer shoppers membership cards. When there are instore specials, if you present your free membership card to the cashier, you'll receive additional "members only" discounts. If you don't already have a card, ask customer service or the cashier for an application.

Freshness Counts

Eating nutritious meals should always be a main objective. In order to do this, however, you need to start by buying fresh food and knowing when it is fresh! Here is what to look for:

- Fish should have clear eyes, shining/slippery skins with definite color and markings.

- Red meat needs to look red, not brown, and the fat must be white and not yellowish.

- Poultry should not look dry and the breast needs to appear to be plump and light in color.

- Avoid salad greens (lettuce, kale, collard, mustard, etc.) that have brown edges or rotting leaves/stems.

- Tomatoes and radishes are fresh if they do not have wrinkles or spots and are very red in color.

- Grapes, cherries, plums, peaches, nectarines, berries should be firm to the touch and brightly colored.

- Only select bananas that are yellow because they are ripe (green-skinned bananas are under-ripe and brown/mushy ones are over-ripe).

"Shopping for fresh foods enhances healthy thinking!"

Safe Storage

If food items are stored properly they will be safe to consume for longer periods of time. Canned foods (once opened) should be kept in the refrigerator, in a covered dish, and eaten within a maximum of 2 days. Avoid even opening a dented can. By doing so, you risk the possibility that its contents is contaminated and might lead to food poisoning. Dried and packaged foods (pasta, beans, rice, flour, etc.) should be stored in tightly sealed containers in a dry place. Meat, poultry and fish need to be tightly wrapped in mois-ture- and vapor-proofed material like heavy foil, freezer bags, freezer plastic wrap or freezer containers and remain frozen until ready to thaw out and use. Onions and potatoes will be perfectly all right if you store them in a basket or wire rack that allows air to circulate. But, be sure to place them in a dry, cool and dark place.

Cheese, milk, cream, sour cream, yogurt, margarine and butter absolutely have to be stored in the refrigerator.

> **Tip**: Always look for an expiration date and do not use past that date!

Eggs are easy to keep. Simply, remember to keep them in their orig-inal carton and in the refrigerator. Breads need to be kept in a bread box, container or cabinet that allows some air to circulate. If you do not, look forward to seeing a pretty-colored "mold" begin to form and spread rather rapidly!

Cooked foods? Left-overs? Store immediately and begin making out your menu, that night, about how to use them the very **next** night.

> **Hint**: If you have planned your menu wisely, you won't have to worry about having too many leftovers for the next night's meal—that is, of course, if you have prepared it—correctly!

Using the Right Tools

The kitchen should be the one place where the necessary tools to perform a job can be found! Did you know that for both safety and efficiency reasons, you need to be more prepared and mindful of items-on-hand, than in any other place in your home? Let's look at a few examples:

- ❑ Buy the best, first! Cheap kitchen tools do not last long and will require you to replace them over and over and over again.

- ❑ Purchase knives and utensils that are dishwasher safe, that have blades made of carbon steel or stainless steel which can be easily sharpened and be sure knife handles have a firm grip to prevent slipping.

❑ Chopping boards made of plastic or acrylic plastic are better than wooden boards. Wooden boards cannot be placed in a dishwasher for thorough cleaning and tend to retain harmful bacteria from raw meats or poultry, no matter how many times you wash them!

❑ Use saucepans that "fit" the item you are preparing. Be sure that pots, pans and skillets are the appropriate size, have the ability to spread heat evenly and are easy to clean.

> **Hint**: Aluminum spreads heat evenly; stainless steal is really durable and easy to clean; cast-iron is very heavy to handle but good for cooking at a slow pace; and, glass cookery is ideal because it can go from the freezer to on-top of the oven and, then to the table.

Selecting multi-purpose items is the way to go! It is soon to be the way of the future and very much worth serious thought if you intend to become a serious kitchen participant!

Setting Up Shop

Whether you are living at home or in your first apartment, there are several items which you need to be sure are available in the kitchen. Below is a very brief list of many of the basics you will need.

❑ Set of mixing bowls, dry measuring cups, clear glass liquid measuring cup
❑ Measuring spoons
❑ Wooden spoons, rubber (and metal) spatulas (3 assorted sizes)
❑ Knives (assorted for different uses)
❑ Vegetable peeler
❑ Long-handled fork/spoon (flexible steel)
❑ Slotted spoon (steel)
❑ Pancake turner (flexible steel)
❑ Bottle/can opener

- ❏ Grater/shredder
- ❏ Small and large strainers (plastic or steel)
- ❏ Kitchen timer
- ❏ Cutting board (plastic)
- ❏ Meat thermometer
- ❏ Wire cooling rack
- ❏ Saucepans (miscellaneous sizes)
- ❏ Skillets (miscellaneous sizes)
- ❏ Baking sheet, muffin pan
- ❏ Cake pan (miscellaneous sizes)
- ❏ Casserole dishes (miscellaneous sizes)
- ❏ Roasting pan with rack
- ❏ Refrigerator dishes (assorted sizes)
- ❏ Vapor/moisture-proof containers for freezing foods
- ❏ Foil, clear plastic wrap, large and small plastic bags
- ❏ Juice and water pitchers
- ❏ Potholders, ice cube trays, wastebasket, wastebasket liners
- ❏ Kitchen cleaning supplies
- ❏ Dishwashing/dishwasher detergents
- ❏ Broom, dustpan, mop and bucket

Some of the optional equipment you might want in your kitchen include: a blender, food processor, slow cooker (also called crockery cooker) and a toaster.

Once, again, this is a very brief list of the many items you will probably need to get started. Keep in mind that you might not have a need for several of these items. At some point, when you become more familiar with cooking, however, you *will* find and *appreciate* having many of these items already at hand. And, with a properly stocked kitchen, over half of your frustrations and fears about being in the kitchen can be avoided.

Safety Stuff!

Preparing food and keeping foods safe are an absolute **must** for you or anyone else doing the cooking.

Wash Your Hands

Nothing can spread germs quicker than **not** washing your hands! Use water that is as hot as you can handle. Soap your hands (up to just past your wrists) and scrub for a minimum of 20 seconds. You may want to keep a nail brush handy in case you need it. Rinse after the 20 seconds and use paper towels to dry your hands **and** to shut off the water.

Washing Dishes

Did you know that there really is a system for washing dishes *by hand*? Well, there is!

■ **Immediately** or very soon after the meal, scrape each dish to remove left-over foods and rinse **all** dishes with cool water **before** washing them.

■ Use a plastic dishpan to prevent chipping of glassware and plates. Fill the dishpan with hot sudsy water (as hot as you can handle).

■ Wash dishes in the following order: (a) glassware and cups; (b) silverware; and, (c) pots and pans. Rinse as you go along using hot water (as hot as you can handle).

> **Hint**: Depending upon how many dishes you have to wash, you might have to change the water a couple of times. Try this little routine: first, wash the glassware, cups and silverware, then change the water; second, wash the plates, wipe off the refrigerator, stove top and microwave oven, then change the water; and, third, wash pots, pans and any appliances that were used and don't forget the table!

■ Yep! You definitely have to remember to put the dishes away, wash out the dishpan, wipe out the sink, fold the dish clothe and put it in its appropriate place—as the *final* step!

Miscellaneous Precautions

Where food safety is concerned, it is impossible to know too much! Following is a "take heed" chart which lists several odds and ends to keep in mind.

Take Heed!

Item	Tip
Eggs	Do not purchase or use eggs that are broken or have cracked shells. They could have become contaminated with a dangerous bacteria which will make you extremely sick! When buying eggs choose either **Grade A** or **Grade AA**. Grade A eggs are good for use in many recipes. Grade AA are the eggs you would use most often to fry, scramble or boil in the shell. **Always** refrigerate eggs immediately when you get home. Cooked eggs (including those pretty, decorated Easter eggs) should **not** be kept out of the refrigerator for more than 2 hours.
Poultry	Avoid buying poultry that has darkened wing tips or appears to have soft or sticky flesh. This could mean it is not fresh, has become contaminated with a bacteria or has been frozen, thawed out and re-frozen, again!
Fruits/ Vegetables	**All** fruits and vegetables must be washed in clear, cool water **before** prepared and/or eaten. This will reduce the amount of possible contamination or residue from pesticides. When storing fresh fruits and vegetables, never wrap them tightly because they will spoil faster! Grapes, plums, pears, bananas and tomatoes will be perfectly all right, to ripen, at room temperature, before refrigerating. Onions and potatoes do best when stored in wire baskets, in a dry, cool, well-ventilated and dark place.

Dry Foods These are items like cereals, rice, flour, sugar, dried beans and dried fruits. Put in a tightly-sealed container that is placed in a dry place and out of direct sunlight or other heat sources.

Canned Foods Like eggs, do not purchase items that are in a can (or glass container) that has dents, cracks or bulging lids. Once you open a can, immediately, put the food item in an appropriate refrigerator-proof container. Leaving can items, in the can once it has been opened, could cause the metal (from the can) to affect the food in either a loss of nutritional value or open the door to the growth of contamination!

Thawing Since bacteria can grow very quickly, especially, at room temperature, avoid thawing-out food items over-night or on the counter. Instead, allow the thawing-out process to occur in the refrigerator (the night before) or in the microwave (just before cooking)!

Cutting Boards It is strongly suggested that utensils and cutting boards be washed in very hot soapy water **after** using it for raw meat or poultry! Plastic cutting boards can be easily washed and sanitized. Wooden ones, cannot!

Meat Thermometers Use them! Purchase one or two. Really read the instructions. Then, make sure that you are food-safety-interested enough to monitor the appropriate "done-ness" level so those who eat your food do not have to be worried about their health or your level of cleanliness in the kitchen!

"Safety in the kitchen yields safe eating!"

Microwaving

Zip, zap—your food is either completely done or completely thawed out—in a matter of minutes!

Proper and safe usage of your microwave oven will save you a lot of time. In fact, with the amount of time saved, you might even be able to devote more—**you-time**—to yourself for a few moments of leisure.

Like cooking in a conventional oven, microwave ovens also have a few particulars to keep in mind. You need to make sure, for example, that you:

- ❏ **Only** use ovenproof ceramic, glass, or china dishes

- ❏ **Only** use "white" paper towels and/or plates (colored patterns might have dyes which could contaminate the food item)

- ❏ Stick with dishes that are **round** so food items will cook evenly

- ❏ Avoid using containers that are **not** microwave-safe

    Tip: some plastic containers like butter tubs can melt very easily!

- ❏ **Absolutely never** use metal or metal-trimmed containers because "metals" and microwaves do not "mix" and can cause sparks that could damage your microwave oven!

Additional tips to observe, according to some experts (USDA Consumer Education Office) are:

- ❏ Remove food from store wrap prior to microwave defrosting.

- ❏ Cook meat and poultry immediately after micro-thawing.

- ❏ Remember to take food out of the microwave.

    Note: "Food should not be left out of refrigeration more than two hours.

❑ Safe utensils for microwave cooking include glass and glass ceramic cookware, and those labeled for microwave use.

❑ Do not use cold storage containers. Margarine tubs, whipped topping bowls, cheese containers, and others can warp or melt from hot food, possibly causing chemical migration (growth).

❑ Cover foods to hold in moisture and provide safe, even heating.

❑ Due to the possibility of uneven heating, microwaving baby food and formula is not recommended. If microwaved, stir food, shake bottles and test for "lukewarm" temperature.

Keep these tips in mind when microwaving. Visit a bookstore or the library to get a book on microwaving safely. Many grocery stores carry pocket-size booklets that provide many of the basics mentioned above, giving even more details. Be a safe and successful microwave cooker who is also informed!

Cookbooks

The secret to cookbook shopping is to purchase cookbooks that feature **only** those items you like to eat! Initially look for cookbooks that are designed for a *beginner.* As your cooking skills progress, search for more challenging cookbooks and recipes. A good cookbook library should include books (or small booklets) on: soups, stews/casseroles, salads, meats, fish, vegetables and desserts. Added to this list you might want to have cookbooks on pizza-making, pasta recipes and chocolate treats. It is always a good idea to purchase cookbooks which have recipes that can be prepared "quickly".

"Quick recipes save time, money and frustration!"

Cookbook Shorthand and Methods of Cooking

Knowing how to read a recipe is the first step in following the directions. You will find recipes, not only in cookbooks, but also in magazines, newspapers and on products you purchase.

> **Hint**: Take a moment to look at the labels on some of the can goods and even cereal boxes!

These recipes use a special set of shorthand notations and mention specific ways of preparation. Once you learn these, you will then be more prepared to tackle a cooking challenge!

Recipe Shorthand and Methods of Cooking

Shorthand/ Method	What It Means
Bake	Cooking foods in the oven that are either covered or uncovered.
Boil	Heating until the liquids produce bubbles that rise to the top and then "pop" in a consistent pattern.
Broil	Cooking foods in the "broiler" section of the oven (usually at a very high heat level) for a very short amount of time.
Cup	Measuring cup that indicates you have reached 1/4, 1/3 or 1/2 cup capacity.
Grated	Cutting various food items into very small portions **Hint**: While this can be done by hand, a food processor is quicker!
Poach	Placing certain foods *gently* into simmering water until completely cooked.
Simmer	Use of *low* heat until bubbles form slowly and pop below the surface.

Steam	Use of steam to cook partially or completely. "Steam" is the vapor (mist) that looks like clouds of smoke, but is really liquids changed into a vapor form. Steam is usually given off by boiling water (or seasoned liquids). Many recipes will require that you use the "steam" method to prepare various dishes.
Stir-fry	With this cooking method you cook food very fast over a high heat and in a lightly oiled skillet. The secret to stir-frying is that you have to *constantly* stir the food items, until done.
Tbs	Tablespoon
Tsp	Teaspoon

All recipes, in order to be successful, will require "strict" adherence (attention) to the directions and measurements given. By paying close attention, you **can** be a successful cook in the kitchen!

Menu Planning

Planning a menu means you know, in advance, what you have to prepare. Depending upon the meal (breakfast, lunch or dinner), there are three elements you need to always keep in mind. Each meal should include a main dish, one (or two) side items and a beverage. Here are a few examples:

Breakfast	Scrambled eggs, bacon, fruit and coffee, juice or milk. Cereal, fruit, toast and tea, juice or milk
Lunch	Sandwich, soup, iced tea or milk Sandwich, carrots/celery sticks, fruit, fruit drink or milk
Dinner	Meat, green vegetable, rice or pasta dish, dessert, coffee, tea or milk Casserole, salad, fruit, dessert, coffee, tea or fruit drink

Let your imagination take over. Remember to plan according to the amount of time you have to use. And, be sure that hot foods are served hot; cold foods served cold. Save time by preparing whatever you can the day or night before. When planning your menu, remember also, to take an inventory of what you have available so you will not have to run to the store 30 minutes before preparation time!

Recipes

The *Washington Post* newspaper published a few recipes you might want to try. These recipes came from various cast members in the movie "Soul Food".

Vanessa Williams' (Teri Joseph's) Macaroni 'N Cheese
(6 to 8 generous servings)
2 tablespoons butter, plus butter for the casserole dish
2 tablespoons flour
1 teaspoon salt
1 teaspoon dry mustard
2½ cups milk
2 cups shredded Cheddar cheese (mild or sharp)
½ cup shredded Gouda cheese
8 ounces elbow macaroni
¼ cup buttered bread crumbs
½ teaspoon paprika
Directions:
Butter a 2-quart casserole dish. Set aside.

In a saucepan over medium heat, melt butter and then remove from the heat. Blend in flour, salt and mustard. Add milk and return to the stove over medium heat, stirring constantly, until the sauce thickens a little and is smooth. Add 1½ cups of the Cheddar cheese and all of the Gouda and heat until melted, stirring occasionally. Meanwhile, cook the macaroni according to package directions. Drain and combine with the cheese sauce in the prepared dish. Top with the remaining ½ cup Cheddar cheese, bread crumbs and paprika. Bake at 375 degrees about 25 minutes or until nicely browned and bubbly.

Irma Hall's (Mother Joe's) Salmon Croquettes

(Makes 8 croquettes)

14.75-ounce can red salmon
1 yellow onion, minced
1 green bell pepper, minced
2 slices bread, torn into small pieces
1 medium potato, boiled and mashed
1 egg, lightly beaten
Salt to taste
½ cup yellow cornmeal
1 teaspoon black pepper
Vegetable oil for sautéing

Directions:

Combine the salmon, onion, green pepper, bread, potato, egg and salt. Shape into 8 patties. Combine the cornmeal and black pepper. Coat the croquettes in the cornmeal mixture. Fill a skillet with a ¼-inch layer of the oil. Heat until very hot, then saute the croquettes until they are browned on both sides, about 3 minutes per side.

Mekhi Phifer's (Lem Davis') Sweet Potato Pie

(Makes one 9-inch pie)

1 pound sweet potatoes
¾ cup sugar
1 teaspoon cinnamon
½ teaspoon nutmeg
Pinch of salt
¼ teaspoon vanilla extract
2 drops lemon flavoring
2 eggs, lightly beaten
12-ounce can evaporated milk
½ cup milk
1 unbaked 9-inch pie crust
Whipped cream (optional)

Directions:

Boil the sweet potatoes until soft. Scrape the flesh from potatoes and discard the skin. In a large bowl, mix the potatoes with the sugar, cinnamon, nutmeg, salt, vanilla extract, lemon flavoring and eggs. While stirring, slowing add the evaporated milk and then the regular milk. Mix well.

Pour the mixture into the unbaked pie crust. Cover the edge of the pie crust with foil. Bake at 375 degrees for 25 minutes. Remove the foil and bake for 25 to 30 minutes more, until a knife inserted comes out clean. Serve with whipped cream, if desired.

"Cooking is good for the soul!"

Chapter 13
"Broaden" Your Horizons

You can, pretty much, go anywhere and do anything you want if you take the time to explore! Exploring is not always a physical activity. It can also be a form of mental enrichment. In order to enhance your cultural-side (everyone has one!) you will need to expand your horizons in that direction.

This section is intentionally short because *you* are the only one who can lend length to its purpose! Review the suggestions offered and do something about expanding *your* horizons—beginning today.

Read On

What's going on? Make it a practice to find out by reading the newspaper everyday. See what is happening in your community, city and the world in general. Stay in touch with current events, issues, health, politics and sports. By doing so, you will broaden your mind, improve your reading skills and even become a better conversationalist.

Reading also allows you to become more informed about a particular city, town or country; its history, and its residents. Depending on your reading materials, you can find out details about their government structure, their financial stability, how most of the residents live and how successful they are with the tourism trade. Aim to become an *expert* about a particular location. Make plans (a year or even five years in advance) to save enough money to take a trip and actually see the location first-hand.

> **Tip**: The National Geographic Society has books and magazines that can take you to any part of the world you can imagine!

Start with a visit to your local library; call or write to the Chamber of Commerce in the city/state you are interested in; contact the National Geographic Society and request a list of the materials they have available about your chosen topic. Get started on a personal adventure—immediately!

For entertainment and enrichment, read books on fiction, biographies, mystery novels, poetry or anything that is of interest to you. Look for and *read* as many Black history books as you can find.

> **Tip**: You might want to begin with books written by author and Black Historian, C.R. Gibbs. Of particular interest are his books which deal with Black Inventors and Black Explorers!

Should you decide to focus on black history facts versus myths (false stories) do not be surprised about how *inspired* you will become by the many accomplishments that have been achieved!

Subscribe to one or two of your favorite magazines. Make it a goal to read all of the articles *before* the next issue comes out.

"Reading can ready you to handle many new experiences!"

Listen Closely

Take the time to *listen* to classical and ethnic music. Yes, actually tune-in to one of those stations that does not play the music you usually listen to! Try listening for 15 minutes a day or for an hour once a week. Instead of limiting your exposure to ethnic music that is Black-focused, include several different cultures as well. If you hear a particular piece that makes you react, do some casual research to find facts about the composer. Why did she/he compose this piece in the first place? How many Black composers of classical music can you find? How many are female? Classical and ethnic music can be soothing (making you feel rather relaxed) or charged with excitement and energy! And, you will not know what you do or do not like until you try *listening closely*!

> **Tip #1**: Absolutely do not forget to tune in to the Jazz stations!

> **Tip #2**: Take lessons in learning a particular musical instrument. This will give you a better sense of, not only the instrument, but "why" that particular artist or composer "favored" one musical instrument instead of another!

Television Pluses

Check your television guide for documentaries on practically everything. If you have cable, you have a nice piece of the world right at your finger-tips! Use a highlighter for reminder purposes about those programs that sound interesting to you. Then, be sure to watch the program for enrichment purposes. Some channels not only air documentaries, but also air classroom/congressional sessions, programs on cooking, gardening, consumer-interest advice, self-help, biographical background information on any number of individuals from the past, and present-day achievements of many others. Watching these programs can be both interesting and beneficial.

Live Theatre and Plays

There is nothing like it! Excitement is usually generated once the curtain goes up. The scenery, costumes and the lively or realistic roles portrayed by the actors (of course...if they are good!) can keep even the most restless/ "uninterested" seat holder, glued to his or her seat! There is not a whole lot that can be said about attending a live performance, except to say, just go and enjoy the experience! Figure out how you feel after you go the first time. Then, do not be surprised, the next day, when you suddenly find yourself searching the entertainment pages for the next theatre or play opening so you can purchase tickets in advance!

> **Tip**: If you have never gone to a Shakespearean play (a play like Romeo and Juliet), try it at least once. While the dialogue may sound a bit strange, you *will* still be able to follow the story line. And, do not feel shocked that you actually enjoy this kind of entertainment!

Attending a live performance of a musical is almost always going to be exciting, fast-paced and well-worth the amount of the ticket! If you *think* you would like to see a particular musical but do not really know what it is about, simply ask the ticket agent to give you a quick overview about what its about. Then, either, purchase a ticket or ask about upcoming scheduled performances.

Added to this list should be going to a performance of the opera. Yes, it is true that most are performed in another language! Think, however, about the power of body language, gestures (movement and/or position of the actors on stage) and the costumes. All of these elements provide the level of communication that the audience needs to understand the story line—without knowing the language. To be more comfortable, you can simply visit your local library and look-up the opera you will be attending, in order to be more familiar with the story-line.

"Open minds, ready to absorb cultural enrichments, experience positive growth!"

Museum/Art Gallery

Take a tour of your city. Visit museums of history, science, aviation, etc. Go on a tour that features historically black sites. It will probably take several months to accomplish this task, but it will be well worth the time and expense. Contact the Chamber of Commerce and ask for a "visitor's packet". In this packet you will receive the tourism information. This information is usually "free" so do not hesitate to request this material!

Step-By-Step

Get involved in dancing. Not just your culture but a few different cultures as well. Dance, afterall is considered to be a form of communication. Take a couple of courses at a community center or the nearest community college. You will learn not only how to do various dances, but instructors will usually give you the history of a particular dance.

Learn "Ballroom" dancing. This kind of dancing can come in pretty handy. You never know when you will be attending a black-tie event and, you'll be well prepared, whether it's a cotillion, your prom, a family wedding or your job's annual holiday party. You will also be able to meet "new" people and develop "new" relationships when you enroll in ballroom dance classes. In fact, expect to become involved in a completely "new" circle of associates and friends. When you see this happening, know that you are on the road to expanding your horizons!

The Yellow Pages Directory

Take a slow and detailed look under the category of "Associations" to see if any of them "spark" your attention. Call and request information about the associations. Then review the materials you receive. It is quite possible that you will want to become a member. This, will then open quite a few more interesting doors for you.

Do Something!

Broadening you horizons means doing something to enrich your thoughts and actions. It means giving serious thought to doing something that you would not ordinarily do. It means forgetting about peer pressure to do what others do or expect you to do. It also means **not** being afraid to do something that is different and positive. If it feels comfortable to you, then, chances are, it is perfectly okay!

Chapter 14
Be A "More Informed" Teen Parent

Are you juggling being a teenager, a student and a parent, all at the same time? While handling so many different roles can be stressful, there are a few tips that may help you get through this period—especially—the parenting part.

You!

First things, first! Let's start with you. First of all, if you have a baby, that baby is your responsibility—not your parents'—so now you must (if you haven't already) grow up no matter how old you are. To be a good teen parent you need a good plan to use as a foundation. While developing your plan there are a few specifics to keep in mind. Get organized. Have a place for everything and keep everything in its place. Make it a strict habit, on a daily basis, to put all of your school items (books, supplies, etc.) back in their appropriate place. Do not forget to put all baby-stuff (supplies, toys, furnishings) away, too. This includes an orderly closet for your clothes and an orderly drawer arrangement for your child's clothes (so you won't have to wonder about what to wear when you get up)!

> **Hint**: Preparing your clothes the night before can reduce an enourmous amount of stress in the morning!

*"The challenges of teen parenting are worth
the efforts put forth for my child!"*

Use your time management skills to get more done using less time. Make a schedule that includes what you have to do on a 24-hour basis, Monday through Friday. Be prepared to seriously and responsibly stick to this schedule. Set a specific amount of time to devote to your child every day. And, do not forget to plug-in relaxation/quiet time for yourself on a regular basis. Below is a sample schedule to get you started.

Juggling My Time

This is a sample schedule for the busy teen parent. It is based on a 24-hour schedule for Monday through Friday. Since this is only an example, let's say the mom (or dad) are in the 11th grade, still lives at home, has a part-time job and her/his child is about 4 months old.

Time	Stuff to Do
5:30Am – 6:15Am	Get up, prepare a bottle to have ready when the little one wakes up, shower and dress for the day.
6:15Am – 7:30Am	Feed, bathe and dress the little one. Place all items you have to take with you, at the front door. (School and baby stuff in separate bags.)
7:30Am – 8:30Am	Commute time to babysitter or daycare center.
8:30Am – 9:00Am	Commute time to school.
9:00Am – 3:00pm	School time. (Arrange for at least **one** study period so you will be able to complete some of your class assignments before your evening routine begins!)
3:00pm – 3:30pm	Commute time to babysitter or daycare center.

3:30pm - 4:30pm	Commute time to home.
4:30pm - 5:30pm	Get the little one settled in; take care of younger brothers and sisters; start dinner for the family; prepare enough bottles for the little one to last through the night, one for early morning and several to be taken to the babysitter or daycare center the next day. Taking **no less** than 15 minutes to give your undivided attention to your little one. During this very short amount of time you can hold a conversation.
5:30pm - 6:00pm	Commute time to part-time job.
6:00pm - 9:00pm	Work at part-time job.
9:00pm - 10:00pm	Commute time to home.

10:00pm - 12:00 midnight

Get the little one settled in for the night; prepare what-to-wear for both you and the little one (for the next day); pack baby-stuff for the next day; put all baby stuff back in the appropriate place; work on and complete homework assignments.

12:00 midnight - 12:30Am

Prepare for bed and go to bed!

12:30Am - 5:30Am	Sleep

(Saturday and Sunday are up to you!)

"Whenever!"   Spend at least 3-5 hours (each day) with your child, giving her/him your undivided attention. The main point is to make sure that **you and your child** have time alone! Do your weekly laundry/ironing and, in general, get organized for the upcoming week! Schedule a **minimum** of 2-hours (each day) for your relaxation and quiet time. Make plans for how you will use this time on Saturday and Sunday. Don't forget to plug-in school assignment time, as well.

Remember: You will start this **same** schedule all over again, the next week!

Depending on the age of your child, of course, your schedule might begin a little later or even a bit earlier. What you have to keep in mind is that making a schedule will reduce the amount of stress you feel, keep you organized and allow you to do all that has to be done in order to be a successful juggler!

Health-ful Tips

If you are not healthy-minded about yourself, chances are you will not be about your child's health, either! As a teen parent, you will need to keep track of your child's doctor visits, when she/he has to be vaccinated against various childhood diseases and give special attention to your own personal health. Keep a detailed record of all doctor visits. Include the date, time and any other notes about each of the doctor visits. Later on, do not forget to include dentist visits, too.

Tips, Tips and More Tips!

Being your parent's child, you probably do not remember what they did for you. So, what you have to do for your child just might be a bit of a mystery for you! Since there are numerous parenting responsibilities to cope with, give some thought to the few tips provided below. Review them, think about them in terms of your child's age and take the appropriate action.

Annoying Behavior

Some children seek attention by behaving in an annoying manner. How irritating is it when your child deliberately stands in front of the television when you are watching it? Is it annoying when she/he makes lots and lots of noise while you are obviously trying to sleep? Then, there is the classic, when children are told to stop; they do, and minutes later actually do whatever it was all over again! Remember, they are trying to get your attention. So, **do** ignore them when they are showing annoying behavior. But, the minute you get a chance to praise them for doing something good, make it a very **big** praise!

Babysitters

All babysitters are self-employed individuals, regardless of their age. As such, you need to engage their services on a business level.

Make sure that you discuss and mutually agree on the hourly amount you will pay for their services. Be insistent that they arrive on time. Explain what you want them to do, what you "hope" they will **not** do—leave your child unattended, use the telephone for long periods of time, go through the your house on a "snooping" spree, answer the door and allow strangers in, simply because the person at the door introduces her/himself as a relative.

When using a babysitter it is your **responsibility** to give as much information and instructions as you can. Have a prepared list of instructions, directions, the telephone number of where you will be, and emergency numbers. Emergency numbers would include: a relative, the police, fire department and poision-control center.

Add to your list of "must's" for the babysitter: (1) keep all entry doors locked; (2) when answering the telephone, inform callers that you are *"not available at this time; but if you will give me a message, I will ask her/him to call you back as soon as possible!"*

> **Hint**: Babysitters should never say they are babysitting. This gives a hint to outsiders that you are not at home and could make certain outsiders feel that breaking-in will be less of a challenge!

Chores

Even a toddler can do chores. Putting their own toys away is a very good start. Depending on the age of your child, of course, she/he can also help set the table, do their version of making the bed, put their dirty clothes in the appropriate location, dust or tidy-up the living room, take clothes out of the dryer, separate clothes, fold certain items and put their own clothes away.

This will give her/him a sense of responsibility and pride when you praise them. And, make sure to praise a lot!

Sit down together and discuss the chores you have in mind. Ask for their suggestions. The key here, is to have a *mutual* understanding and agreement that what she/he has to do is not a game but a *needed* responsibility. Let her/him know that you have so much to do, *it would make you very happy if they helped you just a little bit!*

> **Hint**: Turn some of these chores into learning activities. For example, when your child is helping you with the dishes, say: "Olivia, I think there are six spoons. Will you count them and let me know?"; "Please bring me four towels. I need two white towels, one blue towel and one pink towel."; "Tonight I am supposed to balance my check-book. Since I have so much homework to do, will you help me if I show you how?"

This is a great way to help your child develop the skill of following directions, make her/him feel needed and be able to work on decision-making skills.

Classes

Enroll in a "parenting" course. Do a bit of research to find out who sponsors such courses. Talk to your school counselor or the pastor at your church. Search through the Internet. Carefully look at the Yellow Pages Directory under "Associations" and call those associations that **might** be able to help. Contact the YWCA/YMCA in your area for assistance. And do not forget to call the community colleges in your area, too.

Daycare Basics

When it is time for daycare be mindful of the kind of information your caregiver needs to know. Prepare a fact sheet. List not only your child's name and date of birth, but also: information about allergies, medical problems, special needs and their food and toy preferences. Facts about you should include: name, address, telephone numbers (home and work), place of employment, work hours, when you typically go to lunch, who to call in case of an emergency and who can or cannot have permission to pick-up your child.

> **Hint**: It is a good idea to give the caregiver a picture, to keep on file, of those who have your permission to pick-up your child. Then, there will be no mistake about whether the person is who she/he say they are!

Fun Time!

Fun time should be filled with choices. And, these choices should **not** always include television, automated toys or computer games. Add to their list of fun-stuff-to-do: board games, educational videos (not just cartoons!), taking *you* for a short walk or reading *you* a story.

Gifts

Be extremely careful to examine gifts given to your child. Make sure these gifts meet your required safety level before letting her/him play with their new toys or wear their cute new outfits. Are any parts of the toys loose? Do some of the outfits have buttons that could become loose and end up in your child's mouth, thus causing her/him to choke?

Listening

During those times when your child is talking to you, give your undivided attention. They will, more than likely, feel that what they have to tell you is very, very important. She/he needs to know that what is important to them you think is very important, too! Yes, you will need a lot of patience and discipline to be a successful listener. At the same time you will help your child to develop trust in you, confidence in themselves, conversation and communication skills.

> **Hint**: Give as much eye-contact as you can. Children understand body language and can sense when someone is really not listening to them!

Manners

It is never too early to teach your child to have good manners. The magic words they **must** learn are: *please, thank-you* and *excuse me.* Too few children use these words, today. Do not let your child(ren) be among them!

No!

Saying "no" and getting your point across can be both uncomfortable and frustrating for a parent. There will be times when *you* have had such a busy day that saying "yes" will allow you a few moments of peace and quiet. Do not be surprised if, the next day, you regret having given in to this moment of weakness.

A good portion of your child's behavior pattern will depend on how strong you are as a parent, especially, in your ability to say "no". Getting the meaning of this tiny, little two-letter word across to your child, is extremely important. She/he will have to face this word every day, every year of their life. So, when you say "no", mean it and stick to it! Being strong will mean keeping calm when she/he keeps saying please, whines, throws a tantrum, screams or holds their breath to scare you into saying "yes". Do not fall for these tricks. It is never easy to say "no" regardless of your child's age. But, you need to always be the parent figure who stands firm for the protection and well-being of your child!

Reading

Designate a specific amount of time to read to your child on a daily basis. Ten to fifteen minutes a day is really all you need. It will be good for their educational growth and be a form of bonding between the two of you. It does not matter if your child is an infant, toddler or a pre-schooler. You can read a story from children's books or *combine* your student and parent role by reading a portion of your homework assignment out loud! You will benefit from the reading for understanding. Your child will benefit from this bonding period. Eventually, your routine—at the same time each evening—will become a routine that she/he will begin to look forward to. Again, depending on her/his age, make comments about the stories and encourage questions. Above all, be sure this reading time is a fun and enjoyable experience!

Responsibility

Parents want their children to be responsible and accept responsibilities. Being responsible, depending on your child's age, would initially include: never telling a lie, being honest and open with her/his parent and feeling comfortable with being an honest person. As a parent, you should also want your child to feel a sense of responsibility about completing their homework assignments, making their bed, keeping their room in order, and, handling assigned household chores. Once you notice that a sense of irresponsibility is starting to surface, you might want to prepare a "Things-to-Do" list. Discuss each item on the list with your child. Explain what they have to do and when a particular task needs to be completed. Should it be handled daily, weekly or once a month?

As an important note, be sure to let your child know that completion of certain tasks is a responsibility that they have to handle on their own. And, they should not expect to be given either special privileges or money.

Sick Time

Does your child constantly put up a fuss about going to the babysitter or school? Is her/his excuse quite often that they are "sick?" Have you observed in most instances that they are **not** sick? If this happens too frequently, you need to visit the babysitter, daycare center or school. It could be that she/he is being teased, harrassed or frightened by another youngster. It could be that they do not want to be away from you. It could be just to get attention. Or, it is also possible that some form of inappropriate activity is occurring that makes her/him uncomfortable. Give serious thought to all of these possibilities, immediately!

Tantrums

Isn't it just awful when your child decides to have a tantrum or throw a fit in public? You have probably seen this happen many times with other children at the supermarket and department stores. It is really a familiar sight in toy stores when these children get a case of the gimmes (gimme this or gimme that)! Instead of losing *your* temper or shouting "no!" try saying "no!" in a calm and final voice tone. Or, say:

- "No, we can't afford it!"
- "You have one at home that is much better than this one!"
- "No, it doesn't look safe, you might hurt yourself!"

Again, remember not to shout. Remain calm. Speak in a calm tone of voice. If necessary, simply give your child a *time-out*. This will mean leaving your cart in the store, taking her/him to the car (or sitting outside the store) for a ten-fifteen minute period. While this will require you to participate in the time-out, use this time to write a letter, make notes about a homework assignment or read a portion of your homework assignment.

When you re-enter the store (hopefully, your cart has not been moved!) continue on with what you were doing. Should your child start the same routine again, then *you* should repeat the time-out activity, again. It will not be easy the first, second or even third time, but if you consistently, do this, chances are good that your child will eventually get the message.

"Children use the tantrum method to test their parent's patience; but, parents use patience to over-ride that method!"

Time-Outs

"Time-Out" is really a *sit, be still and do not talk* period for a specific amount of time as punishment for misbehavior. This is a disciplinary action that will allow your child to cool down. When you set the time limit, be sure to keep your child's age in mind. While this might work for a 4-7 year old, you might find that it is a bit more difficult for a little one who is about 1-3 years of age!

> Special Note: Hitting your child as a form of discipline can be dangerous to their health. Children may consider hitting as normal behavior when they are angry. After all, they may think "it must be okay if Mom or Dad does it". They may also consider hitting as a means of instilling fear in someone. Hitting shoul dnever be used for disciplinary action.

> **Tip**: Since you might need a cooling down period, too, join your child during her/his time-out by sitting with her/him!

Travel

Traveling with a child can be involved! The basics to keep in mind are really very general and are sure to help you keep your cool! For instance:

- ❑ Allow your children to help in the selection of what she/he want to pack. Be insistent and explain the "why" of packing items they either did not think about or you know **will have to be packed**. Do not be surprised to find out—at first—that they never seem to remember that underwear, socks and their toothbrush are important items to be packed!

- ❑ A really good way of "limiting the amount" that your child wants to pack, is to tell her/him that they can only pack as much as will fit in their backpack.

   > **Hint**: Naturally, you will have already taken inventory of what your child has packed, and packed these items, elsewhere.

- ❑ Depending on your child's age, it is a good idea to bring along a favorite toy, special pillow or blanket for their comfort. It is quite possible that your child will **not** feel, particularly, comfortable sleeping in a bed that is **not** her/his own.

- ❑ Do not forget about the *safety* of your child when traveling! Child restraint seats are a must! Contact the Department of Transportation to get more information about requirements regarding child-safety seats, whether you are traveling by car, bus, train or airplane.

- ❑ For emergency situations, take along a flashlight and "extra" batteries, a first aid kit that has band-aids, children's/adult vitamins and aspirin, an antiseptic, a thermometer, scissors, safety pins, tweezers, adhesive tape, gauze, cotton balls, eye-drop medication, a good supply of handy wipes, emergency supply of feminine hygiene products and at least two extra blankets to keep an injured family member (or a stranger involved in an accident) warm.

❑ Prayer is also an essential portion of safe travel. Instill in your children and make it a routine to begin **all** trips (short and long) with a *prayer* for safe travel, the safety of each family member and that the *entire* trip end in the safe return of *every* family member!

Remember, you can be a great teen parent with patience, practice and plenty of love, not just for your child, but for yourself, too!

Chapter 15
Coping With "Same Sex" Choices

Let's talk. And share the following on lesbian and gay youth.

"Growing up is a demanding and challenging task for every adolescent. One important aspect is forming one's sexual identity. All children explore and experiment sexually as part of normal development. This sexual behavior may be with members of the same or opposite sex. For many, thinking about and/or experimenting with the same sex may cause concerns and anxiety regarding their sexual orientation. For others, even thoughts or fantasies may cause anxiety.

Homosexuality is the persistent sexual and emotional attraction to someone of the same sex. It is part of the range of sexual expression. Many lesbian and gay individuals first become aware of and experience their homosexual thoughts and feelings during childhood and adolescence. Homosexuality has existed throughout history and across cultures. Recent changes in society's attitude toward homosexuality have helped some lesbian and gay teens to feel more comfortable with their sexual orientation. (More support is still needed!) In other aspects of their development, lesbian and gay teens are similar to heterosexual youngsters. (They experience the same kinds of stress and struggles, for example: become socially isolated, withdraw from activities and friends, have trouble concentrating, and develop low self-esteem.)"

This is what the experts say, What do you say?

Are you a homosexual? If so, have you shared this fact with family members, friends, classmates or co-workers? Are you afraid about how they will react? Do you frequently feel alone? Are you tired, sometimes, about keeping your same sex attractions a secret? Is it *awful* when others around you make jokes about homosexuals? Your answer to many of these questions is probably, yes! Now, is a good time to look a littler closer for a few coping tools.

Who I Am

Let's get specific and directly to the point!

You are a pre-teen or teenager just like your friends. You are a family member with parent(s) who may have sisters/brothers. You attend school and try to get the best grades you can. You are a member of various school clubs, Church committees and/or youth organizations. You participate in sports, go to parties and have friends. You have a sincere interest in your personal growth. This interest includes finding ways to comfortably cope with life experiences, giving special attention to your health/safety, and, taking the necessary steps to ensure you can learn how to feel good about yourself.

All of this sounds like a description of a typical teenager, doesn't it? Well, you are! The only element that separates you from many of your friends is a singular difference. You happen to be a person who is attracted to and interested in a same sex relationship.

What you *really* want, from others, is respect and acceptance about your life-style choice, and **not** have to feel a sense of discomfort about the choice you made!

Some Definitions

Being a homosexual teen, you know better than anyone, about the many challenges and pressures that have to be handled. So, before getting started, a few definitions might be helpful for the sake of awareness.

Sexual Orientation:	A phrase used to describe a person's sexual attraction to their opposite sex, same sex or both.
Heterosexual:	A person who is sexually attracted to their "opposite" sex. A female is attracted to a male; or, a male who is attracted to a female.
	▎ **Hint**: *Hetero* means *other*.
Homosexual:	A person who is sexually attracted to someone of the same sex. A female who is attracted to another female; or, a male who is attracted to another male.
	▎ **Hint**: Homos means same.
Lesbian:	A female who is sexually attracted to another female.
Gay:	A male who is sexually attracted to another male.
Bi-sexual:	A person who is sexually attracted to **both** females and males.
Homophobia:	A fear of homosexuals. (Homophobics: people who have a fear of homosexuals.)

Carefully review this list of definitions. Keep these definitions in mind as you continue to read through this section. By the way, what is *your* sexual orientation?

Personal Problems

As a homosexual teen, you live with an enormous amount of personal pressures every day. Let's look a bit closer at some of these pressures.

Secret-Keeping

Is it *extremely* important to you that no one know you are lesbian/gay? Is the reason because you are afraid of how others might react, what they might say, or, the possibility of loosing your job? If so, chances are high that you will continue keeping this particular secret—secret—for quite some time. Recognize that you are (and have been) experiencing a high level of stress. Then go on to move forward toward self-improvement. Consider selecting a stress-release technique(s) that can help you to cope **and** reduce the amount of stress in your daily life.

"Secret-keeping can cause serious levels of stress to surface!"

Loneliness

There is no doubt that you often feel alone! You feel uncomfortable about talking to family members, a best friend or a close co-worker. There will be times when you really want to talk to someone, but you simply cannot. There will be numerous times when you will want to *approach* the person you are attracted to, but, shy away, just in case she/he will reject you. Fear will tend to take control of your normal (and positive) decision-making skills! What to do about loneliness is strictly up to you. The bottom-line, however, is to get involved with activities that will keep you active and allow you to keep your mind clear so your ability for *positive* decision-making *continues* to be in active mode.

Self-Esteem

Give *particular* attention to your level of self-esteem! You **must** continue to feel good about yourself, in spite of the inner pain, stress, possible confusion and frustrations that you have to cope with on a daily basis. Remember, you are the most important person in *your life*! And, working on your level of self-esteem is **not** a personal challenge, it is a personal obligation for your own well-being.

Pregnancy

This is a strange topic to be included here. Or, is it? In order to keep your secret a secret, many of you engage in activities you would really prefer **not** doing. You date your opposite sex. By a certain age, you are expected to go out on dates, otherwise your family and friends will think there is a problem. For some lesbian/gay teens, how probable is it that you will go a step further to protect your secret, by either getting pregnant or fathering a child?

Children should be conceived in an arena of love. They should not be conceived for the purposes of appearance. In other words, why bring a wonderful gift into the world to prove a point—to others—that you are *not* lesbian/gay?

Depression

If an artist wanted to paint a picture of you, she/he just might paint you as a person who has an important secret to keep; a secret that continuously causes discomfort and stress. The artist's portrait would also show someone who has no one to talk to openly about her/his feelings, and someone who is confused about what to do about all of this.

These are the kinds of thoughts that can bring on depression in homosexual teens. These are also the kind of thoughts that can send you over-the-edge. And, far too often, many of these thoughts are replaced with thoughts of suicide. Don't think about it! Don't do it! Don't make plans for this kind of negative activity!

Work on improvement of your *mental* strength. Carefully guard who you are and protect yourself from those who either do not understand or attempt to remold you in their image.

"Suicide takes me out of the picture
that shows how wonderful a person I really am!"

Parent Reactions

Let's suppose you have *finally* decided to tell your parents you are lesbian/gay. How will they react to the news?

Some parents will be so startled they may not be able to speak for a few moments. Once they regain their composure, a second flood of surprise will probably surface and jolt them right out of the chair! Again, there might be a brief few moments of silent disbelief. Take advantage of those few segments of silence to continue talking. Be as calm and to the point as you can. Remind them that you really appreciated their support about many other decisions you have made; and, you hope they will support you this time, too.

Some parents will be horrified! Their mind's eye will focus, quickly, on the many movies they have seen depicting lesbian/gay individuals, the stories they read about in magazines and newspapers, the kinds of gossip spread throughout their place of work about fellow employees who are lesbian/gay. Then, there is the element of religious beliefs, for **them** to wrestle with—on a *personal* level.

You already know they will (initially) feel embarrassed having a child who is lesbian/gay. You already know the kind of pain this news might bring to them. You also know that you love your parents, respect them and only want them to try to understand, be supportive and continue to love you—as you love them.

Some parents will feel responsible that *they* have done something to make you become lesbian/gay. Many moms might think you *turned out this way* because they took an occasional drink or smoked cigarettes/ marijuana, while they were pregnant with you. A number of dads might feel a sense of responsibility because they had sex with mom, while she was pregnant with you! While this might sound absolutely ridiculous, some parents, probably believe such things. Please know, that for whatever reason (even scientists have not found out why) you are who you are. If *you* feel comfortable with your decision, that is all there is to be considered.

Some parents will, after giving a bit of thought over a couple of hours or days, start to ask a number of questions. The questions will probably be very direct and they will ask for **exact** details. Be prepared to give as much details as you feel comfortable with sharing.

Some parents will feel and/or show anger, disgust, disbelief and hurt about your announcement. Be prepared to remain calm. Consistently repeat the "prepared announcement" (the one you have been practicing mentally for several years!). Keep in mind, that their dream about your future did not include you being lesbian/gay. So, be patient with your parents. They, simply, cannot help themselves where you are concerned!

> **Special Note**: Don't be surprised to find out that one (or both) parents already suspected that you were lesbian/gay. Chances are good, that **one** parent (hopefully, both) will be the supportive-link you need!

Your Health

Taking care of *yourself* should be foremost on your plan for survival. As a lesbian/gay individual, you need to always remember that "special" concern and extra measures are a necessity for your protection and the protection of your partner(s). Here are a few short comments you might want to keep in mind about your health.

Safe-Sex

The possibility of contracting a sexually-transmitted disease should be a major concern for you—a lesbian/gay teen. You need, therefore, to practice safe sex at all times. This includes lesbian/gay and/or sexual activity with those of your opposite sex. Consult a doctor, tell her/him that you are considering (or actively engaging in) sexual activity, you are lesbian/gay and ask for their advice about safe sex precautions to take.

Drugs and Alcohol

Attempting to cope with being a lesbian/gay teen may lead you to seek solace (temporary relief) by using drugs or drinking alcohol. Don't do it! Instead, let your fingers do the walking through the Yellow Page Directory and find a therapist who can help you resolve your problems. Talk to someone who you trust. And, praying, is a definite alternative to consider!

As an added suggestion, join a "Narcotics Anonymous or Alcohol Anonymous" group for support. Contact **any** Church and ask for the number to call for help.

Final Comments

It will be very hard for some family members, friends, classmates and co-workers to understand and accept that you are lesbian/gay. They, also, will have a problem understanding that you are still you, in spite of your sexual orientation. You, after all, know that there *can* be a positive, loving and sexual relationship between individuals of the same sex. The same things can hold true if you find out that one of your parents is homosexual. Or, you might be living in a household with two of the same sex adults and experience mixed feelings or reactions when you come to the realization of what it is all about. If either situation is the case, try to understand your parents' feelings, talk to them if you can, and seek support from an uderstanding adult or counselor, if you need it.

Until everyone can accept this as truth, and stop pre-judging **before** knowing all of the facts and feelings involved, there will simply be **no** unity or freedom of expression, thought, deed or respect for privacy—for anyone!

What should you do about defending your choice of lifestyle? Sit back, be patient, continue to hold your secret—for the benefit of your well-being in a society that is **not** ready to accept your choice of lifestyle. Then, confidently move forward when the opportunity presents itself to say to others: "I am lesbian/gay; not afraid of announcing my choice of sexual orientation; and, I am mentally and emotionally prepared for any situations that might challenge my beliefs or decisions!"

> **Note for your parents:** "Parents need to clearly understand that homosexual orientation is not a mental disorder. The cause(s) are not fully understood. However, a person's sexual orientation is not a matter of choice. It other words, individuals have no more choice about being homosexual than heterosexual. All teenagers do have a choice about their expression of sexual behaviors and lifestyle, regardless of their sexual orientation." (AACAP)

Chapter 16
Learn "Survival" Skills

The final step in your plan for personal growth is to try to become a better *informed* person. What you will find in this section is a little bit of information about a lot of different topics. Since surviving in (and being prepared for entrance to) the adult world is *really* your goal, this section, coupled with the previous sections, will allow you to do just that!

Adult Behavior

Being an adult means acting in a mature manner. It means being responsible for your own well-being, physically, emotionally, socially and spiritually. It also means you will be handling your own problems, will have learned how to respect yourself and others, and understand the difference between right and wrong behavior. You will be very successful in some areas. You will feel a sense of failure in other areas. But, do not be afraid of these failures. Instead, work on improving or correcting them. When you feel ready to take on this new role, allow your actions to show others that you are ready to be treated and respected as an adult.

Aerobic Exercises

Aerobics is a form of exercise that allows you to sleep better, have more energy and reduce the amount of stress and fatigue you probably feel every day. Some forms of aerobics include: running, swimming, cycling, walking, skipping rope, golfing, skating/skiing and playing basketball, football, tennis, soccer and volleyball. If you are **not** involved in doing any of these activities, then get started now...these activities are healthy and can be a lot of fun!

Airplane Earaches

During air travel you will probably experience an earache. This occurs when the pressure in the airplane cabin changes during taek-off and landing. To feel a bit of relief, try swallowing, yawning, chewing gum, sucking on hard candy or exhaling while holding your nostrils shut and closing your mouth. This discomfort doesn't last long. It is just very annoying!

Alcoholic Beverages

Did you know that drinking alcoholic beverages does *not* help in the growth or development of any part of your body? There is no nourishment in alcohol. There are no muscle-building or mind enrichment nutrients in alcohol. It is absorbed directly from the stomach into the blood stream and very quickly has an effect upon the body soon after it has been consumed. The blood stream carries the alcohol to all parts of the body. Alcohol first affects the central nervous system, especially the brain. Then, a person may talk and laugh noisly and say some pretty silly things! This is because their good judgment, common sense, and self-control are affected by the alcohol. Drinking alcoholic beverages reduces a person's efficiency to do work, can make her/him unreliable because it lessens their memory, reasoning, judgment and ability to think clearly.

*"Think **before** you drink!"*

Babysitting Musts!

A responsible "babysitter" always:

- ❏ Takes the time to take notes on instructions given by the parents.
- ❏ Follows the parent's instructions.
- ❏ Makes it a point to have a telephone number of where the parents are, in case of an emergency.
- ❏ Keeps the doors locked.

❑ Makes sure that personal calls are kept to a minimum and **does not** invite friends over to visit.

❑ Stays awake and alert.

❑ Reports to the parents *any* and *all* illnesses or accidents that may have occurred.

Being honest and doing what is expected of you *can* result in repeat business. And, after all, isn't that what you *really* want?

Bad Breath

To test your breath, cup your hands, breathe deeply into them and take a sniff! If that sniff smells *bad* to you, chances are it smells bad to anyone you talk to, too! You can get bad breath from eating foods with garlic, spicy deli meats, some dairy products such as blue cheese dressings, tuna or even coffee. Carry a toothbrush and use it after meals. Make it a habit to brush your tongue so you won't leave food and bacteria behind to breed bad breath. Chew a mint or some gum, eat parsley (**not** a great taste, but it *does do* the job!), and gargle with a minty mouthwash for a *temporary* solution to bad breath.

Belching

Belching is your body's way of giving off air and other gases swallowed on a normal basis. Since some people belch more than others, here are a few tips that might help: try to stay clear of carbonated beverages, eat slowly and be mindful of chewing your food completely **before** swallowing, try to avoid chewing gum and resist the convenience of drinking out of cans/bottles or using a straw. You also need to avoid certain foods like ice cream, omelets, whipped cream, salad oils, margarine and sour cream because these foods tend to have high air content. And, the result of course, will be you experiencing episodes of belching.

Birth Control

There are many birth control items available. Since you have several choices available to you, it is advised that you consult your doctor to see which item is best for you. You might, for example, ask her/him to describe the different items that are available. Then ask her/him for advice about using a diaphragm, foam, IUD, Norplant, pill or sponge.

> **Hint:** The most effective (100%) way to not get pregnant is abstinence or not having sex at all!

Black National Anthem

Do you know all of the words? Perhaps you should learn them!

Lift every voice and sing,
Till earth and heaven ring,
Ring with the harmonies of liberty;
Let our rejoicing rise,
High as the listening skies,
Let resound loud as the rolling sea.
Sing a song full of faith that the dark
Past has taught us,
Sing a song full of the hope that the present
has brought us;
Facing the rising sun of our new day begun,
Let us march on till victory is won.
*

Stony the road we trod,
bitter the chastening rod,
Felt in the days when hope unborn had died;
Yet with a steady beat,
have not our weary feet,
come to the place for which our fathers sighed?
We have come over a way that with tears has
been watered,
We have come, treading our path through the
blood of the slaughtered.
Out of the gloomy past,
till now we stand at least,
Where the white gleam of our bright star is cast.
*

God of our weary years,

God of our silent tears,
Thou who hast brought us thus far on the way;
Thou who has by thy might, led us into the light,
Keep us forever in the path, we pray.
Least our feet stray from the places,
Our God, where we met thee,
Lest our hearts, drunk with the wine of the world,
we forget Thee;
Shadowed beneath Thy hand, may we forever stand,
True to our God, true to our native land.

Braids

Wearing braids are great! They are carefree and convenient. Or, are they? Contrary to what many might think, you can't just have your hair braided and forget about it for 3 to 4 months! You still need to shampoo your hair regularly to make sure your scalp is clean and your braids don't look dull. Remember to wrap your hair in a silk or satin scarf before going to bed at night. And, it will be time for a "touch-up" about every 4-6 weeks as the braids start to grow out.

Car Maintenance

Keeping an accurate record of your car's maintenance can prolong the life of your car! There are several areas of concern that you need to give special and consistent attention to, making sure to always record the dates. These areas include: oil changes, lubrication, changing oil filters, having air filters cleaned, servicing the cooling system, rotation of tires, replacing tires, servicing brakes, engine tune-ups and/or monitoring transmission fluid level servicing.

Added to this list are the following:

- ❑ Checking headlights and break lights.
- ❑ Making sure the air-conditioning system is checked.
- ❑ Giving special attention to the windshield wipers. (Do this **especially** during summer months so you will be more than prepared for winter-weather emergency times!)
- ❑ Check carefully for tire tread depth and inflation pressure. (It is suggested that you do this on a regular basis

for your/your family's safety! Make this particular check a routine on a **weekly** basis!)

In case of an emergency:

Always have, in your car, a fire extinguisher, jumper cables, flashlight, ice scraper, flares and/or highway triangular warning signs, container of water, an approved (and empty) gasoline container, distress flag, warm/clean blanket, pair of gloves, small shovel and a can of sand.

If you work at night and drive home alone, it would be a good idea to carry a cell phone with you for emergency calls. And, just in case your car breaks down or won't start, you should get an American Automobile Association (AAA) membership. They'll send a service truck to you wherever you are, fix a flat, bring you gas, give your battery a boot, or tow your car as part of your membership benefits.

"A healthy car, like a a healthy body
kept in good shape will perform as it is intended!"

Cleaning Your Room

Yes, it has to be done and you have to do it! But, it does not have to be as painful as you think. Here are five steps to follow in order to make this as easy for you as possible.

Step 1:   Gather all of your supplies (cleaning stuff, furniture polish, vacuum cleaner, trash bags, etc.) and place them inside your room (behind the door).

Step 2:   Close the door, set your alarm clock for one hour and turn on some music that has a very *fast* beat.

Step 3:   Begin cleaning in one direction—start cleaning on the wall that is on the right of the door and move on to the next wall, and so on until you have completed a full square (you will end up where you started—at the closed door).

Step 4:   Clear your bed of miscellaneous items being sure to put these items in their appropriate place; clean under the bed, too! Now, make your bed using fresh linens.

Step 5:   Vacuum/sweep the entire room.

Keep in mind that **anything** that is on either of the four walls in your room has to be taken care of as you go through these steps. For example: one wall might have a bookshelf, so you would dust and straighten up the bookshelf as well as put books which are on the floor in front of it, away. Or, when you get to the wall that has your dresser and mirror, the dresser would be cleared/cleaned and left in order, etc.

Once all of this has been done, turn off your music, put your cleaning supplies away and give yourself a *smile* in the mirror, for a job well done—in record time!

Coffee Consciousness

A cup of coffee is simply that—a cup of coffee...or is it? There are many different kinds of coffee, prepared in different ways and served with more than just cream and sugar. Here are a few *coffee facts* to get you started.

Regular Coffee Coffee prepared in a coffee maker that requires finely-ground coffee beans that are usually sold in pre-packaged amounts or that can be purchased in larger quantities (can-size).

Instant Coffee Coffee beans that have been ground to the point that only one teaspoon full needs to be added to your mug along with enough boiling water to immediately begin enjoying your cup-of-coffee!

Espresso Coffee An Italian specialty that is very different from American coffee. It is prepared using an Espresso machine that produces a powerful (strong) drink with the consistency (texture or thickness) of light cream.

Cappuccino   This is Espresso Coffee that is prepared with hot milk, a dash of cinnamon or nutmeg.

Cafe Au Lait   A French coffee that combines equal parts of strong coffee, milk and sugar.

Caffe Latte   *Here is an assignment for you*—find out what this type of coffee is by calling or visiting a Coffee Bar!

Go to a "Coffee Bar" by yourself or with a date. Coffee Bars offer a pretty good atmosphere for having a conversation and for relaxation purposes! While you are there take the opportunity to ask the waiter or waitress to describe the different types of coffees they offer and ask questions about how each of the coffees are prepared. You might also want to go to your local supermarket and purchase many of the different blends they have available until you find the one that appeals most to you!

Cold Treatments

The next time you have a cold keep the following tips in mind:

- ❑ Stay bundled up as often as possible

- ❑ Eat *lots* of fresh fruits and vegetables

- ❑ Sip, inhale and eat chicken soup because it is believed that chicken soup *can* help unclog nasal passages which in turn, helps you (by blowing your nose or sneezing) to release germs from your system;

- ❑ Drink lots of clear liquids (especially juice and water) to help flush out impurities from your system;

- ❑ Take hot and steamy showers which can also help clear your congestion problems; and,

- ❑ Don't forget to medicate at night with the appropriate night-time cold medications you can buy over the counter.

As a special note, make sure that you purchase **only** those over-the-counter cold medications that "fit" your *specific* symptoms! Be mindful, for example, about using over-the-counter cold/flu medications that will make you "drowsy" during the day!

Competition

Competing is not easy for everyone. For some, it means they will *willingly* work harder, and for others it means they will experience a *fear-of failure*! In both instances, there are suggestions available that can be very helpful.

- Competing means that there will *always* be at least one winner and several losers. So, learn to be a good loser. Remember, you tried your best and there is no shame in losing. Also, remember to congratulate the winner.

- The best person to compete against is yourself! Work at getting better and better at whatever your best record is and don't be surprised to find that you are even better than you thought.

- It is all right to feel bad when you lose, but only for a short time. Try not to let your family and friends know *how much* you were counting on winning. In other words, keep your emotions to yourself until you get a chance to be alone. It is important that your parents and friends notice that you are taking this loss in a mature manner.

"Failures are stepping stones to future successes."

Condoms

Condoms help prevent unplanned pregnancies and contracting sexually transmitted diseases. You can easily purchase them over-the-counter. While they do not come with a 100% guarantee, using condoms is necessary in order to engage in safe-sex. So, *use* them for your protection and others. Be *insistent* with your partner. And, stay *prepared* for the unexpected!

Constipation

Being constipated is when your bowel discharge is slow or difficult to pass. Constipation can be painful, cause cramping and lots of discomfort in the rectum when you strain trying to pass hard stools. It sometimes means that: there is a lack of fiber in your daily diet; you have an insufficient amount of liquid intake; you are under unusual stress; you are on special medications; or, you have not been exercising enough. To handle those times when you are constipated, drink lots of water (8 to 10 glasses a day just might help). Include on your daily menu whole grains, fruit and vegetables, cooked dried beans, prunes, figs, raisins, popcorn, oatmeal, pears and nuts. Start, or get back into, exercise mode. And, as soon as the urge to go hits you...hit the nearest restroom!

Conversations

Are you a good conversationalist? Do people like to talk to you about lots of different subjects? Do they appear to enjoy listening to you? Do you give them your attention when they are talking to you? Do they like talking to you because you have a good sense of humor? Do you give compliments to others?

If you can answer "yes" to **most** of these questions, then you are probably a person who is a good conversationalist!

Some of the characteristics of a bad conversationalist include:

- ❏ The person who constantly talks about themselves even when it is obvious no one is interested.

- ❏ The person who only wants to talk about their personal problems—sometimes to the point that they make others uncomfortable in their presence.

- ❏ The person who never lets others finish a sentence. *How awful do you feel when you are telling a joke and this wonderful person gives the punch-line **before** you finish?*

- ❏ The person who never agrees with others about different issues no matter what the issue might be, and continues to challenge the speaker.

- ❏ The person who does not look at you (have eye contact) when they are talking to you.

If you have any of these characteristics, now is a pretty good time to do something about them. What can you do? Well, stop it, of course! Others will appreciate the change and begin to *look forward* to having a conversation with you.

Courtesy

Treating others as you would want them to treat you is the real basis for showing common courtesy. Allow thoughtfulness to be the foundation of how you treat others. For example, staring at others or talking very loud (in an attempt to embarrass someone) is impolite because it can cause them to feel uncomfortable. Making personal comments of a negative nature, to an individual or in the presence of others, is also added to this list. Step into their shoes, for just a moment. How would you feel?

Dieting

To diet safely, diet smart! Examine "why" you feel the need to go on a diet. If, after giving this matter serious thought, you decide to diet, begin by taking a close look at your eating habits. Here are a few suggestions to help you get started.

- ❑ Always go grocery shopping on a full stomach.
- ❑ Reduce how fast you eat by putting your fork down between bites. The slower you eat the quicker you will begin to feel full.
- ❑ Once you have finished eating your meal, immediately leave the table.
- ❑ Skipping meals will cause you to want to catch-up— resulting in overeating later.
- ❑ Sparkling waters (no-calories) are an excellent substitute for alcoholic beverages.

Select a diet program that will be comfortable, not painful; search for exercises that will be fun, not boring; and, above all, get your doctor's opinion and approval *before* starting.

Doors

It is a sign of common courtesy to hold a door open for the person behind you. When entering an elevator, if you see that someone is walking toward the elevator, simply push the "hold" button as a courtesy. No one likes to have a door shut in their face! Do you? Gentlemen are encouraged to open doors and car doors for ladies—at all times!

Eyestrain

For eyestrain (especially if this discomfort occurs frequently) make a quick visit to your eye doctor. Before doing so, however, be sure you have checked on whether or not you normally have sufficient lighting when reading, working on projects or using your computer. Do you usually take a break from your computer for at least 15 minutes or simply shut your eyes for a few moments, several times a day to give your eyes a break? Do you sit very close to your television screen on a frequent basis? Do you suspect that you *really* need to visit your eye doctor and have **not** taken the time to do so? If your answer is "yes" to most of these questions, then, isn't it about time for you to do something about your discomfort?

Exploring the Area

Take some time to explore (investigate) the area where you live so that you will be able to answer the following questions:

- Where is the closest hospital in your area?
- Where is the closest fire department?
- Where is the nearest recycling center?
- How many businesses are owned/operated by Black women in your area?
- Who would you call to find out where to donate food, clothes, toys or used books?
- Where could families, in your area, go if their homes were destroyed by a storm or fire?
- Where would you go or who could you call to get information about obtaining a license for dogs, fishing or starting a business?
- Where would you go to find out the *why* about street names in your area?

Are you surprised that exploring can also apply to more than just going out on a nature walk?

Flowers

Having fresh flowers around is always pleasant. They are nice to look at, smell great and can make you smile. Giving flowers (even *one* in a pretty vase) will almost always make the other person feel very special. If your funds are low, ask a neighbor, if you can have a few flowers from her/his garden. They will probably be more than happy and say "yes"! In fact, by just asking, they will more than likely feel that you have given them a terrific compliment.

Fresh flowers can last longer if you keep them out of direct sun, heat and drafts. Add fresh water to the vase regularly (about every three to four days). Do not forget to remove any dying heads immediately to prevent wilting of the other healthy flowers.

Foot Odor

All right—at one point or another, everyone has a problem with handling foot odors! You, therefore, are **not** the only person in America who has had to go through handling this particular problem.

To tackle the problem of foot odor, try washing your feet on a more than frequent basis, using an antiperspirant directly on your feet, changing your socks frequently, or soaking your feet in a vinegar bath. Use a plastic tub (like the kind used for giving an infant a bath) with about 4 tablespoons of vinegar added. Or, consider using shoe inserts.

Gambling

Gambling for fun is perfectly all right. It becomes a problem, however, when you continuously play for stakes you can't comfortably afford. It also becomes a problem when you find that you simply cannot stop! Did you know that people can become *addicted* to gambling as well as to alcohol and drugs? Think twice, therefore, before taking your gambling activity too far. If you feel that you *might* have a problem (or a friend or relative tells you they think you might have a problem) then, look in the *Yellow Page Directory* for a "Gamblers Anonymous" organization and speak with one of the counselors. You can also get information from your Church, a civic organization or by simply calling a hospital in the area. Do something about your problem as soon as possible...if you don't it will only get worse!

Gift Giving/Receiving

In general, the giving of a gift should be a thought-out project. Purchase gifts that will be useful, reflect the likes, dislikes or hobbies of the individual; or, what the person actually asked for! And, yes, gifts of money are always welcomed...but depending on the occasion might appear to be a little *impersonal.*

If you are the person receiving a gift, always remember:

- When opening the gift to *show* surprise and gratefulness about the gift you have been given (especially in front of the gift-giver)

- To give an *enthusiastic* "Thank You" for the gift, even though you may not like the gift

- Remember to send a "Thank You" card or note at least within the next week.

Gift Wrapping

Did you know that gifts do not always have to be wrapped in gift-wrap paper? You could also use for example, newspaper (sports section, comics, the entertainment section, etc.), a piece of fabric, cellophane, gift bags/boxes, ceramic containers, wicker baskets or cookie jars (with something other than cookies). Be creative and have fun!

Goal Setting

Setting goals gives you something to look forward to and makes you feel a sense of accomplishment once you reach it. In the beginning, set small goals for yourself that will require short periods of time to complete. A short-term goal (requiring a short amount of time) might be to read two books within one week, for example. Or, you might make it a goal to lose 5 pounds within the next three weeks. Or, set a goal to have $100.00 saved by a certain date.

Hint: Always give yourself a specific date—month, year!

Write your goal or goals on an index card and keep it where you will see it every day as a reminder. Once you have reached that particular goal, make another. Eventually, you will be able to set goals for longer than one week, three months to six months, and from one to five years.

"The best day to set a goal is always today!"

Gum

Avoid being an *offensive* gum chewer! It is considered bad taste to chew gum with an open mouth, making loud smacking sounds, popping and blowing bubbles. It is also a sign of thoughtlessness to discard chewing gum in places where someone might sit, step or accidentally touch it. Can you remember how you felt the last time you had gum stuck to your shoe?

Homeless Shelters

Adopt a homeless shelter in your area. Give a bit of volunteer time. Help with the preparation of meals, doing housekeeping tasks and having conversations with the residents. Purchase and donate miscellaneous supplies. You might, for example, collect can goods, clothes and board games in your neighborhood. Since some of the residents in homeless shelters are children (and there are many!) give tutoring sessions to them in math and English. Develop your own booklets and give them homework to complete. Do not forget to provide some sort of reward as proof of their accomplishments!

Remember to always talk positively and be encouraging about their situation. Be a *positive* listener. Do what you can to help. Ask for help and direction from your parents, the pastor at your church and friends/relatives. Decide how often you intend to visit. Include this amount of time on your schedule of thing to do. Whether you go there once a week, or twice a month is unimportant. What is important, however, is that you will be giving your time to help others!

Kwanzaa

Kwanzaa is the African-American cultural holiday that is tradition-ally celebrated from December 26 through January 1. Kwanzaa is recognized by millions throughout America and the world. It is cel-ebrated often in community settings provided by homes, churches, mosques, temples, community centers, schools, and places of work. It allows us to celebrate the season without shame or fear of embracing our history, our culture, and ourselves. It is a spiritual, festive, and joyous celebration of the oneness and goodness of life, which claims no ties with any religion.

The focus of Kwanzaa is centered around the seven principles (Nguzo Sabo) with particular emphasis on the unity of our Black families. It is a time for gathering of our families, and for a rededica-tion to manifesting the principles of Kwanzaa as a way of life for Black Americans. As a living social practice, it is a week of actual remembering, reassessing, recommitting, rewarding and rejoicing. For evaluation of ourselves and our history, we relate to our past, reasssess our thoughts and practices, and recommit ourselves to the achievement of Black liberation and the betterment of life for all Black Americans.

The concept of Kwanzaa, the African-American holiday, is to help Black Americans relate to the past in order to understand the pres-ent and deal with the future.

Library

The next time you need to get away from the house, from school and even from your friends, try going to the public library. There you can take your time to read a book for enjoyment (not for a school assignment), have a little peace and quiet, not have to talk to anyone, and get a chance to relax.

Literacy

Being able to read is something that many take for granted. Did you know that there are thousands of people you pass on the street, everyday, who do not know how to read? A number of pro-grams are available that teach people to teach others how to read. Ask your school counselor or call the public library in your area to find out where these seminars are held. Sign-up today so you can feel part of the pride that the person you help feels!

Loaned/Borrowed Items

You need to keep track of things you loan to or borrow from others. The easiest way to do this is to keep a 3 x 5 card file that has all the necessary information about who borrowed what and when the item is to be returned.

Purchase 3 x 5 cards in two different colors. White, for example could be for items you have loaned to someone; and the yellow 3 x 5 cards would be those items that you borrowed from someone. Keep the cards in chronological (date) order and in a file box that fits the size of these cards. By checking this file box *every day* you will be sure to know when to retrieve (get back) or return all the items on time. Use the format below for filling out the cards. Both cards, regardless of the color, should have the same information.

Date Item To Be Returned:_____

Item Loaned/Borrowed:_____

_____

To/From: _____

Telephone Number:_____

Returned?   Yes   No

With this system you will almost always be able to get back what you gave out and be able to gain a reputation for being a person who "honors their promise" to return what they borrowed.

Maps

Learn to read a map. It will always be helpful to be able to read a map of the area where you live, the surrounding areas and out-of-state areas where you intend to travel. Knowing how to read a map will allow you to save time and a lot of frustration.

> **Hint**: Once you learn how to read a map of local/ state-wide areas, move forward and global to a world-wide map.

Oops! Have you just entered the world of Geography? Think about it for a moment!

Masturbation

Touching or rubbing your vagina/penis for sexual pleasure is referred to as masturbating. It is perfectly normal and personally okay! It is not harmful to you physically or emotionally. What you are doing is simply satisfying your body's urge for sexual pleasure. Masturbating is a very personal activity. As such, you will probably **not tell** anyone that you do this, except your doctor! Know this, however, many feel the same way. Teenagers do this and so do many adults.

While masturbation is a common activity used for the purposes of sexual pleasure, it is **not** an *uncommon* activity. It will **not** hurt you. You should not feel like a "freak" or "sexually-deprived" individual! What you need to keep in mind is that you are perfectly within your personal rights to satisfy your sexual urges in this manner. No one has "official" authority, permission or right to say otherwise!

Money Matters

Strive to be money-wise! Be a bargain shopper. Get in the habit of using a budget. Pay your bills on time, on a regular basis. Avoid being a credit card collector! Ask questions about finance charges, late fees and interest rates.

Contact your local Credit Bureau and request booklets on ways to safeguard your credit rating. No credit or bad credit could prevent you from making major purchases like a car or furniture for your first apartment. Do a little research on money management. There are many books and articles available on the subject. Make it a habit to save at least 10% (20% would be great!) of *all* your earnings. In other words, make sure to calculate the 10% or 20% of each and every paycheck you receive **before** cashing it and that amount should automatically be put into your savings account.

> **Hint**: for every $100.00 you earn (part-time job, tips, gifts or whatever—put $10.00 (or 10%) into your savings account. You will be surprised at how fast it adds up!

Be a smart saver! Do you get an allowance, have you been getting gifts of money from family and friends for graduation, your birthday, etc.? Do you often save loose change in a jar? Deposit these monies in your savings account. At the end of the year your account could be quite healthy. Try it!

It is also suggested that you talk to a bank official about certificates of deposit, savings bonds and the procedure for obtaining a loan.

Neighborhood

Your neighborhood should be the starting point of your involvement with others! Is there a community organization that you join? If not, start one! Do you live in a neighborhood that has lots of children? If so, is there a safe place for them to play? If not, do something about it! Do you have non-Afro Americans in your neighborhood? If so, make it a goal to make them welcome and let them know that you are interested in a mutual exchange of awareness about their culture.

Party Planning

With proper planning your party should be nearly perfect! These are the steps to follow:

- ❑ Pick a theme. What kind of party are you having—birthday, bridal shower, baby shower, graduation or a "Just Because You Feel the Urge"?

- ❑ Select a date and time.

- ❑ Prepare a guest list. Depending on the location, it is not wise to invite too many people. Also, be sure to invite people who are likely to enjoy **each** other's company!

❑ Make a "Party Budget" that you can afford to handle. How much do you want to spend on **each** person you invite? $2.00, $5.00 or $10.00 per person?

Once you have decided how much, multiply that amount times the number of people on your guest list. This per person amount would include the costs of: invitations, postage, food, drinks, decorations, etc.

❑ Plan your menu based on the number of guests.

❑ Now, comes the hard part! List **all** of the expenses you have to handle for this party. How much will the invitations coat? How much postage do you need? What is the approximate cost of food you have to buy (do not forget the cost of the cake)! Do remember to include the purchase of napkins, plates, forks/knives/spoons, table clothes and miscellaneous decorations. What about beverages? Do not forget to include these total costs. After adding up all costs, *divide* your final figure by the number of guests you intend to invite. Should the amount **exceed** what you initially planned to spend on a per-person basis—start again! In fact, do not be surprised that you will have to re-work your figures—several times!

Some ways to "cut corners" and reduce your expenses would include:

— Make your own invitation and simply copy them
— Form a committee or call some of your guests and request that they bring a dish
— Decide that this party will **not** have alcoholic beverages served
— Make your own decorations!

❑ When mailing out the invitations, be sure to put "Please R.S.V.P. by a specific date followed by your telephone number.

Note: R.S.V.P. is an abbreviation for a French phrase that means "please respond."

❑ Set-up a schedule of "things to do". Do not forget to include dates and times for completion! Your schedule needs to include activities for you to do: 3 weeks before, 2 weeks before, 1 week before, the day of, and 1-hour before the party actually begins!

❑ Next, play the perfect hostess/host and enjoy the party **with** your guests.

❑ After all of your guests have left, it is **now** time for clean-up activities! Do this **before** going to bed. If you don't you will wish you had in the morning!

Pet Principles

Does your pet (dog, cat, rabbit, whatever!) have good manners? If not, then you need to be sure that they are not around when your guests come to visit.

Pets that like to greet guests by jumping up on them, those that like to rub up against them, or to be underfoot, *can* make your guests feel either uncomfortable or irritated! Making sure that a guest in your home is welcome and comfortable, is *your* responsibility. A simple solution is to put your pets in another room or outside until your guests leave. Keep in mind that some of your guests may have a phobia (fear) of certain animals. When inviting others to your home, therefore, remember to mention that you have a particular pet ask them if they have a fear or are allergic to certain animals. Just sharing this information and asking the questions, will definitely be appreciated. It will also be a sign of their concern for you and your comfort!

Positive Thoughts

Negative thoughts can lead to depression, loneliness, stress and be linked to certain illnesses. Positive thoughts can make you feel calm, confident and more in control. Make a special effort to replace any and all negative thoughts with—at least—two positive thoughts! Adopting this habit will result in a healthier, more content, you.

Reading Habits

Try to break the habit of reading aloud, reading one word at a time and back-tracking. These habits slow down your reading speed. If you feel the need to improve and/or increase your reading and comprehension skills, take a *course* in some form of "reading improvement." By taking a course you can feel comfortable in knowing that the experts/instructors will have many tips to offer you. Ask your school counselor for suggestions about where to look for such a course.

Religions

A person's religious beliefs are strictly a *personal choice*. As such, it is absolutely inappropriate and a sign of bad manners to make negative comments or jokes, which might be considered *offensive* by some, based on their religious preferences.

Restaurant Etiquette

Are you planning to go to a rather fancy restaurant to impress your date? If so, then please take a look at this short list of *do's* and *don'ts*, first!

❑ **Do** call the restaurant to make reservations. It is a good idea to call at least a few days ahead (3 or 4 days). All you have to say when you call is: *"Good evening. I'm calling to make dinner reservations for two on Wednesday, January 23rd at 7:00pm. My name is Leland Johnson."*

If you find out (the same day you have already made reservations) that you are going to be arriving a little late or that you have to cancel your reservation, do call the restaurant, immediately!

❑ **Do** look for a coat-check room and check hats, coats, umbrellas and any packages you may have with you. You don't want to be bothered with having to store these items on your chair, on the floor or under your table!

❑ **Do** go, immediately, after checking your coats to the Hostess or Headwaiter and say: *"Good evening, I have reservations for two at 7:00pm. My name is Leland Johnson."* At this point, the Hostess or Headwaiter will check their book for your name and then ask you to follow her/him to your table.

❑ Once you have been seated, a waitress or waiter will then appear. You will be presented with a menu and asked what beverage you would like. **Don't** be insulted if they ask for identification to verify your age! It is their job and the **legal** responsibility of the restaurant to make sure they are not serving alcoholic beverages to individuals under a certain age.

❑ While you are waiting for your before-dinner drinks to arrive, take this time to decide what you will order for dinner. If, by the time your before-dinner drinks arrive, you know what you want to order, go ahead and give your order. **Don't** feel pressured to give the waitress or waiter your order right away. If you want a few more minutes to decide, simply say: *"We'd like a few more minutes to decide, please."*

❑ Now what? You have given your order. (Did you remember to put your napkin on your lap?) Your order is placed before you. So, simply enjoy your meal and the special conversation you and your date are exchanging. Feel a sense of the atmosphere that this special restaurant has to offer!

> **Note**: Please review the information in this section under "Table Manners".

❑ After it is obvious that everyone is finished eating and it is time to leave, make a special effort to get the attention of your waitress or waiter and ask them: *"May I have the check, please?"*

> **Note**: The bill you get is never called a "bill", it is called a "check". And, never yell for the waitress or waiter. Simply make eye contact with her/him. Most restaurants have very good waitresses/waiters. Their

▌ responsibility is to their assigned tables. So, chances are they will be there before you can look for them.

The check will be placed in front of you on a special little tray or in a flat wallet-like holder. **Don't** forget to review the check to be sure that what was ordered was received.

▌ **Hint**: Please review "Tipping" in this section.

After making sure that everything is in order, place the correct amount of money on the tray or inside of the wallet-like holder and slide it to the table edge. This will be a sign to your waitress or waiter that they can pick-up payment for your check.

❑ Using cash to pay your check is less expensive. There are no finance charges to deal with at the end of the month! But, using your credit card is quick, easy and allows you to make an even better impression with your date (that is, of course, as long as the waitress or waiter **don't** come back to the table to tell you that your *credit card has "not" been accepted!!*)

A few more do's and don'ts to keep in mind are:

❑ **Don't** put liquids into your mouth when your mouth has solid food in it.

❑ **Don't** leave your spoon in the coffee/tea cup.

❑ **Do** ask your waitress or waiter questions about anything you do not understand on the menu.

❑ **Don't** wave food on any utensil (spoon or fork) that has food on it, while you are talking.

❑ **Do** avoid cutting-up all of your meats and vegetables **in** advance eating. (It makes a mess of what **was** a very pretty presentation of the meal you ordered!) Instead, cut *as* you eat.

Here's a thought...*The next time you go to a Chinese restaurant ask the waitress or waiter to show you how to use chopsticks. You can play around with them for a while but don't let your food get cold! Ask for another set of chopsticks to take with you and practice at* *home. Then, the next time you go to a Chinese restaurant you will be able to impress your friends—and, even better, your date!*

Tipping

Most of the better restaurants have the "tip" already included on your check. On your check you will find the total amount of the meal, beverages and the "gratuity" (or tip). This will usually be about 15% of the total bill. If, after you have paid the check, you feel that the amount of the gratuity was not enough for the very special attention your waitress or waiter gave you, then by all means leave a few dollars more on the table—just as you are about to leave! It's up to you.

What is important to remember is that staff at any restaurant, including the coat-check attendants and parking attendants (when they park your car) rely on tips as a portion of their earnings. So try not to forget to give them a little something.

Tip: Both coat-check and parking attendants should be given a tip of at least $2.00 each! If you had a part-time or full-time job like theirs, you would want to be tipped, too!

Self-Defense

Take a course in self-defense. It does not matter what kind of self-defense course you take. The bottom line is to find a way to defend yourself in case of an emergency!

Sewing

Knowing how to do basic sewing will be very valuable, especially in an emergency. You need to know, at least, the bare basics of hemming, sewing on a button and repairing a zipper. If you don't want to take the time to take a class, ask a parent, someone in your neighborhood, one of your friends or even a friend's parent. You can also go to a book store and purchase a book on sewing basics. Many of these books have clear and easy to follow illustrations that will help you to teach yourself.

Snoring

If you are a person who snores, try sleeping *without* a pillow and on your side. This should reduce the amount of snoring you do. And, offer a set of earplugs to anyone who is sharing your room!

Table Trimmings

With a few extra trimmings, entertaining at home can be a very *special* event!

Aside from the special meal that will be served, your guests (family, friends, your pastor, etc.) will also appreciate the extra time and attention you give to the table decorations for their personal enjoyment. In fact, your *creative* talents can easily transform a "plain" setting for four into quite an "elegant" event! Some of the general tips to keep in mind when you begin planning an informal (but special) breakfast, lunch or dinner event include:

Table Setting "Musts"

❑ Keep it basic, simple and always pretty! All you need to have on your table is a centerpiece, condiments (salt, pepper, butter, etc.), napkins *folded in a decorative way*; a glass for water and one for the main beverage (iced tea, punch, etc.); the appropriate fork(s), knife and spoons, depending on your menu; a bread plate and a dinner plate.

> **Note:** Cups and saucers (or mugs) for coffee/tea can be brought to the table at the *end* of the meal!

❑ Use a tablecloth and/or placemats (solid color, lace or patterned, that matches), and be sure that your (cloth) napkins match both the centerpiece and tablecloth and/or placemats in a *contrasting* (opposite) color or pattern. This will bring a bit of excitement and color to your table.

❑ Be sure to have the appropriate amount of flatware (forks, knives, spoons) to be used for the different courses you will be serving.

Centerpieces

Select a centerpiece that is the appropriate size for your table. It should never be so small that you it makes your table look over-sized! It also should not be so large that others at the table cannot see each other. This would distract from table conversation where everyone should feel comfortable and welcome to partici-pate in the conversations going on! Each guest **must**, therefore, be able to see each other in order to feel included.

> **Hint**: To be quite sure that your centerpiece is appropriate in size and height, simply sit in each of the chairs that your guests will occupy. Then, observe whether or not you feel a sense of discomfort. By sitting in chair one, can you see the person sitting across from you? Does the centerpiece force you to **only** talk to the person who is sitting **next** to you? How comfortable do *you* feel sitting in a particular chair?

Your centerpiece can be almost *anything*! Get creative, get silly or get "theme-minded"! You could, for example:

❑ Use an "Easter Egg Basket" that is filled with different kinds of fresh fruit and few (fresh or artificial) flowers that have lots of green leaves. This can be very pretty and used for a special breakfast or lunch.

❑ Use a clear-glass mixing bowl. Fill it with an assortment of "foil-wrapped" Hershey's Kisses and miniature choco-late bars. Include in this arrangement, bold-colored artifi-cial flowers.

Napkins

Napkins neatly folded into triangles or rectangles are all your table really needs. Should have the time, however, you could fold your napkins into all sorts of sophisticated (creative) shapes which will further enhance your table setting.

> **Hint**: Go to the Library and take notes on "Napkin Folding".

Here is a suggestion: Go to a restaurant or hotel and ask the Banquet Manager to refer you to a waitress/waiter who can actually show you how to do many of the special napkin-folds they use! It is perfectly all right to let them know that you just *want* to know the "how". And, do not be surprised that they will consider your coming to them as a compliment!

Serving Tips

The general rule to follow is: put plates down in front of a guest from their left and take them away from their right. Serve beverages from a person's left. Remove beverage items from the right.

Menu Planning

A typical "informal" dinner menu would include *at least four* of the five courses listed below.

- Soup (or fruit cup)
- Salad (with assorted breads)
- Entree (the main course of either meat/fish and two vegetables)
- Dessert
- Coffee or tea

Good luck with your planning, cooking, table setting and hosting. And, by the way, even though you are hosting the dinner party—keep in mind that it is still possible for you to sit down and *eat* with your guests—as long as you remember to include some time to eat and host on your schedule!

Table Manners

In general, tips about your table manners include:

- ❏ As soon as you are seated at the table, place the napkin on your lap.
- ❏ A gentleman never **tucks** his napkin into his collar, belt or between the buttons of his shirt.

❑ When using the napkin give special attention to "patting" your mouth instead of "wiping" your mouth—like you would if you were using a washcloth.

❑ Once the meal is finished, put your napkin on the left-hand side of your plate.

❑ Do not start to eat until everyone has been served.

❑ If the usual condiments (salt, pepper, butter, etc.) are **not** on the table once your plate has been placed before you and everyone else, it is perfectly all right to *ask* for them.

❑ **Only** reach for those items on the table that are *within* your reach (if not, then simply ask the person who is closest to that item to pass it to you).

❑ If you are at a dinner party always say "yes" to each and every item that the hostess or host has prepared (in very *small* portions)—*except, of course,* if you are allergic to it or you especially dislike it! All you need to politely say in this case is simply: *"No, thank you."* Should you be asked why, just say: *"It looks tempting,* but I am allergic to it." This should be all your hostess or host needs to forgive you for not sampling their specially-prepared dish.

Several More Tips to Keep in Mind

■ **Your posture is important.** Slouching or slumping is very unattractive and should be avoided.

■ **Avoid leaning back in your chair.** This is hazardous to your safety because you could very well break the legs of the chair, fall back and severely bump your head or injure your back!

■ **Saying grace before meals is purely personal.** Some do and some don't! For those who do say grace, however, you need to remember to respect their choice to do so.

Silverware Placement

The general rules to keep in mind about place settings is that forks are always placed on the left-hand side of the plate; and, knives/spoons are placed on the right.

The African-American Teenager's Guide

Using the Silverware

Have you gone to a restaurant and seen *several* knives, forks and spoons at each place setting? Were you confused about which fork or spoon to use? The many pieces of silverware are placed in a particular order and correspond to the different courses that will be served. Here is the trick: use the silverware that is farthest *away* from the plate—in other words, work from the *outside* in!

Let's look at this a bit closer for a clearer understanding. Use a mental picture of a place setting that has several pieces of silverware, a couple of glasses, a cup and saucer and a specially-folded napkin. Believe it or not, each of these elements has a purpose and are placed in a particular order. With a three-course dinner, for example, you might have:

❑ Two forks (one for dinner and one for dessert or salad)

❑ A plate placed in the center of the silverware (or, just a specially-folded napkin because the dinner plate will be brought out—already decoratively-prepared)

❑ A salad plate, placed to the left of the forks

❑ One knife placed on the right of the plate

❑ Two spoons (one for desert; the other for coffee/tea (placed in the following order: dessert spoon to the right of the knife, with soup spoon placed at the far right)

❑ A "butter" plate with butter knife (placed just above the forks on the left)

❑ One water goblet/glass (placed just above the knife and spoons on the right)

❑ One wine glass (if you plan to serve wine; or a glass for any other beverage **except** water)

Tattoo Safety

Here are a set of questions to ask the Tattoo Artist before getting your tattoo:

- Do you use an antibacterial solution to wash your hands before and afer each tattoo application?

- Do you wear latex gloves during the tattooing procedure?

- Is each needle and tube set individually packaged, dated, and sealed? Do you set up and open them in front of the client?

- Do you use sterile disposable needles?

- Do you properly dispose of contaminated materials?

When you get there, make sure the studio looks and feels clean. If it doesn't, or you feel uncomfortable, leave!

Tea Time!

If you really don't like the taste of coffee but want to put something warm and soothing in your mug, try tea! Visit your local Health Food Store (department stores, specialty stores, etc.) and look carefully at the many kinds of blends there are available. Herbal teas are made from the flowers, leaves, berries, seeds and roots of particular plants and *do not contain caffeine*. What you will find are an assortment of teas that will help you stay healthy, help you to sleep comfortably, help you to relax—naturally, and treat your taste-buds to new and different flavors. Try them—you might like them!

Telephone Tidbits

As a basic note, when talking on the telephone you should: (1) use your normal speaking voice; (2) attempt to speak clearly; and (3) always hang-up the receiver gently. Slamming the receiver down when you hang up is impolite and may cause your caller some discomfort if she or he is still on the other end after both of you have said your good-byes!

Some More Tips

❑ If you are the person *making* the call, once your call is answered you should respond by saying: "Hello, this is (give your name). May I speak to (give the name of the person you are calling).

❑ If you are the person *answering* the telephone, the easiest response to use would be a simple: "Hello!" How irritating is it when someone answers the telephone by saying: "Yeah?" or "Is Linda there?" or "Where's Frank?" or "Is Ann home?"

❑ If you are not the person that the caller asks to speak to, and that person is not around to take the call, respond by saying: "I'm sorry but she/he is not available to speak to you at this time. Would you like to leave a message?"

> **Note:** When taking a message *always* write the following information: the caller's name, telephone number (don't forget to get their area code) and, a brief message—if the caller wants to leave one.

❑ Whether you are the caller or the person answering the telephone, make sure to end the conversation with a pleasant-sounding "good-bye!"

Obscene Calls

The best way to handle an obscene telephone call is very easy—hang-up immediately!

If the caller continues to call back 2, 3 or 4 times in a row, this could be an indication that they think they can continue to do so. On the third or fourth time when you answer the telephone and are certain that they are calling back again, blow a whistle into the telephone. Should the caller persist in dialing your number after doing this, contact the Telephone Company or the Police Department for assistance in tracing the call and putting an end to this most uncomfortable situation.

"My telephone etiquette is a reflection of my temperament!"

Television Time

Too much television time could be harmful to you physically and psychologically! Certain programs, especially those which feature death and destruction, can be stressful and ultimately pull on your physical and mental energy. Design a *wise-watching* schedule which includes a healthy assortment of programs that are entertaining, educational and energy-injected!

Umbrellas

It is suggested that you never carry an umbrella in a dangerous position! Not only is it impolite and dangerous to those around you, but for your safety and the safety of others, it is very important to give serious thought to the manner in which you carry and use an umbrella.

What you need to remember and do is: (1) make sure that you carry your closed umbrella close to your side with the point facing downward; (2) gentlemen should hold an opened umbrella in a position that is at a comfortable height and angle which will allow them to see where they are going and, at the same time, promote a feeling of "protectiveness" for the person they happen to be escorting.

Visiting

One area many seem to forget about when it comes to good manners is when it is appropriate to visit someone. A few of the *do's* and *don'ts* include:

❑ **Do** visit a sick friend in the hospital (or at their home) but be sure to make your visit brief, friendly and cheerful. Remember, they need their rest **and** a smile!

❑ **Don't** visit new parents without calling a day or so ahead to find out when it would be more convenient.

❑ **Do** visit a new neighbor and take a small gift of welcome (fruit basket, flowers, etc.). But, be sure to leave them a note in the mailbox asking when it would be a good time for a visit.

❑ **Don't** be an "un-expected visitor"! Even some of your family and close friends would appreciate a call **before** you visit. They could have made other arrangements for the evening or be in the middle of a meal. At least extend them the courtesy of a call **before** attempting to drop by!

Voice Management

It is always nice to know that your voice has a pleasing sound to others. To find out if your voice is or is not pleasing, try tape recording yourself. The next time you are having a telephone conversation with a friend, turn on the tape recorder. If you try to forget it is on, you will speak more naturally and have a better idea of how you sound—normally. Next, tape yourself reading a couple of paragraphs from a book, the newspaper, a magazine or whatever. Play the tape back and listen to how your voice sounds to you. You might find that you speak too low, have a rather high-pitched tone, speak too rapidly or even that you mumble. Decide what needs to be improved and start working on those areas right away.

You can practice improving your voice while taking a shower, cleaning your room or during those times when you are alone and will have very few—if any—interruptions. You only need to spend 5 or 10 minutes for these practice sessions at a time. How often you practice is up to you. Part of improving your speech is improving what you say and how you say it. Don't talk slang or Ebonics just to fit in or impress someone. If you can't pronounce a word properly, ask someone who can teach you how. Proper speech is associated with intelligence, and it can go a long way in your quest to get ahead in life.

> **Hint**: When you are driving alone in your car is a perfect time to practice—other drivers will think you are singing to your favorite song along with the radio!

If your school has a speech therapist on staff explain what you would like to do about your voice tone, level, etc., and ask to be evaluated. Then ask for practice exercises that you can do to meet your goals. If your school does not have a speech therapist, ask your Counselor to refer you to one, or simply contact the nearest hospital to get a referral.

Washing and Ironing

By washing and ironing your own clothes, you can be sure that they are *exactly* the way you want them to be! Follow the directions on the labels of your clothes, the different cycles on the washing machine, dryer, and iron settings to prevent damage to your clothing. Fold each load as you take them out of the dryer (the quicker you do—the less ironing required). Pick one specific day of the week to wash and iron *everything*. When you finish, the only other thing you will need to do is put everything away.

> **Hint #1**: Have one designated place in your room to put your dirty clothes and you won't have to worry about having to pick them up from all over the room on wash day.

> **Hint #2**: Don't forget to sort by color and by fabric. The wash cycle will *definitely* be different if you are washing a few delicate items versus washing several pairs of heavy jeans!

Special Note: Never run the washing machine or dryer when no one is home. Have you put a load of clothes in the washing machine and decided to run to the store thinking it would only take you about 10-15 minutes? Did you happen to see an old friend, start talking and end up being away for over an hour? Lots of things can happen while you are away for 10 minutes to one hour. How would you feel if after returning home you discovered that the washer had an unexpected leak or the dryer short-circuited causing an unsafe condition to your home? Think about it—this is really important!

Choosing an Iron and Ironing Board

- Purchase an iron that feels right for you by weight, but remember that a light-weight iron may not be as effective at pressing out creases or wrinkles as a heavier one. Do you have a lot of clothes that require a heavier iron?

- Irons designed to have the cords out of the way are much safer.

- Irons with a flat heel-rest don't tip over as easily.

- Look for steam irons that have a clear-plastic water level gauge for easier filling. Also, be sure the steam iron you select can be filled with "tap" (straight from your faucet) water.

- When you begin looking for a safe and appropriate ironing board, be sure to select one that: (a) has a secure heatproof surface to stand the iron on; and (b) has a board cover that is made of stain and scorch-resistant material, lined to retain heat, and will allow the ironing to be smoother.

Wills: Everyone Should Make One!

Accepting the reality of death happening by natural causes or by accident is a sure sign of personal growth. Death, after all, is a situation that you cannot prevent or avoid. With this in mind, it is suggested that you take the necessary time—now—to make plans and preparations by developing a list of instructions about your wishes should *you* die.

Yes, this really sounds depressing, a bit scary and too early to even think about! But, are you discovering through comments from friends, your Pastor's sermons, your parent's warnings and in feature items being presented in the newspapers and magazines that the number of teen deaths are rising—every day? If you are a teen-parent, are you concerned about the well-being of your child should something happen to you? While this list of questions could go on and on, you are simply asked to consider making preparations—now—in writing!

Making a Will is not just for those who are rich or famous! *Everyone* has *something of value* to leave to a loved one! And, everyone wants to feel comfortable and confident—now—that their specific wishes and instructions will be handled in a satisfactory manner after they die.

Who can make a Will? Generally, anyone of legal age and sound mind can make a Will. The term "legal age" varies from state to state. In some states **18** is considered to be the "legal age" and the magic age for other states is **21**. Okay, you are **under** the magic numbers, but, you *can* do something called an *"Informal Will."*

This is basically a letter that lists your personal possessions, tells how you wish to have them distributed, outlines your funeral arrangements, specifies who you want to take care of your child(ren), and would include any special message you wish to give to particular loved ones. No...this would **not** be considered by the Courts as a legal Will, but it would at least give your parents and friends a sense of direction (and comfort) knowing that they were fulfilling your wishes!

Below is a suggested format that you might use for your "Informal Will". Feel free to *revise* (or to include additional sections) to fit your *specific* wishes!

My "Informal" Will

I, _____(your name)_____, currently live at ___(your address, city, state, zip)_ ; my date of birth is _____; my social security number is _____; and, I declare this to be an *Informal Will* that I have prepared and signed.

First. The members of my immediate family are __(your mother, father, sister(s), brother(s), your child(ren)__. Below are the special messages I wish to give to the following persons:

(name of person)

Message: _____

_____

_____

(name of person)

Message: _____

_____

_____

(name of person)

Message: _____

_____

_____

Second. It is my wish that ___(name of person)___ be responsible for handling any and all of the monies I have or have coming to me which include my checking account, savings account, savings bonds, employment check(s), tax refunds, payments owed to me for child support, etc. It is also my wish that this person be responsible for paying whatever bills I owe out of whatever monies I have or have coming to me.

Third. It is my wish that any and all monies left over be given to (name of person or persons)___ as a "gift" from me. If, however, I have a child(ren), I wish to have this money equally divided and deposited into a separate savings account in my child or children's name and that it be used for ___(purpose you wish)___ , and, further, that they be able to receive these monies when they reach the age of _____.

Fourth. It is my wish that ___(name of person)___ be responsible for taking care of my child(ren).

Fifth. It is my wish that the persons listed below be given the following items that belong to me:

(name of person)	Item
(name of person)	Item
(name of person)	Item
(name of person)	Item

Sixth. It is my wish that my funeral and burial arrangements be handled by (name of person) and I want this person to know that my *specific* wishes are:

1. That my family provides an arrangement of my favorite flower which is: (name of your favorite flower or plant).

2. That my family makes sure I am wearing: (what you would like to be wearing) .

Additional instructions included the following:

1. _____

2. _____

3. _____

4. _____

The information given above represents my last wishes. I have also asked and received the signature of **one** witness as assurance that my signature was written in their presence and that I was, at the time, of sound mind, fully understood what I was preparing and what I was signing.

Your signature:

_____Date:_____

Witness signature:

_____Date:_____

Witness Name: _____

Witness Address: _____

Witness Social Security Number:_____

Witness Date of Birth:_____

Use these survival tips to do just that...be more prepared and survive!

Sources

American Academy of Child and Adolescent Psychiatry, Fact Sheets (Washington, DC, 1992-96).

American Academy of Child and Adolescent Psychiatry, "Children of Parents with Mental Illness" Fact Sheet #39; 1997.

American Heart Association, "African Americans and Cardiovascular Diseases" Biostatistical Fact Sheet; 2001.

Benkov, Laura, Ph.D. *Reinventing the Family* (New York, NY: Crown Publishers, Inc.)

Bluestein, Jane, *Parents Teens and Boundaries: How to Draw the Line* (Florida: Health Communications, Inc., 1993).

Bolander, Donald O., Director of Education, *Instant Quotation Dictionary* (New Jersey, Career Institute, Inc., 1972).

Bolton, Robert. *People Skills* (New York, NY: Simon and Schuster, Inc., 1979).

Byrd, Oliver E., MD, Jones, Edwina, Landis, Paul E. and Morgan, Edna. *Growing In Health* (River Forest, IL: Laidlaw Brothers Publishers, 1960).

Clemes, Harris and Bean, Reynold, *Self-Esteem: The Key to Your Child's Well-Being* (New York: G.P. Putnam's Sons and (simultaneously) Academic Press Canada Limited, Toronto, Canada, 1981).

Eimers, Robert and Robert Aitchison. *Effective Parents/Responsible Children: A Guide to Confident Parenting* (New York, NY: McGraw-Hill Book Company).

Elevator Escalator Safety Foundation. "Safe Rider Rules" (Mobile, AL: Coordinated Effort of the Vertical Transportation Industry, 1994).

Federal Highway Administration. "Everyone is a Pedestrian" (Washington, DC: Publication No. FHWA-SA-93-058; HHS-11/8-93 (20M)E).

Federal Railroad Administration. "Railroad Trespassing Facts" (Washington, DC: U.S. Department of Transportation, 1996).

Frank, Steven. *The Everything Study Book* (Holbrook, MA: Adams Media Corporation, 1996); pp. 35-36.

Frolkey, Carol Ann. "Single Parenting" (U.S. Behavioral Health: Emeryville, CA; vol. 7/no. 9, October 1993).

Fry, Ron. *Manage Your Time* (Hawthorne, NJ: The Career Press, 1991).

Guralnik, David B., Editor-in-Chief, *Webster's New World Dictionary for Young Readers* (New York: Simon and Schuster, 1979).

Harris, Robie H.. *It's Perfectly Normal* (Cambridge, MA, Candlewick Press, 1994).

Hyde, Margaret O., *My Friend Has Four Parents* (New York: McGraw-Hill Book Company, 1981).

Kemper, Donald W., *Kaiser Permanente Healthwise Handbook* (Idaho: Healthwise, Inc., 1994).

Kemper, Donald W., Healthwise Staff and Physicians. *Kaiser Permanente Healthwise Handbook* (Boise, ID: Healthwise, Inc., 1997).

Knox, Gerald M., Editor. *Household Hints and Tips* (London, England: Dorling Kindersley, 1990).

Knox, Gerald M., Editor. *Better Homes and Gardens* (London, England: Dorling Kindersley, Ltd., 1990).

Mackenzie, R. Alec, *The Time Trap*, McGraw-Hill Book Company (New York, New York, 1975), pp. L73-l76.

Metropolitan Police Department, Community Relations Division. "Preventive Measures Against Rape" pamphlet (Washington, DC: The Advertising Council, Inc., 1979).

National Network of Runaway and Youth Services. "Runaway and Homeless Youth: Fact Sheet" (Washington, DC, (package distributed/ received 1998).

National School Transportation Association. "School Bus Rider's Guide" (Springfield, Virginia, 1996).

Temes, Roberta, *Living With an Empty Chair: A Guide Through Grief* (New York: Irvington Publishers, Inc., 1980)

Rose, Yvonne and Rose, Tony. *Is Modeling For You?* (Phoenix, AZ: Amber Books, 1997).

Savage, Peter. *The Safe Travel Book* (Lexington, MA: Lexington Books, 1988).

United Media Enterprise, *"Where Does the Time Go?"*, Newspaper Enterprise Association (New York, New York, 1983), pp. 16-23.

U.S. Consumer Product Safety Commission, Office of Information and Public Affairs. "Bicycles" pamphlet (Washington, DC: Publication #346:009603, 1996).

United States Department of Agriculture, Food Safety and Inspection Service, Food Safety and Consumer Education Office. "Consumer Information From USDA" (December 1996).

Vanzant, Iyanla, *Acts of Faith: Daily Mediations for People of Color* (New York: Simon and Schuster, Inc., 1993).

Vickery, Donald M., *Take Care of Yourself: Your Personal Guide to Self-Care and Preventing Illness* (Massachusetts: Addison-Wesley Publishing Company, Inc., 1989).

The Washington Post, "Some Real-Life Recipes From the Cast of *Soul Food*. (September 24, 1997), p. E8.

About the Author

A native Washingtonian, Debrah Harris-Johnson is the mother of two, grandmother and a neighborhood mom of many. While currently a working mom, some of her other hats include: self-employment consultant, seminar presenter, meeting planner, author of several articles which appeared in local publications, and she is also a trained mediator. Her entrepreneurial spirit has afforded her the opportunity to focus energy on helping youth make the transition to adulthood a little easier. Debrah and her husband of 32 years, Leland, currently reside in Maryland.

Index

K

Kwanzaa 300

L

Lactose Intolerance 44
Library 300
Literacy 300
Loaned/Borrowed Items 301
Lying 85

M

Maps 302
Masturbation 302
Methods of Cooking 254
Microwaving 252
Mixed Race Families 83
Money Matters 302
    Starting a business 234
Motivation 166
Multiple Moves 17

N

Name-Callers 18
Negative Activities 113
    Alcohol 115
    Drugs 116
    Eating Problems 119
    Gangs 121
    Graffiti 122
    Guns and Firearms 122
    Playing jokes 124
    Profanity 125
    Railroad trespassing 125
    Running Away 126
    Sex 127
    Smoking 130
    Suicide 132
    Violent Behavior 133
Negative Thinking 167
Neighborhood 303

O

Overweight persons 22

P

Parenting, Teen 265
Parents 77
Party Planning 303
Peer Pressure 19
Pet Care 94
Pet Principles 305
Pledging 199
Poison Precautions 147
Positive Thoughts 305
Prejudices 20
Problem Solving 15
Procrastination 71
Punishments 23

R

Rail Crossings 157
Rape 150
Reading 259
Reading Habits 306
Relationships
    Family 79
    Healthy 78
    Unhealthy 78
Religions 306
Responsibility 77
    Inappropriate actions 84
    Signs of 88
Restaurant Etiquette 306
Resume 209

S

Safety 141
    at School 148
    at Work 149
    Driving 156
    Personal 149
    Skateboard 158
    Travel 155
Scheduling Time 73
Schoolwork 163
Self-defense 309